The Victorian Governess

'Not a love affair, I hope?'

A young governess faces a grilling from an inquisitive agent as to why
she left her previous situation (1890s). (*Mary Evans Picture Library*)

The Victorian Governess

Kathryn Hughes

Hambledon and London
London and New York

Published by Hambledon and London 2001
102 Gloucester Avenue, London NW 1 8HX (U.K.)
838 Broadway, New York 10003 (U.S.A.)

ISBN 1 85285 002 7 (cased)
ISBN 1 85285 325 5 (paper)

A description of this book is available from the
British Library and from the Library of Congress

Typeset by The Midlands Book Typesetting Company,
Loughborough.
Printed on acid-free paper and bound in Great Britain
by Cambridge University Press.

Contents

List of Illustrations

The interview   *Frontispiece*

Between Pages 48 and 49

An idealised version of home education

An apprehensive child is urged to shake hands with her
    new governess

'The Governess' by Richard Redgrave

Small boys were perceived as a disruptive element in the
    home schoolroom

Mary Bazlinton

Edith Gates

May Pinhorn

FOR MY PARENTS
ANNE AND JOHN HUGHES

Acknowledgements

This study would not have been possible without the generosity of the many listeners to BBC Radio 4's *Woman's Hour* who wrote to me with their recollections and impressions of individual Victorian governesses. In particular, Mrs Charis House, Mrs Anne Schulte and Lady Elisabeth Walley were kind enough to trust me with precious family manuscripts and to allow me to quote from them. I would like to take this opportunity to ask anyone who would be prepared to lend me diaries, memoirs or other material relating to the Victorian governess to contact me via the publisher.

I am extremely grateful to Professor David Vincent of the University of Keele who supervised the original research upon which the book is based and whose encouragement, criticism and continuing interest in the project were invaluable. Thanks go, too, to the University of Keele's Department of Victorian Studies headed by John Briggs. I would also like to acknowledge the financial support I received from the British Academy and the University of Keele during the early years of this project.

Martin Sheppard of The Hambledon Press is the person responsible for making this book a reality. His enthusiasm, efficiency and judgement made the whole editorial process highly enjoyable, and I owe him a great debt of thanks. Over the years the following friends contributed criticism, encouragement and infinite patience: Philip Clough, Helen Corlett, Glenn Patterson, Karen Simpson and Karen Wilson. Finally, I am indebted to my brother Michael Hughes, who brought his customary wit, insight and erudition to seemingly endless drafts of this book. His criticisms and suggestions have been adopted almost without exception, although responsibility for errors of fact or judgement remain mine alone.

Preface

The history of the governess class has yet to be written.

Alfred W. Pollard, *Murray's Magazine* (1889)

The figure of the governess must be one of the most familiar and abiding images in nineteenth-century literature. We know her best in the form of the scandalous Becky Sharp of Thackeray's *Vanity Fair*, or as Charlotte Brontë's Jane Eyre, the plain orphan who eventually marries her employer, the mysterious Mr Rochester. In addition, she appears in scores of other novels from high literature to sensationalist shockers and from *Emma* to *The Turn of the Screw*. Yet it is one of the great ironies of Victorian history that we know virtually nothing about the 25,000 women who actually worked as governesses during the middle years of the century. Indeed, it is the very power of these fictional representations which has blunted our curiosity about the practice of educating girls at home during the Victorian period.

This study aims to rectify matters by reconstructing the life of the governess using a wide range of sources. It has not always been easy. There are, for instance, no great Royal Commissions or parliamentary reports on which to draw. Domestic life, and particularly the domestic life of the middle classes, has always remained opaque to the prying eye of the social investigator. While an historian of female education or employment can rely on the reports of the proceedings of various institutions, commissions and societies, little material of this type pertains to the governess. Nonetheless, some bureaucratic sources have yielded valuable information. These include the published annual reports of the Board of Management of the Governesses' Benevolent Institution for 1843-53,[1] the Report of the Schools Inquiry Commission of 1867-68,[2] and the census enumerators' handbooks for 1861.[3]

More plentiful, although altogether more problematic, is the steady stream of etiquette manuals which appeared between 1840 and 1860, advising the governess and her employer upon their dealings with one another. Many of those who wrote these manuals had started their working lives in the schoolroom and were dependent on selling their books if they were to avoid returning to it.[4] The fact that in many cases these writers produced not one but two or more manuals on home education indicates the scale of the demand for such material. It also suggests that a substantial number of those people employing governesses during the 1840s and 50s were doing so for the first time and felt themselves in urgent need of practical advice. It is difficult to imagine the Duchess of Devonshire pouring over Mary Maurice's *Mothers and Governesses* for clues about how to treat her daughters' teacher;[5] it is far more likely that this book and the many others like it were read by middle-class matrons looking for help on how to cope with the new and, in many ways, alarming experience of sharing their home with an employee who was neither a servant nor a family member.

Whether these women obtained much comfort from reading advice manuals must remain open to question. The way these texts worked was to construct an ideal governess-employer situation and then represent it as actual practice. The effects on the morale of the readers of these manuals can only be imagined: feelings of inadequacy and despair must have surfaced as they learned of the harmonious arrangements of households apparently so much better regulated than their own. Yet if a manual advises an employer and governess to meet every day to discuss any problems which have arisen with the children, care must be taken not to assume that this was actually what happened in the majority of households. This is not to suggest that these conduct books are invalidated as historical sources, rather that they warn against assuming that various forms of representation – including fiction, art and even journalism – accurately reproduce social conditions. Reading these manuals can still give us valuable information about the ideals, desires and aspirations and, conversely, about the anxieties and frailities of both governesses and their employers. In some instances it is those points of greatest assertion in the text which mark the place where the ideal is most in danger of breaking down to reveal the chaos and contradiction of everyday life. In other cases it is what is denied or omitted which gives us the best clue as to what may really have been going on.

Much of the same also applies to the use made of popular

journalism throughout this book. During the 1840s and 50s one of the favourite subjects for a whole range of middle-brow periodicals was the governess' 'plight', which was described as a mixture of low pay, poor working conditions and patchy preparation. Yet the overwhelming majority of readers neither worked as governesses, nor employed one to teach its children. Nonetheless, what these articles do illuminate is the way in which the tensions which the governess seemed to embody – concerning social respectability, sexual morality and financial self-reliance – touched a raw nerve with a whole swathe of middle-class Britain. The figure of the governess took on a significance to her contemporaries out of all proportion to her actual numbers. Exploring the way in which her situation gripped the imagination tells us as much about the aspirations and anxieties of the mid Victorian as it does about the governess' actual working conditions.

Next, and perhaps most obviously, there are the novels. From 1830 to 1865 there appeared in fiction every type of governess imaginable.[6] From the panoramic sweep of Thackeray to the domestic confines of Elizabeth Sewell, it sometimes seemed as if no novel of the period was complete without its governess. But just as one cannot assume that advice manuals reflect anything other than an ideal of life in the home schoolroom, so it is dangerous to assume that novels can what it was like give us a faithful account of to be a governess. A reminder of the folly of using fictional texts as unproblematic sources for social history is suggested by a glance at the very different lives of Jane Eyre and her creator, Charlotte Brontë. While Jane Eyre was pursued by her employer, disappointed at the altar and left to roam the moors as a beggar, Charlotte Brontë found herself ignored by her employers, courted by men who did not excite her and obliged to leave the schoolroom in order to keep house for her ailing father. It is into this yawning gap between fact and fiction that so many previous accounts of the Victorian governess have fallen, peddling as they do a careless stereotype of the plain clergyman's daughter, obliged to spend her time fending off slights from both servants and employers, before escaping a prim middle age by a last-minute marriage to the curate.[7] Nonetheless, governess novels have proved to be a valuable source of material for this study. For while they may not exactly reproduce social reality, they do something just as important, by providing us with an insight into the imaginative impact of the governess upon her contemporaries.

By way of counter-balance, I have made great use of first-hand accounts of the schoolroom, written from the perspective both of the governess and her pupils. First, there are the many autobiographies produced by women during the inter-war decades which include an account of a childhood spent under the supervision of a resident governess.[8] Considerable caution needs to be taken when handling this kind of evidence, not least because it is so vulnerable to fantasy and forgetfulness. For example, some of these autobiographers were actually professional writers exploiting the public's demands for a nostalgic recreation of 'a Victorian childhood'. Another problem is that those women who had the confidence and the leisure to sit down in middle age and write an account of their lives tended to be drawn from privileged backgrounds. While their texts provide a valuable insight into the schoolrooms of well-heeled households, there is virtually no material available from the considerable number of farmers' and shopkeepers' daughters who were educated by governesses during the middle years of the century. Throughout this study, autobiographers are referred to by the name under which they wrote their memoirs. In the cases of those who were married, this is not usually the name by which they were known as children.

The second group of autobiographical material consists of memoirs produced by a group of remarkable women – poets, religious writers, missionaries – who started their working lives as governesses and whose subsequent experiences were considered sufficiently significant to find their way into print. The chief problem in dealing with autobiography produced by exceptional women is that of typicality: to what extent can their experience, even while working as governesses, be assumed to be representative of their mute sisters? In one sense this quandary extends to the use of any autobiographical source, since the act of writing about one's life, and then having the luck or talent to get it published, isolates an individual from the general mass of humanity which remains silent. On the other hand, the material circumstances which propelled women like Elizabeth Ham,[9] Mary Smith[10] and Mary Cowden-Clarke[11] into the schoolroom shaped the experience of all governesses working during the first half of the nineteenth century.

The final category of material consists of three unpublished documents written by governesses whose lives did not subsequently fall under public scrutiny. This is not to suggest, however, that these accounts were not shaped, distorted even, by a set of personal and public pressures. For instance, Edith Gates, a nineteen-year-old governess working in Reading in 1876, filled her diary with stylistic flourishes, as well as assessments of books she had read, in a way which suggested that she was more interested in trying out the identity of 'writer' than giving an account of her life as a governess.[12] May Pinhorn, meanwhile, maintained that in deciding to write her memoir she was responding to an article in a 1913 issue of the *Spectator* which suggested that there was a great need for the middle classes to set down their experiences for the benefit of their grandchildren. Yet, as she herself admitted, 'when I had once begun I found that my motives became more complex'[13], and it is impossible to know what emotional drives lay behind the immaculately written account of her time as governess to some of the most prominent families in the late Victorian Liberal establishment. Finally, Mary Bazlington used her diary, as so many other devout Christians have done, to chart her relationship with God rather than to make a permanent record of her time as governess during the years 1854-59.[14]

Considerations of space have obliged me to confine my attention to those resident governesses who worked within England and Wales. During the Victorian period British governesses were much in demand by wealthy overseas families who wished to provide their offspring with a smattering of what was still the world's most prestigious culture. From New York to Bangkok British governesses laboured to instill the manners and attitudes, not to mention the literary and historical references, that would turn small Prussians or Thais into ersatz English ladies and gentlemen. The way in which these women were responsible for transplanting a particular type of Englishness to the four corners of the globe offers material rich enough to merit a study in itself.

Also omitted is any consideration of those governesses who decided to escape the over-supplied domestic market by emigrating to the colonies. A series of philanthropic initiatives between 1840-90 aimed to help single, educated women start a new life, chiefly in Australia and New Zealand. Having endured an uncomfortable and sometimes perilous three-month sea journey, many of these women found that their new employers expected them to perform a range of duties, including house and farm work, which would have been unthinkable in Britain. The manner in which these women either succeeded or failed in embracing the social conditions of colonial life has already been told in two excellent books, Patricia Clarke's *The Governesses*[15] and A. James Hammerton's *Emigrant Gentlewomen*.[16]

What this study will do, however, is show how an understanding of the governess' situation throws light way beyond the door of the

Victorian home schoolroom. Becoming a governess was the only acceptable way of earning money open to the increasing number of middle-class women whose birth and education defined them as ladies, yet whose families were unable to support them in leisure. Yet while avoiding a total loss of caste, being paid to educate another woman's children set in play a series of emotional and social tensions which governesses, as well as their employers and society at large, were obliged to negotiate. The governess was a surrogate mother who was herself childless, a young woman whose marriage prospects were restricted, and a family member who was sometimes mistaken for a servant. By exploring these contradictions in detail, we can gain insight into the ideology operating in the lives of all those who considered themselves, and wished desperately to be considered, ladies. It is no coincidence that the governess' 'plight', and the impulse to relieve it, became a catalyst for the most important educational and employment reforms to effect middle-class women during the second half of the nineteenth century.

1

Reader, I Married Him

> Reader, I married him. A quiet wedding we had: he and I, the parson and clerk, were alone present.
>
> Charlotte Brontë, *Jane Eyre* (1847)

> It is a curious proof of the present feeling towards governesses, that they are made the heroines of many popular novels.
>
> Mary Maurice, *Governess Life* (1849)

If we think we know the Victorian governess it is because we have read her story – or something which purports to be her story – in numerous novels of the day. For that reason any investigation into her life and times has to begin with the popular images, the confusions and the fantasies which have both familiarised the governess as an historical subject and, paradoxically, made her more remote.

The year 1847 marked the governess' arrival at the very heart of the English novel.[1] While she had been hovering on its edges since the end of the previous century, it was not until that year that a middle-class woman employed to teach the daughters of those better off than herself appeared as the central character in a major work. First on the scene was Becky Sharp, heroine or anti-heroine of William Thackeray's *Vanity Fair*, a governess who learns to rise through Regency society by means of her own energetic and amoral efforts.[2] Employed by a country baronet, she manages to carry off the son of the house before abandoning him when greater prizes beckon. Devious beyond dreaming, Becky manages to cheat, steal and lie without getting caught by the agents of social, moral and economic order who pursue her throughout her disreputable career. She ends the novel as the self-styled Lady Crawley, a raddled *demi-mondaine* condemned to live out the rest of her days in second-rate resorts, having long since been shunned by decent people. Her story is told in the third person by a buoyant, all-knowing narrator who sweeps his way confidently through the jostling, promiscuous panorama which is Vanity Fair. The tone is detached, ironic. Characters reveal themselves in their behaviour towards others, conceived by the narrator as puppets whose interior life remains opaque if, indeed, it exists at all.

That same year there appeared a book on a strikingly similar subject, for it too told the story of a young orphan obliged to go out as a governess who eventually marries a man of higher social status than herself. Yet Charlotte Brontë's *Jane Eyre* treated its material in a very different way.[3] Told in the form of an autobiography, the drama of the book lies in the way in which Jane processes and then reacts to the fantastic events unfolding around her. Courted by her employer, she discovers at the altar that Mr Rochester is already married to the madwoman in the attic whose screams have previously disturbed and puzzled her. Fleeing to the moors, Jane takes refuge with her cousins before returning a year later to discover that the house where she once worked has been burned to the ground and that Mr Rochester, though blind, is now free to marry. Essentially an account of the social, moral and sexual development of its central character, *Jane Eyre* depends for its dramatic interest upon the densely plotted consciousness of its first-person narrator. The latter's quietly emphatic 'Reader, I married him' confirms the sense that her story has been told in the form of an intimate conversation between two individuals, between Jane and her reader.[4]

While contemporaries insisted upon seeing the two novels as bound together both by subject matter and by the real-life friendship of their authors, the marked differences in their conception and execution should warn against trying to identify a coherent genre of governess fiction. One has only to look at the vast array of novels featuring a governess which appeared between 1814 and 1865 – one estimate has put the figure at around 140 – to see the difficulties of classification.[5] These books span virtually every category of fiction, including melodrama, morality tale and silver-spoon, as well as the more general territory into which both *Jane Eyre* and *Vanity Fair* fall. Fictional governesses are, according to the demands of the story in which they appear, wicked and pious, French and English, victims and schemers. They play both major and minor roles, are observed from the outside, and minutely plotted from within. They were created by men and by women; by women who had themselves once worked as governesses, as well as by those who had not. While the way the governess was portrayed in the novel shifted as the century progressed – in response to changes both in the conditions of her historical model as well as to internal developments in the form itself – what remains is a sense of the sheer range of fiction in which she appears. Far from defining a particular type of novel by her presence, the governess seems to have provided a figure or space in the fictional landscape which could be used by writers for a whole variety of literary ends.

The transformation of the governess into a major literary character was inseparable from the wider process of feminisation which the novel had been undergoing since the middle of the eighteenth century.[6] Burgeoning levels of literacy amongst middle-class women, combined with the greater leisure time now available to them, fuelled a hunger for fiction which concerned itself with female experience. This, in turn, created a market for middle-class women writers only too happy to find a way of supporting themselves without having to embrace the stigma which came with waged work. Yet almost immediately a tension arose in the demands which these female writers and readers made upon the novel form. The novel had historically concerned itself with the social, moral and, above all, economic, journey of a man obliged to make his own way in the world without the normal resources of kith and kin. For female writers and readers these conventions presented problems, since women lacked access to the public world, the domain of action and doing, in which the narrative was necessarily set.

It was to ease this tension that the governess began to appear as a central character in the novel. On the one hand, she was an orphan, propelled by economic circumstances into taking a moral, geographic and social journey similar to that of any male hero. On the other hand, she was a middle-class woman who could be re-incorporated at the end of the narrative into the domestic sphere, the proper realm of women, by means of a conventional marriage plot. Winning a husband who could restore her to her rightful social position, if not advance it a little, represented a reworking of the hero's goal of economic self-sufficiency, while still resisting any challenge to a social order which insisted upon women's financial dependence on men. Thus the governess provided a point of entry into the novel for both the female writer and reader. For the former, she was the economically precarious woman who, like herself, was obliged to make a living whilst clinging to the status of a lady. In this case the governess' triumph in winning social and economic security functioned as a wish-fufilment for the woman writer anxious about her own ambiguous status. For the reader, the governess became a daring alter-ego who could wander the world in a manner quite unthinkable for a young woman in more comfortable circumstances.

That the governess functioned within the novel as a symbol for *all* middle-class women, including those whose actual circumstances were far removed from her own, is clear from *Emma*, Jane Austen's novel of 1816.[7] Although not yet working as a governess, Jane Fairfax has been educated explicitly with this end in mind. As a result she is prodigiously accomplished, able to sing, play and speak French with an ease which is secretly galling to Emma Woodhouse, who, as a young lady of independent means, is expected to excel in these subjects without any financial motivation to spur her on. As it turns out, Jane's secret engagement to Frank Churchill, a young man of some fortune, means that she will not have to seek work in the schoolroom but can instead look forward to the socially and financially secure life of a married woman. Within the terms which Jane Austen sets out in *Emma*, the highly-skilled and accomplished governess represents both an ideal of refined ladyhood and, in her likely spinsterhood and poverty, its antithesis. The only thing which divides governesses from ladies is the attainment of a husband (Emma's own governess has recently quitted her post on her marriage to the gentlemanly Mr Weston). Far from being some remote horror, becoming a governess is revealed within the novel as the fate which shadows all middle-class women except for those lucky few who, like Emma, are absolutely assured of their own fortune.

Once this elision had been made between the governess and all middle-class women, the way was open for novelists to use her to explore far more than life in the schoolroom. As a lady who was nonetheless exempt from some of the more constricting aspects of ladyhood, she represented the perfect place to mount an enquiry into the social and moral codes which middle-class women were increasingly obliged to observe. The governess' situation within the household, her relationship with her pupils, her choice of a marriage partner, could all be represented as a discussion about the governess' unusual and uncomfortable situation, while at another level functioning as an examination of genteel femininity in action. The following passage from *Jane Eyre* shows how the process worked. At its opening the ostensible subject is Jane-as-governess, but two thirds of the way through the more radical possibility emerges that it is actually Jane-as-woman who is under discussion:

I climbed the three staircases, raised the trapdoor of the attic, and having reached the leads, looked out afar over sequestered field and hill, and along dim skyline – that then I longed for a power of vision which might overpass that limit; which might reach the busy world, towns, regions full of life I had heard of but never seen; that then I desired more of practical experience than I possessed; more of intercourse with my kind, of acquaintance with variety of character, than was here within my reach. I valued what was good in Mrs Fairfax and what was good in Adele; but I believed in the existence of other and more vivid kinds of goodness, and what I belied in I wished to behold.

Who blames me? Many, no doubt: and I shall be called discontented. I could not help it; the restlessness was in my nature; it agitated me to pain sometimes . . .

It is vain to say human beings ought to be satisfied with tranquillity: they must have action; and they will make it if they cannot find it. Millions are condemned to a stiller doom than mine, and millions are in silent revolt against their lot. Nobody knows how many rebellions besides political rebellions ferment in the masses of life which people earth. Women are supposed to be very calm generally; but women feel just as men feel; they need exercise for their faculties, and a field for their efforts as much as their brothers do; they suffer from too rigid a restraint, too absolute a stagnation, precisely as men would suffer; and it is narrow-minded in their more privileged fellow-creatures to say that they ought to confine themselves to making puddings and knitting stockings, to playing on the piano and embroidering bags. It is thoughtless to condemn them, or laugh at them, if they seek to do more or learn more than custom has pronounced necessary for their sex.[8]

Jane starts with a set of grievances which appear to arise from her position as a governess: that she lives in an isolated region with only a child and an old housekeeper for company; that she has no access to people of her own temperament; that she longs for more 'practical experience'. These are complaints which are familiar from the public discussion of the governess' 'plight': Jane's revolt, as articulated in the first paragraph of this extract, can be accommodated, understood and even excused. Only with the sentence beginning 'women are supposed to be very calm generally' is it revealed that Jane is talking not about herself as a governess but herself as a middle-class woman. In this case, the companionship of children and old domestics becomes the lot of bourgeois women generally while the 'busy world' Jane longs for is not so much a position in an urban household but rather the public world of literature and the professions, the world occupied by men. It is only once the subject is made explicit – 'women are supposed . . . .' – that the pent-up torrent of puddings, stockings and pianos is released. Early in the passage Jane asks, disingenuously, 'Who will blame me?', anticipating that while many will, many will not: everyone knows that being a governess is a rotten deal. Only subsequently, when it becomes clear that her discontent arises from her experience as a middle-class woman, does that question 'Who will blame me?' take on an altogether more urgent edge.

The fictional governess was not always made to serve such subversive ends. Two novels of the 1840s, *Agnes Grey* by Anne Brontë[9] and *Amy Herbert* by Elizabeth Sewell,[10] both use her ambiguous status as a way of conducting an essentially conservative enquiry into the social and moral responsibilities of ladyhood. In both texts a sharp distinction is set up between the governess, a clergyman's daughter of high ideals and behaviour, and the selfish and, by implication, slightly vulgar people for whom she works. Agnes Grey, for instance, finds herself in the employment first of the middle-class Bloomfield family, and subsequently of the aristocratic Murrays. The Bloomfields indulge their brutish children to excess, then dismiss Agnes when she is unable to exert control over them. Mrs Murray does much the same, keeping up a running commentary of complaints against Agnes while doing nothing to control the infuriating behaviour of her teenage daughters. Interested only in men, clothes, horses and dogs, Rosalie and Matilda Murray refuse to occupy themselves with the church-going and poor-visiting which, as squire's daughters, should be their proper concern. The quiet and sober Agnes Grey, by contrast, carries out these duties on their behalf and is rewarded with the love of the curate, Mr Weston. Rosalie Murray, meanwhile, finishes the story with a loveless match to the wealthy but degraded Sir Thomas Ashby.

Emily Morton, the governess in *Amy Herbert*, undergoes a sensationalised version of the trials of Agnes Grey. Her employers, the Harringtons, may be gentry, but they are more concerned with wealth and status than with their social responsibilities. While the orphaned clergyman's daughter Emily Morton is beautiful and good, her elder pupils Dora and Margaret are rude, dishonest and mainly concerned with getting their governess into trouble. Emily is sacked when her youngest charge is fatally injured and the blame laid unjustly at her door. Her innocence eventually revealed, Emily is taken in by the Herberts (Mrs Herbert is the sister of Mrs Harrington and mother of the eponymous Amy), where she becomes a much-loved member of a thoroughly Christian home. Elizabeth Sewell uses the contrast between Emily Morton's behaviour and that of the Harringtons to dramatise Christian gentility in action. Although Emily may appear shabby (the footman mistakes her for a maid) she has the breeding and virtue of a real lady. Her pupils, by contrast, exhibit all the moral refinement of fishwives. The young Amy's attempt to puzzle out just where Emily Morton stands in the social and moral hierarchy allows the author to present a series of Sunday School homilies, designed to remind her young female readers of the obligations attached to their (assumed) status as ladies.

While she could not be more different from the saintly Emily Morton, Becky Sharp serves a similar moral and literary purpose within the pages of *Vanity Fair*. Like Emily Morton and, indeed, Jane Eyre and Jane Fairfax, Becky is an orphan without fortune who has been educated specifically with her future role in mind. Significantly Becky's late mother was French, a fact which hints at a certain moral turpitude, most particularly with regard to truth-telling and sexual conduct. In the event, Becky turns out to be scandalously wicked, the absolute antithesis of all ladylike virtues as represented by her best friend and schoolmate Amelia Sedley. Far from functioning as a model against which the moral inadequacy of the other female characters may be shown up, the figure of Becky is a measure of just how debased society has become. If a wild and wicked woman such as this has been installed at the heart of the Christian English home, implies the narrator, then all indeed must be Vanity Fair.

The manner in which Becky Sharp became the shadow of the more conventionally heroic Amelia Sedley prefigured a phenomenon increasingly common in the cheap, melodramatic 'railway' novels of the 1850s and 60s. Earlier books like *Amy Herbert* relied upon a generalised contrast between the governess and a series of financially secure women, most typically her pupils and her employers, to create moral and dramatic tension. Others, such as *Agnes Grey* and *Jane Eyre*, used the internal struggles of the fictional autobiographer as a way of voicing the debate over the nature of female experience. As those struggles became increasingly intense the female figure at the centre of the novel split in two and the contradictions which she had previously strained to contain were now externalised and embodied in the twinned figures of the governess and the lady. As with Becky and Amelia, these pairings were used to demonstrate a series of oppositions – dark/light, sin/virtue, virgin/prostitute – which were believed to express the dual aspect of female nature.

This time, however, it was the lady who embodied all the traditional virtues associated with Christian gentility, leaving the governess to represent those darker qualities which had been repressed from the dominant ideal.

One book which sensationally organizes itself around this governess/lady pairing is Mrs Henry Wood's best-seller of 1861, *East Lynne*.[11] It tells the story of the beautiful aristocrat Lady Isabel Vane who, as a result of a momentary madness, leaves her husband Archibald Carlyle and her beloved children for an affair with the weak and wicked Francis Leaveson. Swiftly abandoned by Leaveson in France, and hideously disfigured by a railway accident in which she has been reported dead, Lady Isabel returns to East Lynne to take up the position of governess to her own children. Disguised by her facial scars and the curious costume she adopts, Vane is able to live undetected in the home where once she was mistress. That position is now taken by Barbara Hare, Carlyle's second wife, a model of genteel virtue. Fair where Isabel is dark, faithful where she has been flighty, maternal where she was sexual, Barbara represents the ideal of English motherhood from which the governess has fallen, the Madonna to Isabel's Whore. Significantly, there is only space for the two women in the book as long as they continue to embody these polarities. Once Lady Isabel has been recognised and forgiven by Carlyle, she is no longer required to live out the darker side of female nature, and her harrowing deathbed scene effectively brings the narrative swiftly to a close.

While *East Lynne* stays just this side of melodrama, rooting itself in a recognisable social landscape, *Uncle Silas*, the 1864 novel by Sheridan Le Fanu, represents a flight into the fantastic.[12] Foisted on the motherless Maud Ruthyn by her remote father, Madame de la Rougierre embodies the worst qualities associated with Frenchness or, more particularly, with French governesses. She drinks, lies, uses rouge, wears a wig and steals from her pupil. Worst of all, she doesn't speak English. Within the text she is paired with Maud's fifty-year-old cousin, Lady Knollys. While by no means a pasteboard version of virtue, Lady Knollys embodies the more attractive qualities associated with English gentility. Kind, unpretentious, and completely lacking in guile, she acts as protectress to Maud, warning her against the sinister de la Rougierre, who turns out to be involved in a plot to murder her pupil.

By 1864 the passage of the governess through every type of novel and to every literary end was virtually complete, although she continued to turn up as late as 1907-9, when she appeared in

Henry James' *The Turn of the Screw*.[13] From being the barely-named shadow of the English gentlewoman in Emma, she became the model of genteel virtue to which every lady should aspire in *Amy Herbert*. In *Jane Eyre* she was used to explore the social and intellectual limitations laid upon all bourgeois women, while in *Vanity Fair* her function was to point up the moral feebleness of the existing social order. In *East Lynne* she served as a dreadful warning to those English gentlewomen who failed to live up to the moral responsibilities attendant upon their social position, while in *Uncle Silas* she was the embodiment of evil which threatened the well-being of the genteel Christian home.

The problem remains, however, as to what the fictional governess can be assumed to tell us about the historical figure upon which she is based. The fact that many of the authors of these novels had direct personal experience of the schoolroom only reinforces the confusion about where documentary ends and fantasy begins.[14] Even today, at the end of the twentieth century, our perceptions of the Victorian governess are based on nothing more solid than hazy recollections of *Jane Eyre* and *Vanity Fair*. Yet the fact remains that few of the 25,000 women who were working in the home schoolroom in the middle of the century would have recognised themselves from the fiction of the day. Unlike Jane and Becky the governess seldom married into her employer's family; unlike Emily Morton she did not often find herself accused of causing her pupil's death; unlike Madame de la Rougierre it was unusual for her to embark upon murder and, unlike Isabel Vane, she was not frequently called upon to don an elaborate disguise. In short, the reality of the governess' life was at once more prosaic and more complex than anything experienced by her fictional counterpart. It is to that reality which we must now turn.

2

A Matter of Necessity

Every miss must grind a waltz, daub a piece of paper and chatter bad French. As a matter of necessity, then, they must have a governess.

Anon., *Fraser's Magazine* (1844)

The wealthiest class, as a rule, do not send their daughters to school.

Report of the Schools Inquiry Commission (1867-68)

While the governess was not a new figure in the British social landscape – the aristocracy had been using her services since medieval days – her employment by middle-class families dated back only to the end of the eighteenth century. Her appearance at their table was a direct consequence of the increased wealth of the nation, epitomised by the success of industrialists and financiers, but shared by a growing middle class. As men began to move away from direct participation in the factory and the counting house, their families started to live a life which was increasingly refined and polite. Industrial production no longer centred on the family-run business, shifting instead to larger factories to which labourers walked daily. Whilst a manager – often the owner's son – might continue to live in accommodation adjoining the business, the rest of the family was likely to move out to a residence on the edge of town.[1] In the new suburbs of England's towns and cities, pseudo-rustic villas sprang up complete with landscaped gardens and thick privet hedges. A few very rich families actually bought estates out in the country, setting themselves up as full-scale landowners living off the rents from tenanted farms. More common was the practice of buying a country house with some recreational land attached.[2]

As the richer members of the urban middle class began to make a

11

bid for the moral, political and intellectual leadership of the country they chose to graft certain aspects of the ruling culture on to their own. One of the most significant markers in this process was the way in which the terms 'lady' and 'gentleman' were revised and expanded to accommodate their aspirations. For centuries these terms had been understood to refer to those who had been born into the landed classes and could claim to be of gentle birth. Implicit in this definition was the assumption that social status was immutable, even though during the seventeenth and eighteenth centuries successful money men had acquired titles, younger sons of the gentry had entered commerce and the professions, while the daughters of rich merchants had long provided a source of capital for the aristocracy.[3] Nonetheless the definition of gentility as it stood at the end of the eighteenth century excluded the vast majority of the newly wealthy whose fathers had been men of business, yet whose polished lifestyle was ample qualification, so they felt, for the title of 'gentleman'. It was to accommodate these men that the definition of gentility was expanded so that it became something which could be earned by professional success and displayed through attention to dress, speech and behaviour.

It was the public realm which offered the best opportunity for dissolving tension between these genteel aspirations and a bourgeois inheritance which celebrated work as an essential component of manliness. While the aristocrat continued to live on rents and other forms of assured income, the middle-class man was able to enter one of the newly reformed professions which allowed him a field of endeavour while apparently removing him from the cut and thrust of the market place. No longer in the service of one or two gentry families, the lawyer or doctor drew his clients from the section of society from which he himself came. At the same time, he distanced himself from any sugestion of financial dependency upon them by claiming either a fixed salary or a non-negotiable fee.[4] This, in turn, smoothed the way for mixing and inter-marriage with the gentry. As Matthew Arnold observed, 'in no country . . . do the professions so naturally and generally share the cast of ideas of the aristocracy as in England'.[5] Wealthy lawyers, by virtue of their apparent distance from the money-making process, were particularly acceptable to the landed classes as neighbours, friends and even in-laws.[6]

Yet while the successful professional man could achieve the status of a gentleman through work, the opposite was increasingly true of his wife and daughters, as Mrs Sarah Ellis pointed out in her 1839 conduct manual, *The Women of England*:

gentlemen may employ their hours of business in almost any degrading occupation and, if they but have the means of supporting a respectable establishment at home, may be gentlemen still; while, if a lady but touch any article, no matter how delicate, in the way of trade, she loses caste and ceases to be a lady.[7]

Now that the workplace was usually quite separate from the home, women were no longer called upon to help out in the family business as secretaries, book-keepers or shop assistants. While this shift was a direct response to changing economic conditions, the redundancy of middle-class female labour soon became enshrined as an article of faith in the new evangelical morality which swept British homes during the last decades of the eighteenth century and was taken up by a broad band of the middle and working classes throughout the Victorian period. Writers like Sarah Ellis and her predecessor Hannah More insisted that there were essential differences in the intellectual, emotional and spiritual natures of men and women and that these differences needed to be acknowledged in the organisation of their daily lives.[8] While men were to sally forth into the market place, wresting an income from the economic hurly-burly, women were to remain at home, creating an oasis of domestic comfort where sons and husbands could refresh themselves before returning to the fray. Female economic dependence upon men was ensured by a pattern of inheritance which decreed that while boys might inherit active capital, girls were to be left money either in the form of a marriage settlement or that of a trust to be administered by a male relative. By 1830 the middle-class home had become a female domain, a power-house of moral virtue, the chief purpose of which was to absolve the capitalist world beyond the front door from the sins of greed, envy and lust.

No longer permitted to participate in the family business, women faced a further ban on labour within the home itself. Service areas such as the kitchen, pantry and servants' quarters were tucked away out of sight, as if to emphasise that the ladies of the house now had little direct involvement in the mundane, tiring and sometimes dirty activities which went on there. From the turn of the nineteenth century, the employment of a female servant had become an important qualification for any family which wished to consider itself middle-class, and from the 1850s an increasing number of specialist domestics – parlourmaids, cooks, housemaids and, for the wealthy, footmen – were to be found in bourgeois homes.[9] Significantly, the first servant to be hired was usually a nursemaid to help with small children: by the 1850s the wiping of small noses had become an unacceptable task for any woman who sought to observe these social codes.

Not that the leisured lady was necessarily idle. The diary of a fifteen-year-old clergyman's daughter, Emily Shore, for the year 1833 describes a round of constant activity: there were calls to pay on neighbours, visitors to entertain and younger siblings to supervise.[10] Yet the fact remained that all these activities, by virtue of being unpaid, sent a message to the world about the ability of the master of the house to support a clutch of economically unproductive women. More than this, these women consumed profit in the form of the goods and services with which they furnished their surroundings. By creating a suitably luxurious establishment complete with coffee, wine, pianos, carriages, holidays, carpets and servants – a panoply which twentieth century historians have dubbed 'the paraphernalia of gentility'[11] – a woman was making a statement to the world about her husband's credit. She herself became a status symbol, dressing in a series of elaborate and expensive outfits. The point about a fashion such as the crinoline was not simply that it proclaimed the wearer (or rather her husband or father) to be rich enough to afford yards of expensive material, but that, by virtue of its cumbersome dimensions, it prevented her performing any practical activity around the house. Increasingly specialised types of clothing not only suggested that the lady of leisure employed someone else to keep her wardrobe clean and mended, but that she had sufficient time at her disposal to wriggle in and out of three or four outfits every day.[12]

As well as becoming a site for the display of financial wealth, the female body also became the place where unruly desires of all kinds were contained and subdued. The Victorian lady learned from an early age how to refine both her accent and the contents of her speech, how to keep herself and her clothing scrupulously clean (with the help of others), how to move gracefully, sing sweetly and eat very little in public. She was held to have very little interest in sexual intercourse, although part of being a good wife involved allowing her body to be used as the ever-available recipient of her husband's sperm. It was motherhood, rather than marriage itself, which was represented by doctors and moralists alike as the most valuable and pleasurable component of female experience. While the Victorian lady was required to develop her reading and expertise in certain subject areas, she was to shy away from anything which might suggest that she was a blue-stocking.[13] As the moral (though never the spiritual) guardian of men, her behaviour was to be patterned along a highly conventional notion of the good. Ladies did not lie, swear, steal or read other peoples' letters over their shoulders.

The penalties for those who refused or were unable to live out these ideals were harsh. The woman who dared to express sexual desire, who failed to have children, who preferred reading to afternoon calls, who showed signs of courage and independence, was swiftly condemned by a whole range of experts as 'unnatural'. Thus for the medical man the rebellious woman was a victim of a whole host of gynaecological problems from 'hysteria dependent on a morbid state of the uterine system' to self-abuse;[14] for the lawyer she might be a dangerous lunatic whose husband had every right to keep her locked up in an asylum for years; for the evangelical moralist she was, quite simply, on her way to hell. All these interpretations consigned the unconventional woman to a social and sexual wilderness. It was here, in an urban landscape depicted by the popular art of the day, that the unregulated female sexuality of the prostitute, factory girl and madwoman simmered in unspeakable degradation. In the place of well-kept homes and pink-cheeked children could be found only hovels of dirt and decay.[15]

So great was the economic power and social prestige of the middle class that by 1850 its particular brand of gentility, and especially its ideal of ladyhood, had started to rub off on those social groups above and below. Definitions of female nature incorporated many of the prescriptions of moral and social behaviour just noted, yet sought to apply them to all women of whatever class or, indeed, country. Since the late eighteenth century, the shift associated with the evangelical revival had gone a long way towards purging aristocratic life of its concentration on public display and had encouraged the wives and daughters of the nobility and gentry to concern themselves with domestic and private affairs. Supervising the servants, checking the accounts, visiting the poor were all duties which the upper-class woman no longer felt beneath her. Working-class women, meanwhile, especially those no longer directly involved in paid labour outside the home, also came under pressure to conform, as far as possible, to an ideal of genteel femininity. While there can be no doubt that the task of cooking and cleaning for a household of ten without paid domestic assistance left little time or energy for social niceties, women of this kind still wished to be thought ladylike. Keeping oneself clean, attending church or chapel, avoiding bad language or intoxicating liquor were all ways of demonstrating respectability, particularly in relation to the class immediately below one's own. In this way the ideal of ladyhood came increasingly to be used as the measure against which the moral and social worth of all women, of whatever social or economic class, would be judged.

These changes in social attitudes and ideals set in motion a reassessment of how middle-class children were to be educated for their new roles and responsibilities. From the mid eighteenth century, Dissenting academies had provided the sons of nonconformists with an education which prepared them for a life spent at the head of the family business.[16] Science and technical subjects were emphasised over the classical curriculum which predominated at the older grammar and public schools, where the sons of gentlemen were prepared for entry to the ancient universities. As the subsequent generations of successful business families pulled away from direct involvement in the family firm, they too began to require an education that would fit them for their new role as gentlemen.

From the 1840s the public schools provided a veneer of gentility for those boys not born into the landed classes.[17] At the newer institutions, such as Marlborough or Wellington, a businessman's son might learn all he needed to take his place in polite society. Although the introduction of entrance examinations by the universities, the professions and the civil and military services obliged public schools to raise their academic standards, any attempt to give a higher profile to science on the syllabus was severely resisted, not least by parents who were unwilling to let their sons study anything which might equip them for a life in commerce. They were well aware that an intimate knowledge of Latin, Greek and the cultures they represented remained the essential qualification for Law, the Church and even Medicine. When a technocrat like Isambard Kingdom Brunel sent his sons to Harrow he did not expect them to be taught how to build bridges. On the contrary, parents were clear about what they expected a public-school education to give their boys: Homer, Euclid, and the chance to make the right sort of friends.

In the meantime the education of girls was undergoing a parallel shift. Before 1830 the daughters of even quite substantial tradesmen and businessmen were expected to help their mothers with the running of the household, learning in the process how to 'work, cook and housekeep to perfection'.[18] Basic literacy and numeracy were taught either by the mother herself or by an elder sister or other female relative.[19] A nearby day-school might provide a year or two's more systematic instruction, although attendance might be interrupted at any point if the girl was needed at home – perhaps because a new baby had arrived or a maidservant had left without being replaced. Only those girls who were lucky enough to have fathers, frequently clergymen, who kept large libraries found themselves embarking on an education, sometimes shared with their brothers, which was both wide-ranging and rigorous. Such was the experience of Emily Shore, who was taught Latin and Greek by her clergyman father and English and history by her mother. In addition, she managed to master zoology, botany and geology with the help of her father's textbooks and a home-made microscope.[20] Emily Shore was an exception: the vast majority of girls in the early nineteenth century were unlikely to get much beyond the Three Rs.

The trend for wealthy households to employ more domestic servants meant that there no longer seemed any point in teaching daughters how to cook and clean: indeed to do so would be to cast doubt on their ability to marry a man who could provide them with a sufficiently large establishment. Far more suitable in the circumstances was an education devoted to attracting a solvent husband. Rather than learning domestic skills from her mother, the genteel girl of the 1830s and beyond was to acquire a set of accomplishments which included the ability to speak French and perhaps Italian, play the piano, dance and show a proficiency in fancy needlework. At the age of eighteen she was expected to take her place in her parents' social circle, using her carefully acquired sophistication as bait to land a husband from the pool of available young men. In *Vanity Fair* William Thackeray spelled out the part that accomplishments played in the competitive business of catching a man:

> What causes . . . [young people] to labour at pianoforte sonatas, and to learn four songs from a fashionable master at a guinea a lesson, and to play the harp if they have handsome arms and neat elbows, and to wear Lincoln Green toxophilite hats and feathers, but that they may bring down some 'desirable' young man with those killing bows and arrows of theirs?[21]

The question remained of how and where a girl was to acquire these accomplishments. Newly genteel mothers could no longer teach their own children for fear of losing caste and, in any case, were unlikely to be sufficiently prepared to impart an elaborate syllabus. The most obvious solution was to use the services of one of the small boarding schools which had been a feature of the English landscape from the mid eighteenth century. Unlike the later generation of academic boarding schools which came into being from the 1870s, these schools aimed to take girls for no more than a couple of years during their mid teens. The task of an institution such as this was to 'finish' their pupils by equipping them with the social gloss that would allow them to take their place in their parents' drawing-room. Rather than a standardised syllabus with regular examinations, there was continuous instruction in modern languages, music, dancing and painting. While general moral and social supervision was provided by resident female mistresses, tuition in more specialist subjects was given by visiting masters whose fees varied with their reputation. Girls who had received all their education at home in the country were particularly likely to be sent to boarding schools in the larger spa towns so that they might benefit from the advanced instruction these men could offer.

With their dozen or so pupils, these ladies' seminaries were felt to cultivate genteel femininity in the same way as the refined household on which they were modelled.[22] The school itself would be housed in the lady proprietress' own home, the drawing-room often doubling as the classroom. The assistant mistresses – typically, there might be one or two – acted as elder sisters or aunts to their pupils: when the novelist and advice writer Elizabeth Sewell and her sisters started a school on the Isle of Wight, their pupils referred to the trio as 'Aunts Elizabeth, Ellen and Emma'.[23] Adolescent insurbordination was hardly a problem in a community where ties of personal affection bound the inhabitants in mutual obligation. On being asked how she dealt with disruptive pupils, one lady proprietress replied, 'I say that I don't love them, that is always enough'.[24]

Giving evidence to the 1867-68 Schools Inquiry Commission, the educational reformer Emily Davies was dismissive about the quality and quantity of instruction on offer at these institutions: 'they are obliged to profess French and music, and I do not think they do much besides'.[25] The commission found that while advances had been made in the quality of schooling available to working-class children of either sex, as well as to middle-class boys, as far as middle-class girls were concerned, standards had improved little from the eighteenth century and may even have been falling. At the vast majority of these institutions, the teaching of etiquette and accomplishments took precedence over academic subjects, although the more expensive schools did make some effort to teach history, literature, geography, drawing and general knowledge. Even here, however, the instruction could be patchy. In the 1820s Elizabeth and Ellen Sewell were sent to boarding school in Bath, specifically so that they might have the benefit of advanced tuition. Elizabeth Sewell later reported in her autobiography:

> We were not well taught at this Bath school. The French master was an indifferent one, and professed to teach Italian also which I question if he was at all competent to do. We had a second-rate dancing mistress, a fairly good sentimental singing master (who showed his grief for his child's death by playing psalm tunes on the piano in the short interval between the lessons to the several pupils), a very inferior drawing master, whose artistic talent was not at all equal to that of Miss Aldridge herself; and a music master with a great reputation, a violent temper, and an amount of conceit and vanity which made him tell us that he slept in white kid gloves to keep his hands white . . . As to the more essential subjects of instruction, we were not bound by strict laws. We had a master for arithmetic and were carefully taught; but the lessons we were expected to learn by heart were repeated according to the sense and not the exact words, and those who were quick got them up in a few minutes, said them fairly well, and forgot them immediately afterwards.[26]

Academic incompetence was only one of the reasons why boarding schools provided a less than satisfactory solution to the problem of how young ladies were to be educated. Fear of the social mix that might be represented by the other pupils attending the school prevented well-heeled parents keeping their daughters there longer than was necessary. From the 1820s a craze for ornamental education swept through the entire ranks of the middle class, with the result that even the daughters of shopkeepers were sent away for a year or two to pick up a smattering of French and good manners. The scorn of conservative commentators was aimed particularly at farmers' daughters who, returning home from a stint at boarding school, spurned the delights of butter-making in favour of embroidery and afternoon tea with their friends.[27] Behind such criticism lay the paradoxical fear that once able but low-born girls were given an ornamental education, it would be impossible to tell who was a lady and who was not. As it turned out, worries about the type of girl that might be encountered at these schools were exaggerated, since the variation in fees charged by different establishments ensured a high degree of self-selection on the basis of wealth, if not of class. Headmistresses were only too aware of the need to generate as high a social tone as possible: Miss

Crooke, who ran a school during the 1820s and professed to be a radical in politics, nonetheless took great pains to prevent pupils from different backgrounds developing 'undesirable intimacy' by insisting that these little girls should refer to each other as Miss Smith, Miss Jones and so forth.[28]

Other worries about sending girls away to be educated focused on the fact that even the most home-like school could not provide the close moral supervision of the genteel Christian household. Those unfortunate orphans who were sent to boarding schools for up to ten years were often, like Jane Eyre at Lowood, obliged to stay on in the holidays since they had no other place to go. Deprived of a mother's guiding hand, these girls were felt to have suffered irreparable moral damage. There was a perception that boarding schools constituted a breeding ground for the 'bad habit' of masturbation which might be passed on from girl to girl in the large shared bedrooms (and beds) which were a feature of these establishments.[29] There was a feeling, too, that insufficient time was allowed for the saying of private prayers. Prudence Hackworth, headmistress of a school in Keswick during the 1850s, reported how one of her young teachers, Miss Smith:

> tells me she has been a pupil in two or three large schools, and complains very much of their laxity of morals particularly at Miss C.'s. She says she was perfectly miserable there. On the Sabbath Miss C. never came into the room where the young ladies sat, nor did the head teacher, and the young ladies amused themselves in munching sweets or in playing with each other and made such a noise that she could not read to profit.[30]

This criticism of girls' boarding schools was fed by a sense that whereas a boy needed to be hardened against the corruption he would encounter in the outside world by being sent to *public* school, his sister was a delicate flower best cultivated in a devout home environment. Christian teaching, reiterated in pulpits across the land, made the middle-class mother believe that it was her particular vocation to guide her daughters in their journey towards confirmation and first communion.[31] The idea of a stranger, a schoolteacher, fulfilling this function was abhorrent.

The theory and practice of genteel female education in the first decades of the nineteenth century was marked by a deepening tension. As women increasingly derived their social and moral power from exclusive association with the domestic sphere, it became clear that the only satisfactory place to educate girls was at home. Yet this was also the time when women were coming under pressure to give up the domestic labour – including responsibility for the rearing of children – which had formed a large part of their grandmothers' lives. Even if teaching one's daughters had not now been considered *infra dig*, many women would have found themselves unequal to the task of instructing in the new range of female accomplishments.[32] The aristocracy had for centuries dealt with this problem by using the services of a resident female teacher to relieve the mistress of the house of her pedagogic duties.[33] Chosen as much for her moral as her intellectual qualities, the governess was responsible for the total welfare of her young charges. While she was competent to instruct in a wide range of academic subjects, her main task was to provide the round-the-clock moral and social supervision that her employer was unable to supply. Far from being a mere teacher or instructress, her role had often been that of moral guide and sympathetic older friend. Since ladyhood could only be absorbed from a suitably refined home environment, it was essential that the governess, as stand-in for her pupils' mother, should be a gentlewoman. For that reason she was most likely to be either the daughter of a local clergyman, or perhaps a cousin or niece on the edge of the family network. In return, she seems to have been regarded with consideration by her employers, receiving a salary and conditions of employment which were far from mean: for instance, Selina Trimmer, who was governess to the daughters of the Duchess of Devonshire during the last two decades of the eighteenth century, was said to have been 'treated in every respect like one of the young Lady Cavendishes'.[34]

From the turn of the nineteenth century the richest members of the middle class began to copy the gentry's custom of employing governesses to educate its daughters. For many of these families one of the most important functions of the governess was to show off their own wealth and social prestige.[35] Her presence in their midst was proof that the lady of the house could afford to absent herself from even the least degrading aspect of womanhood and dedicate herself instead to social duties and charitable pursuits. Yet the situation was not without its tensions. While aristocratic families had long since evolved codes for dealing with the anomaly of a gentlewoman who was also an employee, the middle-class woman had no such accumulated custom upon which to draw. It was to help her negotiate a situation entirely new to her that a stream of manuals with titles such as *The Relative Social Position of Mothers and Governesses,*

Governess Life: Its Trials, Duties, and Encouragements and *Observations on Governesses* appeared on the market during the 1840s.[36] Such texts were evidence that a new governess-employing class, not to mention a new class of governesses, had come into existence.

Just what sort of family employed a governess for its daughters? At first glance it needed to be rich, since the governess was one of the last additions that an aspiring family would make to its staff, completing a household already serviced by at least three, but usually five or more, domestic servants. Although patterns varied, a typical domestic staff in one of these households might consist of a cook, two housemaids, a nurse and a footman. According to Mrs Beeton's 1861 manual, *Book of Household Management*, such a staff was affordable by those households with an income of at least £1,000 – rich merchants, gentry and successful professional men.[37] More information about the occupations of those men who in 1861 were employing a governess for their daughters may be found in Table 1 (below, p. 205).[38] According to the census enumerators' handbooks for that year, in well-heeled metropolitan Paddington, thirty-three out of a total of a 148 governess-employing households were headed by merchants, eleven by lawyers, and seven were in the army or navy. In Edgbaston, a smart suburb of industrial Birmingham, governesses were found exclusively in the homes of manufacturers, merchants and wealthy tradesmen. In agricultural Crediton, as might be expected, governesses were employed in households headed by farmers, gentry and clergy.

The census of 1861 lists 24,770 governesses living in England and Wales.[39] It seems fair to assume that the gentry and aristocracy – which accounted for around 50,000 households in 1867 – would have had first claim on the available pool of governesses.[40] If it is estimated that one quarter of these families had daughters between the ages of five and eighteen, this leaves twelve thousand governesses to service the entire middle class, suggesting again that it was only the very wealthiest who employed a resident teacher for their daughters.[41] Confirmation comes from the fact that in 1861 the highest concentration of governesses in relation to girls aged between five and twenty in the population was to be found in the agricultural shires where the gentry lived, as well as in the counties which were close enough to London to make them attractive to successful business and professional men.[42]

Yet those commentators who made a living writing for the scores self employed widowers 5

e-brow periodicals that lined the Victorian newstands were that the practice of employing a governess was no longer confined to the very wealthy, but had spread to some very modest homes indeed:

> Mothers in frugal parsonages have learned to think that their girls must be taught. The wives of country apothecaries and lawyers will give their girls the shreds and patches of those acquirements which become the daughters of wealthy patients and clients. Every miss must grind a waltz, daub a piece of paper and chatter bad French. As a matter of necessity, then, they must have a governess.[43]

The puzzle is whether this jibe was any more than a piece of polemic, fuelled by the same social insecurity that marked attitudes towards tenant farmers' daughters going off to boarding school, or whether it really was the case that country apothecaries and lawyers hired governesses for their daughters. A glance at the household accounts suggests that the commentators may have based their observations on more than popular prejudice. During the 1860s the typical annual boarding school fee in Bath was £70 to £80,[44] while a governess might cost as little as £25 a year. With three girls to raise, employing a resident teacher for a few years to finish an education begun at a cheaper local day school might make sound financial sense. In her book *How Girls Should be Educated* Jane Loudon put her finger on the mixture of pragmatism and idealism which might lie behind such a decision when she maintained that a governess was 'the safest, the healthiest, the pleasantest, the most effectual, and cheapest form of education'.[45]

An altogether more urgent reason for a family of modest means to hire a governess was to replace an absent mother. The 1861 census enumerators' handbooks for Paddington reveal that, of the six tradesmen employing a governess for their daughters, five were widowers. It was these men, drapers and jewellers, who used the governess much as single women had been used for centuries – as a way of plugging a gap in the household's available personnel. In these modest homes the governess was not simply a teacher, but a housekeeper, stepmother and even parlourmaid rolled in to one. Those widowers who had failed to marry again, and who had no female relative living nearby, were obliged to pay a woman to live *en famille* to carry out the duties formerly performed by their wives. A typical instance in Paddington was Andrew Campbell, a jeweller of Woodfield Terrace who employed forty-eight year old Eliza Morris to look after his three young daughters and two sons.[46]

The Campbell household had in addition two general servants. It is difficult to believe that Eliza Morris did not combine her schoolroom duties with a more general responsibility for the smooth running of this little household.

A further reason why the governess appeared in homes which were far from wealthy was suggested by the Bishop of Bath and Wells in evidence to the Schools Inquiry Commission of 1867-68: he suggested that farmers in his diocese were increasingly employing governesses because of the lack of good cheap schools in their sparsely populated counties.[47] Given that up until the 1860s there were women prepared to work for nothing more than board and lodging, it may have been the case that comparatively modest families took advantage of this buyer's market: those Crediton farmers who employed governesses, for instance, had average holdings of only 200 acres and were clearly far from being members of the gentry. Their households were still organised on a pre-industrial scale, with assorted family members, farm workers and domestic servants living under one roof and contributing their labour without too much concern for social distinction. Throughout the seventeenth and eighteenth centuries farming families had sent their children to work as servants in neighbouring households, a custom which continued into the nineteenth century in the form of sending girls out as governesses. Within the sprawling set-up of a small farming household it would have been comparatively easy to find an extra bed and a place at table for a local girl able to combine teaching the children their letters with helping out at harvest time. For instance, William Wreford of West Southcott farmed 150 acres and employed three men to help him.[48] He and his wife had four daughters of ten, eight, five and two and, in addition, Wreford's mother shared their accommodation. Only one domestic servant was employed in the house, although three farm labourers boarded with the family. Into this tangle of a household came a seventeen-year-old local girl called Jessie Austin, who described herself to the census enumerator as 'governess' but whose duties must surely have spread beyond the schoolroom.

Families like the Wrefords had been used for centuries to incorporating extra household members; those such as the Blyth family of Paddington were coping with a situation that was entirely new to them. At 24 Hyde Park Gardens lived merchant James Blyth, his wife, four daughters, one son and a governess, thirty-seven-year-old Charlotte Williams. The household was serviced by a staff of nine, comprising a butler, footman, nurse, two lady's maids, a kitchen maid, scullery maid, cook and housemaid.[49] It was in households like these, the opulent homes of bankers, barristers and brewers, that the ambiguities, strains and tensions generated by the governess were most clearly set in play. For while the governess represented a potent status symbol to the wealthiest sections of the middle class, she also embodied a delicate unpicking of those codes of bourgeois gentility on which it partly based its claims to power. On the one hand, the urban middle class constituted that section of the population which had benefited most spectacularly from Britain's shift from a traditional to a market economy and from the transition of the personal relationship of master and man to the limited contractual obligations which existed between employer and employee. On the other hand, these were also the people who had invested most in emphasising the fact that their daughter's teacher, of necessity a perfect lady, was to be treated as a family member in a manner which reproduced the labour arrangements of an eighteenth-century country house. More crucially, the governess' presence in a wealthy middle-class household unsettled the assumed relationship between genteel femininity and a life of leisure. For if, as her entry on the family's pay roll suggested, not all ladies were leisured, then might it not also follow that not all leisured women were necessarily ladies? For the newly genteel woman who based her claims to ladyhood less on her pedigree than on the spectacular non-productivity of her body and home, this represented a challenge to all that she held most dear.

3

Take a Lady

Take a lady, in every meaning of the word, born and bred, and let
her father pass through the gazette, and she wants nothing more to
suit our highest *beau ideal* of a guide and instructress to our children.

Lady Eastlake, *Quarterly Review* (1848)

What a woman *is*, not what she *knows*, is the test by which a governess
should be chosen.

Mary Maurice, *Governess Life* (1849)

The social and economic conditions which created a new governess-
employing class in the first half of the nineteenth century also
produced a pool of labour to satisfy (and, indeed, to exceed)
the demand for genteel home teachers. While Britain's swell into
affluence brought prosperity to the middle class as a whole, individual fortunes could be lost as quickly as they had been made,
bringing even the wealthiest to overnight destitution. In an article
which appeared in 1858 in the first issue of the feminist periodical,
the *English Woman's Journal*, the editor Bessie Rayner Parkes declared
that

> while *all* our lady readers have received instruction from some class
> of governess, there is probably not one who has not also some relative
> or cherished friend either actually engaged in teaching, or having
> formerly been so engaged ... from the highest to the lowest rank
> in which a liberal education is bestowed, we shall find some cousin
> or friend who is a governess.[1]

It was a testimony to the insecurity of the times that Parkes, writing
for a social and economic elite, could assert without fear of offence
that every one of her readers would have 'some relative or cherished

27

friend' who had been driven into the schoolroom. Close to the surface of her text lay the warning that this fate might all too soon become the reader's own. Just as the ancient Romans etched skeletons on the bottom of their drinking cups to remind them of their own mortality, so the governess' hovering presence on the edges of middle-class society acted as a warning that the most glittering of debuts in the drawing room could end in the shabby anonymity of the schoolroom.

The occupations of governesses' fathers most frequently mentioned in the 1848 Report of the Board of Management of the Governesses' Benevolent Institution (hereafter the GBI), a charitable body set up in 1843, were, in descending order, merchant, surgeon, military or naval officer, civil/government servant, solicitor and clergyman.[2] It was the daughters of men such as these who had been brought up in anticipation of a life of leisure, an expectation which, for a variety of reasons, their fathers had been unable to fulfil. Some men were doubtless incompetent or unlucky in their professional lives, while others found themselves falling foul of a culture which required lavish expenditure in order to prove personal and public worth – a phenomenon which one commentator dubbed 'the canker of Gentility'.[3] Others again were burdened with the support of an unusually large number of daughters: while sons could be trained to support themselves from the age of sixteen, their sisters had to be maintained in leisure before being married off handsomely, if the whole family were not to lose caste. A man of modest means who was unlucky enough to produce a brood of seven girls could offer his daughters little beyond the near certainty that they would one day be responsible for their own support.

Those families which depended for their incomes on capital investment rather than the professional skills of their male members were no more secure: the high rate of banking and business failures between 1820 and 1850 meant that many found themselves sliding from prosperity to destitution overnight, especially in the years before the Limited Liability Act of 1855. Fraudulent 'men of business' also served to deprive women who had been left reasonably secure from enjoying their economic independence. Such was the case of Miss Mary C. whose sad life history was set out in the GBI's annual report for 1853: 'her father having entrusted his affairs to a relative, his property was dissipated, and he died broken-hearted, leaving six orphans. The same relative appropriated, as their guardian, the money which should have come to the children'.[4] In cases like these, where the family was 'reduced from extreme affluence to extreme distress',[5] there was no choice but to send the girls out as governesses immediately, regardless of whether they had finished their own education. On the other hand, the popular conception of the governess as a suddenly destitute girl plucked from her own schoolroom needs qualification: according to the 1861 census, only one in eight governesses was under the age of twenty.[6] More typical seems to have been the situation where a family experienced a slow trickling away of funds together with the gradual realisation that its daughters would one day be obliged to work for their living.[7]

The single most likely circumstance in which a middle-class girl found herself facing destitution was following the death of her father. Even those men who occupied the most prestigious posts during their lifetime could not necessarily expect a pension for their dependents after their death: in 1848 the GBI recorded the case of 'Miss Mary Ann G; Father, principal of the Interior Office, Bank of England; his income ceased with his life, and she became a Governess'.[8] The practice of insuring one's life, which became commonplace by the end of the century, was not widespread during this earlier period, although this was certainly not for want of public debate on the subject. Commentators as different as the statistician William Farr, the journalist Harriet Martineau, the novelist and headmistress Elizabeth Sewell, and the feminist campaigners Barbara Bodichon and Bessie Rayner Parkes were all agreed that if only fathers could be persuaded to take out life insurance 'it will be the brightest event in the history of the governess class'.[9] Yet even those cautious souls who followed this sound advice in an attempt to provide for their daughters could find themselves the victims of economic circumstances beyond their control. Many of the 500 or so life insurance offices which were established between 1800 and 1870 collapsed through bad luck or fraud, and it was not until the passage of the Life Assurance Companies Act of 1870 that a policy holder could be certain of reaping the rewards of his prudence.[10]

In addition there were a few unusual cases where the death of a mother, rather than a father, forced a middle-class girl into becoming self-supporting. Millicent Fawcett, a sister of Elizabeth Garrett Anderson, recalled in her autobiography the sad case of their cousin Rhoda, a clergyman's daughter from Derbyshire:

> Her mother had died in her early childhood, and after several years of widowhood her father had married again, and a fairly

rapid succession of babies appeared once more in Elton Rectory. The three children of the first marriage were almost by force of circumstances pushed out of the parent nest.[11]

As a result of her father's inability or reluctance to support two families, Rhoda was left with no option but to seek work as a governess.

As middle-class men tended not to marry before the age of thirty, yet often died before they reached fifty, young women scarcely out of their teens frequently found themselves in the position of chief breadwinner and turned to governessing to support not just themselves but a whole tribe of brothers, sisters and nieces. Those whose parents were still alive found themselves in an altogether more ambiguous position. Although they could ill afford it, parents urged their daughters not to 'go out' for fear that they would lose a status, particularly with regard to future marriage prospects, that could never be regained. Yet the knowledge that they were a financial burden on their families was enough to spur on conscientious women like Mary Smith to look for a job: 'I was now very anxious, and thought it my duty, being twenty years of age, to relieve my father altogether for the future count of any care on my account.'[12] Nearly fifty years later, in 1887, a young clergyman's daughter called May Pinhorn experienced that same burden of obligation towards the aunt and uncle who had brought her up:

This year I was really launched into the world with no experience of my own and no advice to guide me ... I was cool, cautious, and reserved, with an overwhelming sense of duty and responsibility and of the crying need that I should support myself, and so lighten the burden of poverty on my family ... My aunt and I set to work, during the Christmas holidays, to find a post ... and we were both worried by anxiety, for we knew there would be storms from my uncle if I were not soon launched into the life's business of bread winning. I was particularly indebted to him, for in addition, to all he did for me in my earlier days, he gave me £100 to help in the last part of my school life.[13]

At the opposite end of the spectrum, and even more pitiful, were the cases the GBI recorded of those women like Mrs Frances C. who had been forced into governessing at the age of thirty-five 'having been left with three children under four years of age quite unprovided for'.[14] In 1861, according to the census, one fifth of all governesses were over the age of forty and there were even forty-three women still working at the age of eighty or more.[15] To make matters worse, the older a woman was, the less likely she was to find a position which paid a reasonable salary. Twenty-five to thirty-five was perceived as being the optimum age for a governess, although in a buyer's market, employers could afford to be even more exacting: 'A lady told an agent she wanted a governess, not under twenty-eight, nor over thirty-two: we suppose her apprenticeship was to have been served elsewhere, and this lady wished for the quintessence of her powers.'[16]

Destitution was not, of course, the inevitable consequence of losing a father or a fortune. Marriage to a solvent man, the goal for which every middle-class girl had been educated, was still the most satisfactory solution to the problem of where and how to live. Yet the 1861 census revealed that the population comprised 1,053 women for every 1,000 men.[17] Not only were contemporaries dismayed by the fact that there was a pool of 'redundant' women unable to fulfil their destiny of marriage and motherhood but, on a practical level, it was now clear that some women were destined to remain unmarried all their life. Although there was really no way of telling, contemporaries were adamant that the causes of this gender imbalance – the tendency of professional men to marry late, the greater proportion of male to female middle-class emigrants – meant that a high proportion of 'redundant' women came from the professional classes. While it now appears that the number of 'excess' women was more evenly spread between the ages of ten and forty than the enumerators believed,[18] the overriding impression of distressed gentlewomen was still that of women who had failed to marry.

Yet even marriage was no guarantee against life's more uncertain aspects. The illnesses and financial disasters which befell fathers could just as easily happen to husbands. The situation was even more difficult if there were young children involved. A woman widowed at thirty might be obliged to board her children with relatives and return to governessing or, even more traumatically, to take it up for the first time. Out of seventy-four annuitants listed by the GBI in its 1853 report, seventeen were widows, of whom ten were specifically mentioned as having children.[19]

Lady [Elizabeth] Eastlake offered a succinct definition of the governess' assumed personal history when she declared:

> Take a lady, in every meaning of the word, born and bred, and let her father pass through the gazette, and she wants nothing more

to suit our highest *beau ideal* of a guide and instructress to our children.[20]

Those women who entered the schoolroom for quite different reasons attracted the most vitriolic scorn from Eastlake and her peers:

> Farmers and tradespeople are now educating their daughters for governesses as a mode of advancing them a step in life, and thus a number of underbred young women have crept into the profession who have brought down the value of salaries and interfered with the rights of those whose birth and misfortune leave them no other refuge.[21]

Quite how these farmers' and tradesmen's daughters intended to advance themselves was never spelt out. The census enumerators' handbooks reveal that nine out of the thirteen governesses employed by the Crediton farmers and millers were local women,[22] and it may simply have been the case that working as a governess in someone else's home represented a step up from doing the dairy work in one's own. Theresa McBride has described a pattern whereby domestic servants, returning to their native villages after fifteen years' employment in a middle-class urban household, used their noticeably refined manners and knowledge of how the other half lived to attract a prosperous tenant farmer or tradesman as a husband.[23] McBride's findings suggest the possibility that a country-born governess, returning to her own community after several years in the schoolroom of an urban professional family, may have found it easier to marry a man of higher social status than her father simply by virtue of having steered clear of farm work all her adult life. In this case her newly-acquired refinement and wider cultural references could only ease the way into an upwardly mobile marriage.

As far as governesses from London were concerned, the evidence from the 1861 census data for Paddington seems to support commentators' assertions that a certain number of women were attracted to the schoolroom 'for the sake of social advancement, just as men sometimes go into the Church or the army in order to become gentlemen by profession'.[24] Governesses who were found in the bosom of their own families, perhaps because they were unemployed or on holiday on the night the census enumerator came to call, included those whose fathers were coachmen and ticket collectors as well as the more usual surveyors and leaseholders.[25] It is important to remember that not all of these women were necessarily groomed for the schoolroom from an early age. A proportion of clerks and coachmen's daughters would have taken up governessing only once it became clear that their fathers were no longer able to support them in the leisure to which they had become accustomed. A draper's girl who had been sent away to boarding school before being brought home to sit and paint in the front parlour was likely to feel just as mortified at having to go out to work as the daughter of a once prosperous lawyer. Yet while such a woman considered herself to have lost caste irredeemably by entering the schoolroom, to conservative commentators she represented just one more member of the lower orders who, infected by an all-pervasive 'mania for gentility', was hell-bent on scrambling her way up the social ladder.

Bessie Rayner Parkes captured this sense of governessing as the site of two-directional social mobility when she spoke of 'a platform' on which two classes met, 'the one struggling up, the other drifting down'.[26] Unfortunately, it is impossible to be precise about the ratio of those governesses who were 'rising' to those who were 'falling'. One clue comes from Theresa McBride's calculation that about one third of British domestic servants during the nineteenth century could be said to be upwardly mobile, using the bait of recently-acquired refinement as well as substantial savings to find a husband of significantly higher social status.[27] Significantly, in 1860 Parkes herself estimated that one third of the women who had entered the newly-respectable trades and semi-professions, which she and her colleagues had worked to open up to middle-class women, could be said to be climbing up rather than slipping down the social ladder.[28] Lacking more concrete evidence, the best guess that can be made is that at least a substantial minority of the total governess body was socially ascendant during the middle decades of the century.

When Annabella and Barbara Carlisle found themselves destitute on the death of their father, the family lawyer tried his hardest to persuade them against the 'last and most wretched hope of earning your living as governesses . . .'[29] Likewise when Caroline Helstone, one of the heroines of Charlotte Brontë's 1849 novel, *Shirley*, suggested to her uncle and guardian that she might look for a situation as governess, she met with a horrified refusal which spoke eloquently of the way in which middle-class women were responsible for reflecting and confirming the status of their male relatives: 'While I live, you shall not turn out as a governess, Caroline. I will not have it said that my niece is a governess.'[30] It was a phenomenon which Harriet Martineau, herself the daughter of a bankrupt businessman and sister of a governess, understood only too well:

> Wherever we go among parents of the middle class, we find the one gnawing anxiety which abides in their hearts is the dread of their daughters 'having to go out as governesses'. 'Anything but that!' says the father, when talking confidentially after his day's work at the office, or the mill, or the counting-house, or in going the rounds of his patients. 'Anything but that!' sighs the mother, as she thinks of her own girls placed and treated as she has seen so many.[31]

'Anything but that', did not, in fact, leave much. As ideas about who and what was genteel began to harden from the beginning of the century, the range of work open to middle-class women dwindled to almost nothing. Whereas once they had worked as hairdressers, midwives and pharmacists, without any loss of respectability, the straining towards a genteel lifestyle, even by those who would never have the money to achieve it, meant that by the beginning of the nineteenth century a woman following any of these trades would have found herself *declassée*. In any case, she no longer had the practical training to allow her to earn her living in this, or any other, way. Educated for the domestic sphere, her only real option was to seek a space in someone else's household: Elizabeth Ham was typical in characterising her search for work as a governess during 1819 as 'my wearing search for a *home*' [my italics].[32]

Ham's best chance of finding that home lay in securing bed and board with some financially secure family member, most likely a brother or married sister. As the sprawling kin networks of earlier centuries moved into a tighter nuclear form, families found themselves lacking members to undertake certain key tasks; a single woman might step in to fill the gap, working as an unpaid servant yet still retaining her status as a lady. A family which had lost a mother might provide a warm welcome for an aunt who was prepared to fill the vacant role. Teaching nephews and nieces was another obvious way of earning one's keep: John Ruskin remembered how, as a boy, his young orphaned cousin May, 'took somewhat of a governess position toward me'.[33] Then again, single women frequently kept house for their bachelor brothers, although, as Mary Smith noted wryly, this frequently turned out to be a temporary solution, 'as is the case with women, even the most capable and energetic, the small event of my brother's marrying had stranded me without occupation'.[34]

Another alternative was to try and find some way of making a living within the privacy of one's own home, by marketing an existing skill or talent. All middle-class women, indeed all women, were taught to sew as part of their basic education and the columns of magazines like the *Englishwoman's Domestic Magazine* were flooded with notices throughout the 1850s and 1860s offering homemade lampshades and collars for sale.[35] Even so, this miserably paid work could not be counted on to provide the means of support for anything but the most wretched style of living. Writing – both journalism and fiction – was the other possibility for a few women: it satisfied the essential criterion in that it could be carried out at home, and no one need be any the wiser if the work were signed simply 'by a Lady'. Three of the leading writers on female education during the first half of the Victorian period – Sarah Ellis, Anna Jameson and Elizabeth Sewell – had all started their working lives as governesses or schoolkeepers before moving on to this more congenial and profitable way of supporting themselves.[36]

The two activities for which all women were deemed to be naturally suited were nursing and teaching. Looking after a sick relative was an entirely proper occupation for a lady, but it was to take the reforming work of Florence Nightingale before paid hospital work could even be contemplated as fit for respectable women.[37] Teaching was a skill which built on the experience which so many middle-class women had gained through instructing younger sisters or the local poor. Schoolteaching, however, presented only limited opportunities. Elementary schools which catered for the working class would not be viewed as a suitable place of employment for middle-class women until the end of the century.[38] Posts in genteel boarding schools were hard to come by unless one had first served there as a pupil-teacher or happened to be the sister or daughter of the proprietress. On the other hand, there was nothing to stop a woman who was lucky enough to have her own home from taking in some pupils: this was a particularly popular option with widows who had their own small children to look after. Advertisements placed by these women in *The Times* always characterised their schoolkeeping activites as an extension of their maternal duties:

EDUCATION (Private).– A lady residing in the country on the Great Northern Railway, who is educating her own daughter, aided

35

by a talented foreign governess and a professor, RECEIVES a few YOUNG LADIES as companions in study. Parents leaving England or having delicate children, or those whose education has been neglected, are particularly invited to pay the advertiser a visit. Every home comfort is enjoyed. The house stands in its own beautiful pleasure grounds and gardens of four acres.[39]

Another possibility for those women who still had a roof over their heads was to go out teaching as a 'daily' or 'visiting' goveness. Operating mainly in the town where transport was easier, a daily governess travelled to her pupils' house every morning to supervise their lessons. She might spend the whole day with them or, at lunch time, depart for another family where she passed the afternoons. A woman who was a particularly skilled musician or linguist might work as a peripatetic teacher, although in general male masters were assumed to be better qualified to give advanced tuition. A post as daily governess had both advantages and disadvantages over a living-in post. On the plus side, the private life of the daily governess was not subject to the same degree of control and scrutiny as that of the woman who boarded with her employers. For married women with children, working from home provided a means of keeping the family together while continuing to bring in some money. One of the appeals of a post as a daily governess in 1859 for Mary Bazlinton was that it would allow her to look after her mother while also being able to contribute financially to the household.[40] On the other hand, the fact that the daily governess was a hired hand rather than a family member was emphasised by the journey which she made each day between her own home and that of her employers. To make matters worse, that journey could prove to be extremely difficult. In a letter of 1863 to her half sister the writer Mary Shelley, Claire Claremont, a young woman working as a daily governess in London, described how her whole life revolved painfully around the capital's unreliable public transport system:

> I am so worried I fear I shall go out of my mind – this is now my life – I go by nine to Mrs Kitchener's house where I give lessons until one – then I rush to the top of Wilton Place and get a Richmond omnibus and go to Richmond to the Cohens ... that vile omnibus takes two hours to get to Richmond and the same to come back and so with every giving my lesson I am never back before seven.[41]

Since a governess drew a certain amount of her social status from that of her employers, working for a family which did not have the space or income to accommodate a live-in teacher could only reflect poorly on the visiting governess. The daily governess' fees, at around £24 a year for morning– or afternoon-only tuition, represented a saving on the £25 plus the cost of board and lodging that her resident counterpart represented.[42] What is more, the daily governess who split her time by giving tuition in two or more families gave the lie to the construction of the governess as integrated into the domestic and moral life of the genteel household. As a result the daily teacher seems to have represented a second-rate category of governessing, a fact reflected by the social backgrounds of some of those who opted for this means of making a living. From the 1861 census enumerators' handbooks for Paddington it appears that daily governesses were drawn from far from genteel backgrounds. Typical was Sarah Bottull, who was married to an omnibus driver, and Amelia Frane whose father was a jeweller.[43] It seems very possible that these women were employed not to impart the finer points of French grammar but simply to look after a neighbour's children while their mother served behind the counter in the family shop. By 1861 the label 'governess', with all its connotations of gentility and refinement, may have become a tag which some urban lower middle class-women liked to use to describe activities which consisted of little more than child-minding.

For a middle-class woman considering the limited range of employment possibilities, it was clear that working as a resident governess was 'the one means of breadwinning to which access alone seems open and to which alone untrained capacity is equal, or pride admits appeal'.[44] Every middle-class woman had received some sort of education, no matter how patchy: there was no need to serve an expensive or lengthy apprenticeship or equip oneself with special tools. Most importantly, governessing involved living *en famille*, providing a service that any lady might have offered voluntarily in her brother's or father's house. The fact that the governess received only a tiny salary on top of her board and lodging served to emphasise that she was more concerned with finding a place by someone's fireplace than selling her labour for a profit.

The consequence of this lack of alternatives to home teaching as an occupation for middle-class women was that, for much of the nineteenth century, the supply of governesses far exceeded the demand, although whether it was by as much as the '99 per cent' claimed by Bessie Rayner Parkes remains unclear.[45] Women did not become governesses because they perceived that the service they offered was in short supply, but because they had little choice. While contemporary historians have suggested that the opening up of white-collar work to middle-class women from the 1870s reduced the number of women competing for posts as governesses, what evidence there is suggests that the situation in 1880 was only slightly better than it had been in 1840. No really satisfactory alternative employment for the distressed gentlewoman appeared before the Great War, and many suddenly destitute women found themselves looking for a post as a governess right through the second half of the nineteenth century. Yet while supply remained high and constant, demand continued to be severely limited by the small number of families with sufficient income and space to accommodate an extra member of the household. As we have seen, the ratio of goveneses to upper- and middle-class girls was extremely high and it must have been the case that a large proportion was not working at any one time. Running through the autobiographies and diaries of the Victorian governess is a sense of the sheer difficulty of finding a job, of the necessity of making multiple applications over several months before a post could be secured. Competition for a first post was particularly intense, since the candidate could offer no evidence of her suitability for the task in hand:[46] on returning home from her stay at a German boarding school, eighteen-year-old Edith Gates endured three months of worry and expense during the summer of 1875 before the efforts of herself and her aunt to find her a position finally met with success.[47] Even an experienced governess like Mary Bazlinton could find it hard to obtain a situation in the over-stocked governess market: her diary for 1856 records how over a period of a few anxious weeks she made 'altogether 12 attempts issuing in as many failures'.[48]

Essential to any definition of the governess' role was the under-standing that she had not undergone any special preparation for it. It was bad enough that she had betrayed her own liberal education by using it for financial gain. To have received vocational training as well would imply that she had always expected to go out to work, instead of having this unpleasant necessity thrust upon her. On the other hand, the middle classes' increasing need to display their gentility through the accomplishments of their teenage daughters meant that any woman wanting to work as a governess needed to be quite certain that she was in possession of certain key skills, the most important of which was the ability to speak French and play the piano. In 1842 shoe-maker's daughter Mary Smith found to her dismay that her solid but decidedly unornamental education was simply not sufficient to get her a post:

> I looked over all manner of advertisements, seeking an assistant teacher's or a preparatory governess' situation; for alas! I had no accomplishments, so called. No music, nor singing, nor dancing; no German, Italian, and very little French; nor any fine manners . . .
> Every advertisement I read, even for farmers' families in the country, required music and French, and the various accompaniments of what was called 'genteel education'.[49]

There was a tension between the ideal of a governess as someone who had received no special training and the practical need of such women to be competent to instruct in certain tightly defined subject areas. Perhaps because their gentility was assumed to be beyond question, clergymen's daughters who knew from an early age that they would have to earn their living were exempted from this dilemma, being frequently sent to institutions which concentrated on preparing girls for their future work. By contrast, those girls who had lost their parents in childhood and were similarly 'educated for the profession' by well-intentioned guardians found themselves the object of commentators' suspicions, precisely because they were assumed to lack the refined and stable home background that would offset the vulgar associations of vocational training. The type of school to which both orphans and clergy daughters were sent appeared in sensational detail in Charlotte Brontë's first novel, *Jane Eyre*. Her fictional Lowood was modelled, infamously, on the Rev Carus Wilson's Cowan Bridge to which she and her sisters had been sent in 1824, a year after their mother's death.[50] Yet the Spartan regime, which she recalled for her appalled and fascinated readers, may have been more typical of this kind of school than contemporaries liked to believe. St Mary's Hall in Brighton, which from 1832 aimed at turning vicars' daughters into 'governesses for the higher and middle classes', seems to have offered a similarly rigorous ethos. One ex-pupil recalled 'days spent sitting on the lockers which lined a large schoolroom, hemming dusters; solitary meals eaten at a side table in the dining-room; or being sent to bed frequently throughout the day, and then as frequently being obliged to get up and dress . . .'[51] Despite such horrors there remained a sense in which the pupils at this type of institution received a more realistic sense of their place in the world than those clergymen's daughters who attended a typical ladies' seminary. When Charlotte Brontë was removed from Cowan Bridge and sent, after a short interval, to Roe Head, a small proprietary boarding school, she stuck out like a sore thumb: years later her classmate Mary Taylor still remembered how 'Charlotte, at school, had no plan of life beyond what circumstances made for her. She knew that she must provide for herself, and chose her trade'; and described an anxious, shabby girl who poured over her books while the other girls played on around her.[52]

A more enlightened and unusual school was that run in Tiverton during the 1860s by Mary Porter, which aimed at preparing 'the daughters of professional men who had been reduced in circumstances' for a career as a governess. Pupils received a standard education in French, German, drawing, music and elementary Latin, but on top of this they studied 'the art of teaching'. A small junior school was attached and here the would-be governesses practised their pedagogic skills. Typically girls attended between the ages of sixteen and eighteen, but some women in their early twenties, who had already worked as governesses, enrolled because they wished to improve their skills and enhance their earning power. Porter's school was unusual, which was precisely why she was called to give evidence about it to the Schools Inquiry Commission of 1867-68.[53] There was a strong feeling from witnesses such as Emily Davies and Susan Kyberd that governesses should not receive an education that was radically different in style or content from that of any other middle-class girl.[54] This did not mean that much could not be done to improve the general standard of female education: what was wanted was 'good inspected schools, and girls trained to teach as part of their education'.[55] Training colleges for lower middle-class women intending to work in elementary schools were all very well, but to extend the principle to governesses was to misunderstand the nature of their vocation. A governess was concerned with the social and moral development of her pupils as well as the simply academic, and her qualifications were not merely of the academic variety but were rather part of her birthright as a lady. Lying even further behind this mistrust of special training institutions was the fear of the opportunities for social mobility which they might offer to ambitious lower middle-class girls. Coming down heavily against the whole 'college' principle, Elizabeth Sewell warned that 'in the present desire for the cultivation of the intellect, a clever, though under-bred woman, who really knows what she attempts to teach, will make her way before the refined lady who has only a superficial amount of information'.[56]

Yet there remained the problem of how a young single women was to prepare herself for a life spent supervising children. While her nearest working- class counter-part, the nanny, could learn her trade through a period of apprenticeship as a nursemaid, the governess had no such opportunity to study by example and was left to pick up the necessary skills as best she could. Educated for the most part by her mother, at a small boarding school or at one of the institutions designed specifically to prepare girls for a life spent teaching, the governess was frequently required to provide a type of education of which she herself had no direct experience. Perhaps it was for this reason that by the mid 1860s the low level of competence displayed by so many home teachers, 'refined' and 'under-bred' alike, had become a pressing cause for concern. The compromise of Porter's school which offered a sound general education as well as a small amount of vocational training seemed to offer an attractive solution although, apart from a few individual initiatives, it was not one which was generally taken up.

Instead governesses continued to prepare themselves for their future work on an *ad hoc* basis, paying particular attention to those skills which they knew would bring them the best financial rewards. Given the prime position that the command of French, German and Italian occupied in the ranking of ornamental accomplishments, shrewd governesses equipped themselves with these languages which, for maximum prestige, needed to have been learnt abroad: notices placed in *The Times* always stressed that the advertiser had learnt her French in Paris and spoke it like a native.[57] Families that could afford it sent their daughters to study on the Continent for a year before they started work, although the schools which most of these girls attended usually contained so many British pupils that the chances of getting to grips with another language were slight.[58] A frequent pattern was for a girl to go out as an assistant teacher to one of these schools – a privilege for which she was charged a hefty premium – paying for her keep through the giving of English conversation lessons. The theory was that the cost of acquiring fluent languages abroad would be recouped through the higher salaries that would naturally follow, a point which the young Anna Jameson tried to explain to her father in a letter from Florence where she was working as a governess in 1821:

> My only extravagance (if such it can be called) is having an Italian master regularly, and this I think you would like me to do, as it is not only a great advantage to me now, but will be of the greatest

use to me hereafter ... I denied myself a winter dress that I might have an Italian master.[59]

The result of concentrating on certain profitable skills at the expense of others meant that the majority of governesses during the first half the Victorian period could offer a level of instruction that was patchy in the extreme: 'what lady would study Latin, or mathematics, when the same time bestowed on music and French would, in a mere commercial point of view, produce so much larger a return?'[60] Employers, however, still insisted on maintaining the pretence that they were as keen on their daughters learning geometry as German, with the result that governesses were left with no option but to claim competence in a whole range of subjects with which they were only superficially acquainted. While much aggressive criticism was aimed at governesses during the 1840s and 1850s by commentators who characterised them as incompetent and even fraudulent, a few of the more perceptive realised that blame needed to be laid at the door not of lazy or ignorant governesses but of employers whose unrealistic expectations left applicants with no choice but to make inflated claims about their own abilities:

> The fault lies here with the mother, who will expect to meet with universal geniuses: that master would be considered a pedant who pretended to teach three or four languages, as well as music, drawing, and the circle of the sciences, but from a lady it is thought no unreasonable demand.[61]

One young man, writing to his mother in the 1840s, asked her to let him know when she had finally found the well-qualified governess for whom she had been searching. If such a paragon did indeed exist, he explained, 'he should *not* recommend her as a governess for his sisters, but keep her as *a wife* for himself'.[62]

The recruitment process which every governess was obliged to negotiate in some form or other provided a foretaste of the ambiguities and tensions which she would meet once she started work. Encapsulated here were those illogicalities and downright contradictions which marked the construction of her position as a gentlewoman who nonetheless needed to support herself. On the one hand the polite fiction was maintained by all concerned that the governess was a volunteer who, having unfortunately lost her own family, was obliged to seek a place in someone else's. On the other, the harsh realities of the market place could not fail to shape the way in which individual governesses and employers came together. Given that the supply of governesses far outstripped demand, competition for individual posts was fierce. As a result the whole process of governess recruitment exhibited profound inconsistency. For instance, much of the rhetoric of advertisements and letters of application suggested that the governess was a genteel volunteer who liked nothing more than looking after other peoples' children. Yet, the content, if not the style, of many face-to-face interviews revealed a much franker acknowledgement of what was at stake.

The easiest way for the would-be governess to preserve the fiction that she was a volunteer was to try and find a situation within her own family network. In a few cases, this tie might be further strengthened by the governess actually marrying into her employer's family. Sarah Haselwood, who was governess to the children of her distant cousin, the Revd Charles Kingsley, married his younger brother in 1864.[63] In the course of a few years her status changed from that of distant relative, to paid employee and, finally, to full family member. Another strategy was to find a job with friends or friends-of-friends – an added advantage here was that both sides knew what they were letting themselves in for. When Elizabeth Ham was offered the post of governess by an old family friend in 1819, her chief asset was not so much competence as compatability since '[Mrs Bullock] could not endure the idea of having a stranger, and she had known me all my life'.[64] Those women who worked for well-placed families – whether aristocrats or meritocrats – found themselves profiting from the ties of blood and friendship which bound their employers together. Once May Pinhorn started work for the Kay-Shuttleworth family in 1895 she never again had to look for a job. For the next twenty years, until her retirement, Pinhorn moved around other leading Liberal families on the strength of Lady Kay-Shuttleworth's recommendation. Such an arrangement by-passed the more embarrassing aspects of recruitment – the taking-up of references, the negotiating of a salary – and, by implication, replaced the governess in the role she had occupied in earlier times, as a distant member of the family's kith and kin. Middle-class families, lacking access to this type of sprawling social network, seem to have remained more dependent on newspaper advertisements and employment agencies to find themselves a governess.

For those whose immediate connections were unable to provide them with a job, contacts made at school could prove valuable. Several years after leaving Roe Head in 1838, where she had been both pupil and assistant teacher, Charlotte Brontë was still using her former headmistress' help in her search for employment.[65] Clergymen were another useful link between employers and governesses, while Baptist and Methodist ministers were also likely to be asked by members of their flock if they knew of a suitable candidate for a position.[66] In addition, individual middle-class women, motivated by a sense of charity or duty, often acted as informal employment agencies for governesses, putting candidates in touch with prospective employers within their social and family network.[67]

It was only once all these unofficial networks had been exhausted that the would-be governess was left with no choice but to launch herself unequivocally onto the market place. The cheapest way to advertise was simply to pin up a card on the board of some respectable meeting place: libraries and stationers were a popular choice. Only as a final resort would an advertisement be inserted into a local or national newspaper or one of the many religious periodicals which flourished in the mid nineteenth century. Not only was this often disappointingly ineffective – Mary Bazlinton received only one answer to the advertisement she placed in *The Times* in 1856 – it was also expensive:[68] according to its report for 1846, the GBI reckoned that ten shillings represented a very small outlay for the governess in pursuit of a post.[69] What is more, announcing that one was up for hire broke every rule of genteel behaviour: in *The Times* the governess' entry was sandwiched strangely between advertisements for day excursions and requests for capital loans. Equally distasteful was the fact that placing an advertisement necessarily involved a vulgar act of self-promotion, a listing and amplification of all one's skills and attainments: one governess reported how she had to have her objections to advertising 'overruled by my kind friend who assured me that this step was positively requisite to ensure success'.[70] During the 1840s and 1850s around five advertisements appeared every day in *The Times* from governesses seeking positions, of which the following is a typical example:

GOVERNESS.– a LADY, of considerable experience in tuition, wishes to obtain a SITUATION in a gentleman's family. She is competent to teach the English, French and Italian languages, music, drawing, and the usual branches of a lady's education. The advertiser has resided three years in Paris. Address, post paid, to P. A., at Mr Strange's 14, Broadway, near Queen's-square, Westminster.[71]

Quite frequently the wording of the notice revealed that the advertiser's most pressing concern was not so much to exercise her pedagogic skills but to get a roof over her head by whatever means necessary:

A YOUNG LADY, of the highest respectability wishes for a SITUATION, either to accompany a young lady or little girl in delicate health to the sea-side, whose parents might be prevented from going with her; or as a companion to a lady or a young lady who has nearly finished her education, and from the loss of her mother or other circumstances might wish for a lady to go into society with her; or as Governess to one or two little girls. This lady has lived several years abroad in the best society, and from her amiable manners and gentle disposition, is peculiarly adapted to situations where these qualities are particularly desirable.[72]

Many advertisers went so far as to disclaim any interest at all in remuneration, declaring 'salary a secondary consideration';[73] one would-be governess even informed readers of the commercial columns of *The Times* that 'having a small independence, salary would be no consideration'.[74] Here was a declaration of desperation which employers were only too happy to exploit: several of *their* advertisements, especially for nursery governesses to look after smaller children, offered no payment beyond bed, board and travelling expenses.[75] The fact that even these miserable offers attracted scores of replies testified to the chronic over-supply in the governess market.

The letters which governesses wrote in response to employers' advertisements revealed that many of them did not possess the skills they claimed, including that of basic literacy. Dorothea Beale, in later life headmistress of Cheltenham Ladies College, recalled how her mother set about finding a governess who had at least mastered the basics of the English language:

My mother advertised, and hundreds of answers were sent. She began by eliminating all those in which bad spelling occurred . . . next, the wording and composition were criticised, and lastly a few of the writers were interviewed and a selection was made.[76]

The situation had not improved much by the end of the century. As late as 1890 the periodical *Work and Leisure* was advising governesses that they needed to put far more care into an application if it was to have any chance of success. The following lack-lustre attempt simply would not do:

> Madam – I have seen your advertisements in the –, and beg to offer myself for your situation, which I think is exactly what I am looking for. I am confident that I am in every way competent to suit you. My acquirements are good music, French, German, the rudiments of Latin, and English in all its branches. I am now with Mrs – at –, who I am sure will be most happy to answer all inquiries about me. I shall be much obliged if you will write as soon as possible, and tell me the ages of your children and full particulars about your situation.[77]

Such a bland letter, *Work and Leisure* assures the governess, will fail to stand out amongst the hundreds of other applications. Many more personal details are needed: she should give the profession of both her father and her maternal grandfather; her education should be noted, together with the names of any masters from whom she has taken advanced instruction; the circumstances which led up to her being obliged to go out to work should be mentioned; and she should also stress any additional responsibilities she has undertaken, such as being left in charge of the household while her employer was absent.[78]

On a par with newspaper advertisements were the many scholastic agencies which offered to put parents and governesses in touch with each other.[79] The hefty commission fee was to be paid by the governess – often as much as 5 per cent of a whole year's salary – and even then there was no guarantee that a job would actually be found.[80] Some agencies employed the most peculiar criteria in checking credentials: one gentleman, a keen amateur phrenologist, examined the governess' head for lumps and bumps before recommending her to an employer – a service for which he charged 'five shillings for his manipulation, a percentage on the salary, and a fee from the employer'.[81] Governesses who had to resort to this way of finding work were vocal in their complaints, but it was not until the 1870s that unscrupulous agents like William Bragg of Southwark, the proprietor of 'The General Employment and Advertisement Office' were prosecuted for defrauding women out of sums ranging from 2s. 6d. to 30s. 'by pretending to obtain them situations'.[82]

It was as a much needed alternative to all this that the GBI set up its own registry in 1843, entirely free to governess and employer alike. The system was simple but effective. A series of books was kept on display at the Institute's offices in Harley Street. The pages were divided into columns, each one representing a different skill or qualification: a governess who could produce two satisfactory letters of reference might enter her details. Anyone wishing to engage a governess could then ask to see the book, copy down the details of a candidate in whom they were interested, and then contact her by leaving a note with the Lady Resident. Alternatively, there was a book into which those who were looking for governesses might enter their requirements.[83] Employers and governesses from the country often travelled up to London for a couple of weeks specifically in order to consult the register, organise interviews, and confirm arrangements for a new post. Governesses were obliged, on pain of exclusion from the registry, to let the Lady Resident know as soon as they were suited, so that their names could be removed. Unfortunately, employers were not under a similar obligation and their failure to do so caused enormous frustration: at least one governess reported turning up to see an employer who had left her name in the register, only to find that the lady had returned to the country three weeks previously.[84] Roughly half of the 1,500 or so women registered in any one year eventually found employment through the GBI's registry; this proportion rose to about two-thirds as more employers came to hear about the service.[85] Even so, governesses needed to be quick off the mark for, as these figures suggest, supply outstripped demand. One governess travelled seven miles every day from the suburbs to inspect the register, an undertaking which soon drained her small savings.[86]

Unless geography prevented it, the final hurdle to be negotiated was the formal interview. Exactly what questions the governess was asked seems to have depended entirely on the employer's own priorities, whether she valued music over French, geography over German.[87] Mme Bureaud Riofrey, who wrote no less than four advice books exclusively on the subject of governessing in the space of five years during the early 1840s, recommended the most stringent interviewing procedure to her readers:

> it would be desirable, that governesses should undergo a species of examination, or moral ordeal. It does not for instance suffice to enquire, whether they are good musicians, clever linguists, and able teachers; because generally a short and affirmative answer is given; but an hour should be devoted to unreserved conversation on the principle points of education; and if in this conversation,

47

the governess shews good judgement, and sound understanding; if she express her ideas with order, clearness, and elegance, without emphasis or affectation, she must be calculated for the great and difficult art of teaching.[88]

Despite the rigour of Mme Bureaud Riofrey's appoach, testing intellectual achievement nearly always took second place to investigating the governess' claims to be a lady.[89] As stand-in for her pupils' mother it was essential that she provide a model of perfect Christian ladyhood. A less than genteel accent or family background suggested that a candidate was not only 'not quite a lady' but that she was not quite moral and, on both counts, was a highly unsuitable person to be entrusted with the education of young gentlewomen. Specialist tuition in music and languages could always be provided by visiting masters but there was no way of making good the damage done by a socially and morally inferior governess. For this reason employers had absolutely no qualms about 'making most minute inquiries' as to a candidate's social class.[90] When had the governess' father died? Why had his business failed? Who was her mother's father? What did her brothers do? The applicant's bearing, the way she spoke, whether she remembered to get to her feet when her prospective employer did, all these hallmarks of gentility were carefully scrutinised. A provincial accent would immediately put its owner beyond serious consideration for a position in a gentleman's house,[91] and a shabby outfit, no matter how 'good' it had once been, could easily cost her the job.[92] As Elizabeth Ham discovered, for some employers the question of whether the governess really was a lady bordered on the obsessional:

> I was rather amused, on being shewn into a small room, by the fussy old lady that had advertised for 'a perfect gentlewoman' as companion to her nieces, rising with great quickness and *empressement* to place a chair for me. Her politeness was so very elaborate that it seemed to say 'You may see that I know something about the article I am in quest of . . .'

> After some conversation relative to the duties required, I was told that I should hear from the lady in a day or two. Certainly not more than two days elapsed before the note came, declining my services, *politely*, and informing me that very soon after parting from me she had been so very fortunate as to meet with a *real* gentlewoman, and had engaged her accordingly, or words to that effect.[93]

Almost as important as the governess' social class was the nature and degree of her religious observance. Catholics, by and large,

An idealised version of home education received at a loving mother's knee (*c.* 1840).
(*Mary Evans Picture Library*)

An apprehensive child is urged to shake hands with her new governess (1892)
(*Mary Evans Picture Library*)

'The Governess', by Richard Redgrave, first exhibited at the Royal Academy in 1844. While the governess sits in a dim interior, reading a black-bordered letter, her three pupils chatter in the fresh air.
(*Bridgeman Art Library; now hanging in the Victoria and Albert Museum, London*)

Small boys, chafing under petticoat rule, were perceived as a disruptive element in
the home schoolroom (1873).
(*Mary Evans Picture Library*)

top   Mary Bazlinton
       (*House Collection*)

above   Edith Gates (*c.* 1882)
       (*Schulte Collection*)

right   May Pinhorn (1889)
       (*Walley Collection*)

were not employed in Protestant households unless they were Frenchwomen, in which case the moral threat of their presence was offset by the prestige that came with having one's daughters taught a modern language by a native speaker. Even so, the broad umbrella of Protestantism sheltered a wide range of doctrinal belief and devotional practice and tensions often arose when governess and employer turned out to have different ideas about how and when to worship. Mary Bazlinton suffered greatly during her time with the Bradshaw family in 1854-55 because she had not spelled out the extent and fervour of her nonconformist views before taking up a post in this easy-going Anglican household. The result was constant bickering as Bazlinton's stern and unyielding attitudes – she insisted on spending Sunday alone in her room and would not venture out to walk along the fashionable promenade at Pau – started to irritate and ultimately alienate her employers to the point where it looked as if they would have to part company.[94] Determined never to repeat the experience, Bazlinton decided that she would henceforth make her position quite clear to any potential employer, even if, as often happened, it cost her the chance of a job. On 24 February 1856 she recorded how a correspondence regarding a possible position had been broken off once she made her 'repugnance to the doctrines of baptismal regeneration' clear to the woman in whose household she sought a post.[95] Disappointing though this may have been, Bazlinton had at least been saved the experience that befell Elizabeth Ham some thirty-five years earlier. Although Ham had secured the agreement of Mrs Hutchins before taking up a situation in her household that she might worship at the local Unitarian chapel, the situation changed drastically once Ham actually began work. A stream of snide remarks and outright criticism of her religious beliefs eventually drove her into quitting her situation.[96]

Given that until 1860 the governess was unable to offer any kind of formal qualification as proof of her suitability for the post, great emphasis was put on the nature and the quality of her previous working experience. There was no obvious career pattern for governesses: some who had received only minimal education worked as nursery governesses all their lives, while well-grounded clergymen's daughters tended to teach older girls, not least because the salary was likely to be higher. Yet there were a thousand exceptions to this rule: Charlotte Brontë started work as a nursery governess, although she was perfectly able to teach Latin, while Mary Bazlinton prayed for a post teaching small girls even though she was qualified to instruct older ones.[97] A combination of personal preference and intellectual competence seems to have determined whether a woman taught younger children or adolescent girls. In any case, such categorisation was often meaningless, since a governess very often found herself responsible for teaching girls as young as five and as old as eighteen. Likewise, there is little evidence to suggest that governesses started out teaching the children of poor professional men and then proceeded to the schoolrooms of the aristocracy. By and large the first post that a woman obtained, which was dependent on her proficiency and her social contacts, determined the sort of people for whom she would subsequently work.

It was in this context that questions about a governess' previous situations – including discreet inquiries about the social status of her employers – were as important as those which aimed to test her mastery of irregular French verbs. This did not mean, however, that such inquiries were necessarily easy to answer. When asked why she had left a previous position, it might be difficult to give an honest response: any breach of confidence would immediately reveal her as being 'not quite a lady' and therefore unfit for the post for which she was applying:

> The uncertain temper, constant and unwarrantable interference, and incivility of one of the parents, or the mental deficiency of the pupils, may be a sufficient reason to herself for quitting a situation, but one which she would hardly feel justified in mentioning to others.[98]

Although the practice of giving and receiving references was the object of chronic disatisfaction – 'I have had teachers come to me with the highest testimonials, some from clergymen, who had proved not only incompetent but criminal' – it was still vital to be able to produce a written recommendation from a former employer.[99] It was virtually impossible for a domestic servant to obtain a situation without a 'character', and the same held true 'in this far more important connexion',[100] a fact of which Mary Bazlinton was all too painfully aware when she asked Mrs Bradshaw, whose employment she was about to leave, whether she might mention her name as a referee:

> During the conversation I held with her respecting the time of my leaving I had asked whether I had her permission to refer any lady to her with whom I might be in correspondence respecting a situation, her reply was 'certainly, indeed, you could not do without it'. My

spirit rose at the tone and manner of this answer, but I made no remark. This wish however could not be suppressed that I might be able to obtain another situation without having to be indebted to her for a recommendation. And indeed, as in regards referring any lady to her, I can feel no confidence that she would really do it in such a manner as to *recommend* me.[101]

Maidservants who had been sacked without references were acknowledged by contemporaries to make up the single biggest element of the capital's prostitute population. Whether or not governesses without 'characters' were also likely to find themselves taking to the streets is unfortunately less clear, although there was no shortage of hints that this was, in fact, the case.[102]

For those governesses and employers who lived too far apart to meet face-to-face there was no alternative but to resort to what was effectively an interview by post. During her search for a position in 1856 Mary Bazlinton, who lived in rural Lincolnshire, frequently found herself exchanging two or three letters on the subject of her credentials, teaching methods and salary requirements before receiving a polite but firm rejection from a would-be employer. Such a protracted procedure brought with it its own particular stresses and strains and Bazlinton, not surprisingly, turned into an obsessional post-watcher. On one occasion her anxiety actually lost her a job. Having exchanged a couple of letters with a certain Mrs Betts, Bazlinton failed to receive a prompt reply to her most recent missive. Wondering whether the letter had got lost in the post, she decided to send Mrs Betts a brief note of inquiry. The latter was so offended at Bazlinton's unladylike impatience that she refused to have anything more to do with her and broke off correspondence forthwith.[103]

As Mary Bazlinton's experience suggests, when it came to letting the candidate know whether she had got the job, employers often failed to show the courtesy and consideration which they expected in return:

Once, I met a lady by appointment in the City, and my downcast heart bounded with joy, as she said after a long conversation: 'Well, then, you must really come and spend a long day with us soon; it would be so disagreeable to come to a strange house'. I had returned home and was gaily chatting over a cup of tea, when the postman's knock startled me. Tremblingly I took the letter, handed to me. Was it something good at last? No, alas no! 'Mrs A. presents her compliments to Miss C., and begs to decline'.[104]

51

Eventually the day came when a letter arrived with a formal offer of a position. Relief and joy at the good news quickly gave way to grief as the full implications of leaving one's family, perhaps for the first time, sank in: 'there is something sad and melancholy in the thought of leaving the home of my childhood, and all the endearments that are associated with that word *home*',[105] wrote Harriet Jukes wistfully in 1831, a few weeks into her first post. Novice governesses frequently took advantage of Britain's burgeoning railway network to choose positions far away from their native neighbourhoods in order to avoid inquisitive neighbours witnessing their 'humiliation'.[106] The price of such anonymity was long and often arduous cross-country travel undertaken without a companion and often, to add insult to injury, at one's own expense. When nineteen-year-old May Pinhorn obtained a post in a small Welsh vicarage in 1887 she found herself negotiating a journey of epic proportions. Her experiences of the trip – which included travelling third class and fending off over-familiar men – pointed up the social as well as the geographical distance that the governess travelled in her progress from leisured lady to working woman:

At last an appointment was secured in the depths of Wales at £25 a year, and I started off on a cold winter day on a long journey to Aberystwyth, where I was to be met and driven to Aberayron, a distance of 16 miles. The time seemed endless, as I sat cold and alone in a poor third class carriage of a Welsh train. When I got to Aberystwyth I was met by a rubicund little carrier, who told me in barely intelligible English that he was to take me to my destination an hour or two later. Meanwhile he deposited me in the back kitchen of a little inn, where the old Welsh women made comments upon me in their own language. By the time we started the wind was getting up and went on increasing in violence as we pegged along in a canvas-covered van on an exposed coast road. The sea and winds roared, and nothing could be seen through the impenetrable darkness outside. At intervals the whole cart load descended and went into a public house; I refusing to accompany them, was left alone in the cart with the storm threatening every moment to blow away its cover. After each visit the company became merrier and the flow of Welsh freer, while the carrier began to make familiar remarks suited to his ideas of young women.

At last I arrived at the Vicarage, which seemed to be in darkness, but presently a strange, gaunt figure, with a partly bald head crowned by a knobbly growth, emerged holding up a little lamp which just made the darkness visible. This proved to be the Vicar, who ushered me into a very shabby drawing-room, where I was introduced to his wife, Mrs Edwards, who gave me a shock by groping towards me. Nobody had prepared me for her being blind. Three plain girls next appeared, the eldest suave and rather humbuggy in manner, the other two awkward and uncouth, the third having the appearance of a wild, wicked little elf. Then the young only son entered, but promptly retired in a paroxysm of laughter, which was not reassuring to a tired and shy girl. I was then taken up a grease bedaubed staircase to my room, which had only been half cleaned for my reception.[107]

4

A Perfect Treadmill of Learning

We had eight hours a day of lessons, and sometimes even more,
getting up at six o'clock, summer and winter, and commencing work
at seven . . . [it was] a perfect treadmill of learning.

> Georgiana Sitwell, recalling her schoolroom of 1834
> Osbert Sitwell (ed.), *Two Generations* (1940)

Many mothers . . . will gladly engage a governess who will do
the great work of education and will employ masters for the less
important one of teaching.

> Mary Maurice, *Governess Life* (1849)

Throughout Victoria's reign motherhood was regarded as the most
valuable and natural component of female experience. By the
middle of the century the evangelicals' earlier teachings on the
duties and rewards of maternal love had spread through all the
Protestant denominations until they had become an established part
of bourgeois culture. As the guardians of the home and hearth,
women were charged with responsibility for the moral health not
only of the next generation but of the nation and, later on, the
Empire as a whole. In return they were to enjoy the giving and
receiving of a love so intense and pure that it came to stand as a
model for all other human relationships. As the century progressed,
motherhood became a subject for celebration in a wide variety of
cultural forms, from popular song to high art, as the linch-pin of
civilisation and salvation alike.

The central place which motherhood occupied in 'woman's mission' was sanctioned not only by the teachings of the various churches
but also by an appeal to Nature: maternal instinct was represented
as an essential and unchanging component of femininity. From the
end of the eighteenth century doctors urged mothers to abandon

the custom of hiring working-class women to feed their babies and encouraged them to perform this function themselves instead. The cholera outbreaks and political crises of the 1840s provided ample breeding ground for fears about all sorts of 'contamination' which might seep from the working to the middle class via the tainted milk of the wet-nurse. As a result 'breast-feeding was re-defined as a natural and healthy practice for the responsible middle-class mother, and childcare became a site for the separation and insulation of the middle class from corruption by the class below it'.[1]

Although it was represented as universal and eternal, the Victorian ideal of motherhood was the product of a specific place and time in history. It depended on the assumption that a woman took no part in the market economy but was confined and defined by her place in the domestic sphere. Not only did she not sell her labour outside the front door, the effort she put in to bringing up her children was represented as the flowering of instinctual love rather than a pragmatic response to her social and economic circumstances. A mother's work was perceived to be of a natural kind and, as such, beyond price.[2] Any woman whose material situation made it difficult for her to live out this ideal – because her attendance in a factory or a ballroom prevented her from devoting herself to her children – was characterised by a range of professional discourses as immoral, criminal or ill.

The challenge that the governess represented to this ideal of motherhood was profound. Her presence in the household signalled that some women chose not to dedicate themselves to full-time child-rearing but preferred to hire other women to carry out these duties on their behalf. Moreover, the fact that the childless governess could perform many of the functions of a mother suggested that, far from being instinctual, maternal affection was something which might be bought. To contain the damage thus done to a definition of motherhood as rooted in enduring female nature, the advice writers put great time and energy into setting out guidelines within which home teaching was to operate. According to these, only those women whose gentility and morality were beyond question – the upper class and the upper middle class – were justified in employing governesses. These were the women who were obliged to concentrate on their social and philanthropic commitments – activities which themselves represented a sort of institutionalised mothering – at the expense of immediate involvement in their daughters' education.[3] In these circumstances there was no alternative but to employ a genteel

te to carry out those duties which had been abdicated only
: greatest reluctance.

Those women who were not justified in employing governesses,
by contrast, were those who had no duties beyond that of wife and
mother. In this case it was feared that the governess' task would not
so much be to oversee the moral, social and intellectual education
of young women as to cram them with showy accomplishments
designed, at some future date, to be displayed to others. It was
the wives of small-time professional men and impoverished clerics
who, failing to display proper moral behaviour, were believed to
be most likely to hire governesses from the lower middle class who
also fell short of the ideal of bourgeois-Christian womanhood. The
motivation which led such women into becoming governesses was
assumed to have less to do with a need to keep body and soul
together than with a hunger for social advancement by means of
association with the genteel home schoolroom. In this case, the
labour of love that comprised middle-class motherhood had been
displaced by the paid work of the lower-class woman; moral and
class stability would only be restored, suggested the manual writers,
by 'ladies of the middle rank resuming the instruction of their own
children, as God ordained they should'.[4]

Even where advice writers agreed that a woman was justified in
hiring a governess, considerable effort was expended in upholding
the primacy of motherhood:

> the duties and the cares of a mother are of that kind that no one
> else can estimate, and she has no right wholly to cast off the care
> of her children. She has a helper, but she cannot have a substitute.
> What God has given her to do, she can never devolve on any other.
> Such conduct, would, indeed, be sinful.[5]

Such a construction set in play as many tensions as it attempted to
resolve. The insistence that it was a mother's duty to remain in charge
of the schoolroom left the governess no role save that of a cypher,
a stand-in who was neither to think or act for herself. Once the
governess had been stripped of the autonomy that might have made
her work interesting, the real reasons for her seeking employment
could no longer be avoided: nothing but financial desperation could
have driven her into such an unrewarding situation. This recognition
was a worrying one, since it threatened to collapse the boundaries
between the public and the private spheres, the economic and the
moral worlds. Motherhood, the pinnacle of all that was pure and

good about the domestic sphere, was in danger of con~~tamination~~ on by the social and material hungers which seeped from ~~the figure~~ re of the governess.

One way of getting around the problem was to assign the governess a new motive, that of love. The problem with this reading was that it threatened to displace the mother as the central figure in her child's life. In the end the advice writers reached a compromise whereby the governess was permitted to love her pupils, but with two important qualifications attached. First, she would have to *learn* to cultivate those feelings for her pupils which came naturally to their mother.[6] Second, she was not to expect or, worse still, solicit any love from her pupils in return. Even at the beginning of the twentieth century manual writers were still warning the home governess that:

> Sometimes there is a temptation to win power and affection for yourself, and you seem to do more good to the child thereby – but that was not your job, and there will be no blessing on it.[7]

The governess found herself expected to lavish emotional energy on her pupils,[8] yet to expect nothing more than mild affection in return. Such a situation hardly made for a happy life although, in practice, such injunctions were softened by the myriad circumstances of every day existence. The relationship which a governess developed with her pupils inevitably depended less on what the advice writers said ought to happen and more on the range and quality of the other emotional outlets available. In those households where parents were emotionally or physically absent, the governess found herself meeting all the needs of her pupil, a situation which gave rise to feelings of claustrophobia: when Rose Stanley 'scratched Mlle B.'s hands till they bled' one senses the pitch of a schoolroom where governess and pupils were forced into each other's company twelve hours a day, for at least five and a half days a week.[9] On the other hand, in those households where parents took an active part in their children's lives, the opportunities for jealousy and rivalry were correspondingly greater: when her three-year-old charge gushed to Charlotte Brontë that he loved her, his mother exclaimed with horror and hurt, 'love the *governess*, my dear!'[10]

For those governesses who were isolated from their own family and friends, there was a strong need to love and be loved in return. Nineteen-year-old Edith Gates, for instance, was certain that, 'I cannot esteem myself sufficiently happy in having such dear affectionate pupils, how much of my happiness I owe to their love, for without it, what would my life be?'[11] Experienced governesses, like Sybil Lubbock's Miss Cutting, responded to the situation by cultivating an emotional distance so that 'the little barrier that had been set up was a valuable check to the emotional sensibility so often seen between an affectionate pupil and her teacher'.[12] Gates, by contrast, charged on impetuously, winning from Harry Wiggett the affection which she craved:

> Harry is really a funny little boy, he sometimes says such funny things. Whatever Latin verb he is saying to me the English has always been *to love* for some time past. So yesterday I asked him if he did the same with his Papa to which he said no. I then asked him what made him do so to me, and he answered he: 'supposed it was because he was always thinking about loving me'.[13]

To try and generalise about the nature of the bond between governess and pupil is, ultimately, an impossible task. Contained within memoirs of the period can be found relationships characterised by every nuance of emotion from fierce love to passionate hatred, with a fair amount of indifference in between. Sybil Lubbock even dedicated her autobiography to Miss Cutting, her much-loved governess.[14] Some autobiographers spent pages on glowing testimonials to their teachers, while others dismissed theirs in a couple of lines. Lady Dorothy Nevill, for instance, broke off the narrative of her life story to record her thanks to Eliza Redgrave, sister of the famous painter Richard Redgrave, in the strongest terms:

> She was a woman of great cultivation, besides being possessed of a certain distinction of mind . . . Her tender care and companionship – in childhood a preceptress, in after-life a much-loved friend – I have always felt to have been an inestimable boon, for thus was implanted in my mind a love of the artistic and the beautiful which during my life has proved a certain and ever-present source of delight.[15]

On the other side of the coin, Loelia Ponsonby spent several pages describing the pain and unhappiness of her time in the schoolroom before concluding, '. . . I had reached middle-age before I overcame the complexes that were the legacy of those years of misery'.[16] Finally, the Countess of Asquith and Oxford recorded, without a hint of embarrassment, that: 'I detested my nursery governess with such intensity that I remember writing on a piece of paper which I put under my pillow one night: "I hope Mlle will die, and go to Hell"'.[17]

The further a family travelled up the social scale, the more likely it was to employ specialist servants – parlourmaids, footmen, and cooks – rather than general domestics.[18] Likewise, in the most elevated homes, several governesses might be employed in succession as the children's needs changed and developed. The nursery governess was concerned with the earliest education of children, both boys and girls, from the ages of four to eight: her most important task was teaching her pupils how to read and write. Although not to be confused with the nanny, some of her functions might tip over into generalised childcare and, if there were no nursemaid employed, she might be required to look after the children's wardrobe and help them dress. The nursery governess' great appeal was that she was cheap (she might cost nothing more than her bed and board). Commentators criticised employers for hiring inferior women to supervise their children at this most impressionable of ages, thinking to make good the defects at a later stage when a more experienced and therefore more expensive governess could be employed.[19]

A preparatory governess was responsible for girls from the ages of eight to twelve and taught the basics of English grammar, history,

LATE FROM THE SCHOOL-ROOM.

Minnie. "I AM READING SUCH A PRETTY TALE."
Governess. "YOU MUST SAY NARRATIVE, MINNIE—NOT TALE!"
Minnie. "YES, MA'AM; AND DO JUST LOOK AT MUFF, HOW HE'S WAGGING HIS NARRATIVE!"

Punch's humorous view of life in the home schoolroom.

'use of the globes', French, perhaps Italian or German, piano, singing, drawing, together with whatever other skills she happened to possess. If she was not strong in modern languages, a French maid might be employed to speak to the children in her native tongue;[20] alternatively, a little girl might be brought over from the Continent to share the schoolroom and provide practice in conversation.[21] Once pupils reached the age of fourteen, outside male teachers were increasingly employed – either they attended the schoolroom or the children visited their premises – to instruct in languages, music and art. Typically these 'masters' were political refugees from Europe, educated men and even aristocrats who had fallen on hard times and were obliged to make ends meet through giving tuition. Wealthy families were able to pay men of the very highest calibre from institutions like the Royal Academy of Music to teach their daughters.[22] Masters provided a source of romantic excitement and speculation (rarely more than that) for adolescent girls: in the 1840s Jane Panton was bewitched by the melancholy Italian count who gave her conversation lessons before disappearing one night in fear of his life;[23] while in the late 1850s Annie Rothschild was equally fascinated by Dr Kalisch who taught her Hebrew.[24] The governess was usually present at these encounters not simply to act as a barrier to any illicit intimacy but also so that she might supervise homework more effectively. Shrewd women used this opportunity to improve their own skills and qualifications: 'I endeavoured to pick up a little French from the master that attended my pupils . . .' is a constant refrain in the governess' letters, diaries and memoirs.[25] It was only in modest middle-class homes, where there was little money available to spend on extra tuition, that the governess was expected to struggle along trying to teach everything indifferently.

When a girl reached her mid-teens she might either be sent away for a year to a fashionable boarding school or, alternatively, be entrusted to a 'finishing governess'. Less concerned with the nuts and bolts of academic instruction, it was the job of a 'finisher' like Miss Tenniel (the niece of the illustrator and artist) who worked for Mary Carbery's family in the 1880s to put polish on her charges, preparing them for adult life in the drawing-room.[26] Piano, singing and dancing now took precedence over history and geography. If languages were especially valued, girl and governess might be sent to a genteel boarding-house in some European city to brush up the girl's vocabulary and generally extend her cultural horizons.[27] By the age of seventeen or eighteen, a girl's education was deemed to be complete, regardless of the proficiency she had reached in her various subjects. For upper-class girls presentation at Court, followed by one or more seasons as a debutante, would mark the period until marriage. Young women from more modest homes followed a scaled-down version of this schedule, immersing themselves in a programme of morning calls, charity work and visits to relatives in other parts of the country, the main point of which was to expose them to a pool of eligible men from which they might one day find a husband.[28]

When it came to the day-to-day reality of schoolroom life, these distinctions and specialities were often blurred and even ignored altogether. Since her pupils might range from five to fifteen years old, a governess was frequently obliged to cater for all age groups. If she was in charge of small boys then it was part of her job to bring them up to the point where they were ready to enter a preparatory school at the age of eight.[29] Later in the century, those women who were particularly gifted in one subject could find themselves expected to teach children from neighbouring households whose own governess was weak in that field.[30] Once a governess had been taken on she was at the disposal of her employers and could be borrowed or shared between friends: by the 1880s Milly Acland was far from unusual in setting off every morning for the local vicarage where her cousins and their governess awaited her in the schoolroom.[31]

In a large family, where elder sisters were already under the supervision of the governess, the transition from nursery to school-room was in the natural order of things, as much a part of turning five as a birthday cake with candles. If the nursery was overcrowded with new babies, promotion might come at the age of three or four. For others, like Mary Carbery in the 1880s, the waiting could seem interminable: her elder sister's governess, Miss Moll, was adamant that she should not start lessons until she was five. Desperate to learn to read, Mary turned to the butler for help instead.[32] Yet Miss Moll's hard-line attitude was essential if she was not to find herself overwhelmed with extra responsibilities. Governesses frequently complained that 'those who were too young to be my pupils were not thought too young to be turned into the schoolroom to play'.[33] The more assertive amongst them made it clear to their employers that they were not prepared to have the schoolroom used as nanny's dumping ground.[34]

In those cases where the arrival of the governess coincided with the departure of a much-loved nurse the transition could be traumatic. Sybil Lubbock remembered how, one summer in the early 1880s:

'The bottom fell out of my small safe world':[35] returning from her summer holidays, she found that her beloved nanny had departed to Australia, leaving only a note on her dressing table: 'Do not grieve. It is right that you should have a lady to teach you – and I know you will be good and obedient to her'.[36] Despite nanny's gentle advice, and her mother's attempts to distract her from her grief, the distraught Sybil could see the incident only as a sort of betrayal and, 'It was years before I had any confidence in life again.'[37]

Not every nurse was so generous in their dealings with the in-coming governess. Responsible for the children's emotional and physical needs virtually from the time of their birth, nanny had formed a bond with her young charges that frequently went deeper than anything they felt for their natural parents.[38] Not only did the nurse share the working-class background of the other domestic servants but, in rural areas, she was very often a local woman whose family had been known for decades, if not centuries, to her employers. Jealousy and insecurity grew as, one by one, 'her' children left the nursery for the supervision of a 'foreigner' whose claims to authority seemed to rest on nothing more than a highly contestable class position. Of all the domestic staff, it was the nurse whose life was most intimately bound up with that of the governess. A girl of seven or eight might remain under nanny's general jurisdiction while attending lessons in the schoolroom, a state-of-affairs which required a high degree of co-operation between nurse and governess if the child was to accomplish smoothly her daily time-table of sleep, play and lessons. Not surprisingly, such co-operation seems frequently to have been lacking: strife rather than harmony marked the dealings between schoolroom and nursery. Children often became pawns in a power struggle between the adults who were paid to look after them. Nanny had a head start, in that she had enjoyed five years of unchallenged supremacy during which she could fill her charges' heads with all manner of stories about the horrors which awaited them beyond the nursery:

> the idea of a coming governess was held up to children as a terror, a sort of judgment about to fall upon them; she was expected to be thin, middle-aged, and spectacled, fearfully strict, and wielding a sharp-edged ruler with which cold, stiff fingers were soon to become acquainted whilst trying to play scales on wintry mornings.[39]

Such myths played upon the child's anxiety about exchanging an existence marked by the rhythms of sleep and play for one that was structured by an outside and possibly hostile force. It was no wonder that initial impressions of the schoolroom confirmed it as the hostile and alien place which nanny had so graphically described. Sonia Keppel remembered how her Edwardian schoolroom

> was a dreary room after my bright day-nursery. It looked out on to colourless backs of houses, and through it rattled an aggressively belicose pipe. No one seemed to know the pipe's source or destination and, some days, it rattled worse than others. It added a martial emphasis to my first lessons, as though Moiselle had hidden reserves of troops at sabre-drill which she could call to her aid if I proved obdurate.[40]

Despite the manual writers' far-from-practical suggestion that the governess could disarm the nanny by pretending to ask her advice,[41] a state of war frequently continued to rage for years between the schoolroom and the nursery. When, in the late 1870s, Angela Forbes burst into tears of anguish on catching a glimpse of her beloved former nanny, her governess 'inveigled me into her room with the promise of chocolate and when she got me safely there, gave me a sound smacking'.[42] Bathing and dressing the younger schoolroom children remained the responsibility of the nursery, and nanny made certain that she extracted every possible advantage out of the situation. In the ensuring scuffles children were sometimes, quite literally, pulled in two directions.

> With [Eddie] . . . the nurse was horrid. She stood him up and tickled him. She was not seemly. Eddie fled with a yell into the arms of Miss Moll, who had been lurking in the passage . . .
>
> '*My* little boy, if you please', said the nurse, trying to snatch him. Molly chaséed aside.
>
> 'Little boy indeed!' she snorted, 'That is not the way to speak of a young gentleman! Behave yourself', and she gave another chasée as the woman snatched again. Just then Mama came on the scene.[43]

The different roles which the nurse and the governess played in the life of their charges were reflected in the names by which they were known. The nurse was always 'Nurse' or 'Nanny' – a convention which defined her in terms of a function rather than her own identity. This label might be personalised to the extent of adding either her own surname or that of her employers.[44] The governess, by contrast, was *always* known by her own name,

Miss Smith (not 'Smith' which would have put her on a level with an upper servant). The formality of this arrangement implied a certain emotional distance between governess and pupils and emphasised the former's personal identity over her occupational role. Nonetheless, affectionate children found 'Miss Smith' too daunting and substituted a nickname, most often a corruption of the governess' surname, which they confidently used to her face. Thus Sybil Lubbock's Miss Cutting became 'Scutty',[45] Cynthia Asquith's Fraulein von Moskovicz turned into 'Squidge' (because she looked like a squirrel),[46] while the Maynards had 'Ditchie'.[47] Nor did the flights of fancy stop there: in 1876 young Harry Wiggett lavished on his beloved governess, Edith Gates, every pet name that he could think of:

> dear, darling, sweet, duchy and even jolly, being everyday expressions prefixed to my name which is often so varied as scarcely to have any resemblance with the original.[48]

In return governesses seem generally to have called their pupils by their Christian names, although there may well have been exceptions to this rule. In Elizabeth Sewell's novel, *Amy Herbert*, for instance, Amy noticed how

> her cousins addressed Miss Morton by her Christian name, but that she in reply always spoke of Miss Harrington and Miss Margaret: indeed, in every possible way, there seemed to be a determination to show her that she was considered quite an inferior person.[49]

Likewise the ill-bred Bloomfield family of Anne Brontë's *Agnes Grey* referred to their children as 'Miss' and 'Master' in front of the governess, thus subtly implying that her situation in their house was no different from that of a domestic servant.[50] Such a jibe would hardly be lost on even the youngest children, so that maintaining authority in these circumstances became, as Agnes Grey discovered, an uphill struggle.

The governess found herself in the unenviable position of being a mother-surrogate, yet without any of the delegated authority that normally goes with being *in loco parentis*. The problem was that while mothers fully intended to concern themselves with supervising their daughters' education, the structure of their lives meant that they had only the vaguest idea of what went on in the nursery and the schoolroom. The off-hand yet intrusive way in which some women reacted to events in the home schoolroom suggests that they set very little store by the governess or by her activities. For instance, while the advice writers gave elaborate descriptions of how the schoolroom *ought* to look – 'It need not be carpeted all over, but it should have a centre carpet on its partly polished floor'[51] – all too often it turned out to be the ugliest, noisiest and darkest room in the whole house. What is more, if the family travelled a great deal, and especially if it stayed in hotels, then the governess might find that she was deprived of a permanent place altogether. During the Bradshaws' sojourn at the Hotel de l'Europe in Pau in April 1854 Mary Bazlinton discovered that she was expected to set up her schoolroom in the dining-room, although the nanny had been assigned a very large room for exclusive use as a nursery.[52] This failure to allow Bazlinton autonomy over her own space spoke eloquently to the whole household of just how little importance her employers attached to her activities. From here it was a short step to deducing how little they valued her too.

On a practical level, this type of disruption made it difficult to keep children's minds fixed on their work. Upper-class life remained essentially peripatetic throughout the nineteenth century. Working for the Kay-Shuttleworth family during the 1890s, May Pinhorn found that 'I was sometimes settled in one place for only a few weeks'[53] – the constant packing up and settling in could disturb the most placid child's attention. Other governesses complained of employers who thought nothing of re-arranging the children's day at short notice, taking them out of the schoolroom for an impromptu expedition to the park or to receive visitors in the drawing-room. Even Queen Victoria was not above popping into the schoolroom of her youngest daughter and insisting that she needed Beatrice's help or attention, much to the annoyance of the governess.[54] Only occasionally would a governess, such as the fictional Maria Young from Harriet Martineau's *Deerbrook*, have the confidence and the authority to turn visitors away from the schoolroom on the grounds that such intrusions disturbed the children's concentration.[55]

Many governesses found themselves at the mercy of fond and foolish mothers who had little idea of the difficulties involved in keeping children in good order. In very large houses where the schoolroom and nursery were housed in a distant wing, parents might encounter their children only by prearranged appointment. Even in more modest households it was common for a woman to be with her children for only an hour or two a day. It is no wonder that many mothers came away with the idea that their children were little angels who could be controlled with nothing more than a firm word and a winning smile. As a consequence many governesses were instructed not to punish their pupils themselves but to refer any occasional matters of discipline to their mother.[56]

An experienced woman like Miss Cutting who taught Sybil Lubbock by-passed this problem by annexing the authority of her employer – 'if your mother doesn't mind untidy hair or inky fingers . . . neither do I'[57] – without putting herself into a situation where this might be challenged. By contrast, a younger woman like Charlotte Brontë charged straight into a mire of embarrassment, 'A complaint to Mrs Sidgwick brings only black looks upon oneself, and unjust, partial excuses to screen the children'.[58] Working at the end of the century, May Pinhorn decided to say nothing at all about her pupils' bad manners, and was then left in the position of having to witness behaviour which she herself found unacceptable: 'Mrs Wolfe Barry went in for giving her children a good time and not correcting them; owing to her deafness she probably did not quite realise how rude they often were and how inconsiderate of older people.'[59] It is no wonder that situations in motherless families were particular popular amongst governesses.[60]

Young children were quick to pick up on their governess' power-lessness, losing no time in exploiting the situation to their own advantage. The young Lady Muriel Beckwith was delighted when her enraged Fraulein marched her off to her father's study because she knew that her bad behaviour would be treated by him as nothing more than a huge joke.[61] Some mothers even set aside all notions of tact and discussed the governess with the children behind her back – behaviour which could not fail to undermine her already shaky authority even further. Such was the unhappy experience of Mary Bazlinton:

Tuesday 10 April 1855. Troubled again with Tiney. She was again down late. On my telling her I should be obliged to complain to her Mama she was exceedingly rude even insolent – among other things saying 'you are quite welcome to complain – for Mama is as little pleased with your goings on as I am. You cannot be more disagreeable than you are. It would not be possible to speak too badly of *you*'. The whole party went to the races after an early dinner excepting myself who declined and Mrs Bradshaw whom the cold kept at home. I took the opportunity of being alone with her to speak of Tiney's conduct. She expressed herself much displeased at her impertinence and said I ought to have told her of it sooner and she

should not have gone to the races. But this is as she always has done.
I feel quite certain she would not have kept her at home . . .[62]

Metaphorically bound and gagged, the governess was deprived of the authority that she needed if she were to have any hope of keeping up to half a dozen children under control. Although individual women did write to periodicals with their own tried and tested strategies for coping with children of widely differing ages,[63] it was still the case that someone lost out in terms of supervision and stimulation. Keeping order proved even more of a problem if there were young boys in the schoolroom. Victorian autobiographies are full of tales of governess-baiting – a sport in which small boys, chafing under petticoat rule, were only too happy to lead:

> My eldest brother was not strong, either physically or morally, and Mama would never allow him to be sent away to school, and in consequence he was always at hand to help us in tormenting poor Miss Haas, who was foolish enough to make favourites, and had not, alas for her! the very smallest sense of humour . . . Willie and I drew rude pictures on our slates, and read what we liked, and came in and went out as we liked, and no one interefered with us at all.[64]

Other favourite tricks included placing a live crayfish in the governess' bed,[65] putting mice into her tea-caddy,[66] or surreptitiously putting hedgehogs and squirrels in her bedroom.[67] For even the best-mannered children, there was enormous sport to be had in finding the chinks in their governess' intellectual armour. Angela Forbes was delighted when hers came under a fire of questions from her father;[68] kindly Elizabeth Garrett enjoyed asking Miss Edgeworth questions to which she knew she had not prepared the answer;[69] Jane Panton seems to have experienced delight in finding out that Miss Wright's much-vaunted familiarity of France consisted of a stint au-pairing for a chemist in Boulogne.[70]

Denied the legitimate means to keep order, some governesses inevitably found themselves reduced to an indiscriminate slapping and punching, the result of overstrained nerves. While whipping girls became increasingly less acceptable throughout the century, incidents of corporal punishment were still frequently recorded, even in the most elevated households. As a child, Lady Frederick Cavendish seems to have been particularly unlucky with the tyrannical Miss Nicholson who was

> over-severe and apt to whip me for obstinacy when I was only dense,

letting me see her partiality for the other two, and punishing too often . . .

At Brighton I used to be taken out walking on the parade with my hands tied behind me, terrified out of my wits by Miss Nicholson's declaring it was ten to one we should meet a policeman. At home my usual punishment was being put for a time into a large, deep old-fashioned bath that was in one corner of the schoolroom, before which hung curtains, so that I was partially in the dark. I was continually put between the doors and often whipped.[71]

The young Lord Curzon and his siblings were on the receiving end of even harsher discipline from Miss Perelman who taught them during the 1860s:

In her savage moments she was a brutal and vindictive tyrant; and I have often thought since that she must have been insane. She persecuted and beat us in the most cruel way and established over us a system of terrorism so complete that not one of us ever mustered up the courage to walk upstairs and tell our father or mother. She spanked us with the sole of her slipper on the bare back, beat us with her brushes, tied us for long hours to chairs in uncomfortable positions with our hands holding a pole or a blackboard behind our backs, shut us up in darkness, practised on us every kind of petty persecution, wounded our pride by dressing us (me in particular) in red shining calico petticoats (I was obliged to make my own) with an immense conical cap on our heads round which, as well as on our breasts and backs, were sewn strips of paper bearing in enormous characters, written by ourselves, the words Liar, Sneak, Coward, Lubber and the like . . .

She forced us to confess to lies which we had never told, to sins which we had never committed, and then punished us savagely, as being self-condemned. For weeks we were not allowed to speak to each other or to a human soul.[72]

Just in case there is any suspicion that Lord Curzon and Lady Frederick Cavendish had let their memories run away with them when recalling such fearsome schooldays, it is worth remembering that around this time the Queen's eldest child, Vicky, was punished for lying by being 'imprisoned with tied hands'.[73] That children did not complain to their parents about such rough justice is explained, as Curzon implied, by the emotional distance between schoolroom and drawing-room. The benign indifference which characterised upper-class mothers' attitudes to their children could turn into something cooler when the little angels turned out to have inconvenient and potentially disruptive demands. Loelia Ponsonby endured years of misery at the hands of a stream of sadistic governesses because she felt that to 'tell tales' would only make her life 'a nightmare'.[74] Likewise Mary Carbery explained the reticence of herself and her siblings in the following terms:

> We can't break the strictest law of all children by telling tales of her [Miss Moll] to Papa and Mama, who only see her in her charming manners. They have no idea of our troubles. They do not know how deplorably artful we are growing; how in our fear we try to propitiate her with flowers, peaches, and tender inquiries after her relations. They do not notice how pale and anxious our faces are. They have their own troubles, and Mama is occupied with the new baby . . .[75]

As Carbery suggests, the same code of discretion which, in theory at least, prevented an employer publicly complaining about the governess, and the governess complaining about her pupils, also inhibited pupils from carrying tales about their teacher to their parents. In any case, children quickly worked out that since they were obliged to deal with the governess all day every day, while they saw their mother only intermittently, there was little sense in stirring up conflict in the schoolroom unless they could be certain that it would be resolved permanently in their favour.

In the main the home schoolroom was run along lines as formal as the local elementary school, with terms and timetables, a bell and a blackboard. The school week was usually five and a half days long with lessons continuing until lunchtime on Saturdays – a regime which Georgiana Sitwell wearily remembered as 'a perfect treadmill of learning'[76] Lady Frederick Cavendish was typical in recalling that during her schoolroom days of the 1850s, 'holidays were very rare, and it was seldom we were let off a lesson. I have often worked till bedtime, and always after tea, finishing what had been left undone'.[77] Forty years later, things had changed little. Winifred Peck sketched out the timetable she followed between the ages of three and eight:[78]

Practice	Dinner (lunch)
Breakfast	Rest (using a backboard
Copy books	Bible reading and reading
Arithmetic	aloud from a novel
History	Walk
Break	Tea
Geography	Sewing/reading aloud
Poems	

Around the the age of eight French and possibly German would be added to the timetable; if a foreign governess were employed, whole portions of the day might be spent practising these languages.[79] Music played a central place in the curriculum from the day a child entered the schoolroom until the day she left. Piano, violin and singing were practised on a daily basis, with lessons from visiting masters once or twice a week. Lunch would be served in the schoolroom when the children were small,[80] but once they reached the age of twelve it could be taken downstairs with their mother (a separate table for children and governess might be provided if there were visitors present).[81] Physical exercise was a large and important part of the schoolday: too much concentration on brainwork was thought to overtax growing girls. Until the age of thirteen this recreation could be as boisterous as anything enjoyed by their brothers, although the assumption was always that running, jumping and playing cricket would take place behind the park or garden fence, well away from prying eyes. Once a girl was older, riding and gardening were recommended though, in practice, the most frequent sort of exercise taken by girls and their governess was the daily walk which usually lasted two hours.[82] Even then the time was to be put to good use, either practising French or German conversation,[83] or observing and identifying flora and fauna.[84] An almost obsessive fear that growing girls might develop spinal deformities meant that the backboard was a familiar fixture in the schoolroom and one that would be recalled with dislike in later years.[85]

Arithmetic remained a weak subject with governesses and their pupils until the end of the century.[86] According to Lady Muriel Beckwith, her governess Moffy could not see why there was any need to teach such a vulgarly utilitarian subject at all:

Such arithmetic as might be necessary for the balancing of household accounts she would impart, but for the rest of the tiresome and bothering business, simply let it remain a closed book.[87]

A housemaid interrupts a lesson to deliver a message. While the governess' dress and deportment announce her to be a lady, the housemaid's sulky deference suggests that the status of the governess, as far as the servants are concerned, is open to challenge. Note the schoolroom paraphernalia, including globe, blackboard (complete with elementary geometry) and wall chart (1882). (*Mary Evans Picture Library*).

Science of any type was also unknown to the Victorian home schoolroom. The nearest that girls, and indeed their brothers, got to the subject was a series of passions for butterfly and egg collecting, enthusiasms which might be encouraged by the governess, but which retained the status of a hobby.[88] One clergyman's daughter, who later won a scholarship to Girton, recalled how, in the 1860s:

> Science we learnt from *The Child's Guide to Knowledge* and *Brewer's Guide*. All I now remember of these is the date at which black silk stockings came into England and 'What to do in a thunderstorm at night', the answer being: 'Draw your bed into the the the middle of the room, commend your soul to Almighty God and go to sleep'.[89]

Latin was included on the syllabus only if the governess was a clergyman's daughter or if a father decided to take on this responsibility himself. Other omissions included modern literature, which was not studied during class time because, following the lead of public schools and universities, contemporary novels were not considered a subject suitable for sustained critical attention. Reading Scott aloud (Dickens was a little dubious) made a pleasant accompaniment to an evening's sewing session, but positively light-weight fiction was to be avoided since it encouraged day-dreaming and led to a softening of the brain.[90] Texts used in the schoolroom varied according to preference, but they were likely to include a mixture of specialist books like the infamous *Mangnall's Questions*[91] – row after row of general knowledge questions and answers – as well as classic and contemporary works by authors as varied as Bossuet, Clarendon, Coleridge, Racine, Arnold and Macaulay.[92]

When it came to deciding what should be taught in the school-room, and how, mothers had an unpleasant knack of interfering in matters which they did not understand: Sir George Stephen, who wrote a *Guide To Service* for governesses in 1844, sketched in two of the worst types of offenders. First there was Lady Halton who was adamant that life should be made as pleasant as possible for her girls:

> Language was to be acquired without grammar: history without chronology: geography without globes: music without the scales: drawing without copies: and everything in the way of study was resolved into irregular accumulation of odds and ends of knowledge, because system was ennuyant, and labour should be amusing to be continuous.[93]

Even more irritating was Mrs Watson who insisted unnervingly on sitting and sewing in the corner of the schoolroom.[94] Most common of all, however, was the mother who insisted that her daughters concentrate on one subject at the expense of others – an obsession which was almost certainly the product, as Stephen pointed out, of her own insecurities:

> The mother may be very conscious of her inferiority in some art of accomplishment, and hence she attaches an overweening importance to excellence in it. 'Everything must be sacrificed to *that*.' No matter whether it is painting or music, French or Italian. Some time or other she has failed to pleased, and vanity has told her that it was because she had failed in the desiderated accomplishment. It may be music – then, the piano *must* be practised, at least, three hours a day.[95]

Yet while manual writers were swift in their condemnation of women like Lady Halton and Mrs Watson, they were adamant that this did not give the governess the right to take matters into her own hands. Even by the beginning of the twentieth century manual writers were still warning her that:

> The Mother's suggestions on teaching may seem to you old-fashioned, or you may disagree on even more important matters, but you do more for the child's moral stability by loyally upholding the prestige of the mother as such, than by being right yourself on any special point.[96]

Whether or not this programme captured the imagination depended, inevitably, on the way it was put across. A clever governess might turn out to be a poor teacher since, as Harriet Martineau stressed, 'the faculty of developing and instructing inferior minds is wholly separate from that of acquiring, holding, and using knowledge . . .'[97] Certainly not everyone was as skilled as Jane Panton's Miss Wright at capturing the imagination of small children:

> If anything exciting were going on in any part of the world, we had to know all about that part of the world, and to learn day by day how things were progressing, and thus we fought our way through the Crimea, the Mutiny Bowdlerised, the coming of Garibaldi, and the tremendous war in America that saw the death of slavery.[98]

It was an approach which more literally-minded governesses found suspect. When the German-born and formally-trained Miss Cutting started work in Sybil Lubbock's schoolroom during the 1880s, she discovered that, while Sybil and her sister could argue passionately for and against the Cavaliers and Roundheads, they were unable to tell her when Charlemagne ruled.[99] The only solution, she suggested, was to start again from scratch using a more orderly method of careful reading, abstract-making and rote learning. It was this unimaginative approach which characterised the most rigorous home teaching during the nineteenth century. Constance Maynard, a studious girl who went on to Girton, seems to have been typical in experiencing the schoolroom of the 1870s as a temple dedicated to the learning and reproduction of facts:

> So many pages of Mrs Markham to read aloud, a French verb to repeat (and the accent taught was excellent), ten examples from *Colenso* to be worked, six questions of *Mangnall* to answer, and two pages of *Child's Guide* to prepare. This latter book was easy and also varied; it told you what tapioca was, and why the thunder did not precede the lightning. I do not think I remember a spark of real interest being elicited, except when one governess (otherwise unsatisfactory) taught us to collect, press, and name the beautiful ferns of the neighbourhood; neither do I recollect any sort of explanation – no, not even to correct the spelling of the word Mediterranean, which had been rendered with two t's and one r . . . The strain was on memory and perseverance only, and neither reason nor imagination was called to co-operate. Of all the arithmetic I learned, and there was a little every day for several years, I can call to mind only one single rule, and it ran thus: 'Turn the fraction upside down, and proceed as before'. It was no wonder that children were not interested, and it is not much wonder that a little boy, economical of effort in learning his share of *Mangnall*, miscalculated his turn, and when asked 'What was the character of Henry the Eighth?' cried out enthusiastically 'Round and flattened at the poles'.[100]

Compounding the tedium of the home schoolroom was a sense of its pointlessness. While the assumption was always that a girl's accomplishments would one day be tested in the semi-public arena of the drawing-room, still there was no formal point of reckoning towards which she could channel her efforts. Education terminated at eighteen regardless of what level had been reached, and many girls seem to have spent the last couple of their schoolroom years looking forward to the day when they would 'come out' and start their adult lives.[101] Although by the 1870s a few writers in specialist magazines were suggesting that girls educated at home could be entered for the Cambridge and Oxford Local Examinations, which tested attainment from the age of sixteen,[102] this remained an extremely unpopular option. Dorothea Beale, the headmistress of Cheltenham Ladies College, explained to the Schools Inquiry Commission of 1867-68 that her pupils' parents did not wish their offspring to enter 'the Locals' because 'those who go in for the Local Examinations occupy a much lower place in the social scale, and our pupils would not like to be classed with them'.[103] Competing for certificates was all very well for high school girls, who would one day have to earn their living as schoolteachers, but for girls with any pretensions there was nothing to be gained and much to be lost by participating in anything so utilitarian.

So great was the stigma against any sort of examination for women that even informal tests in the schoolroom had to be handled with care. There was a feeling that the competitive element made them intrinsically unladylike, and there was always the danger of fanning existing sibling jealousies into something altogether more combustible. Despite warnings of its dangers from advice writers, favouritism was rife in the home schoolroom. Mary Carbery, Jane Panton and Lady Frederick Cavendish all mention in their autobiographies that their sisters – good, studious, clever little girls – were the ones who got all the attention, leaving them feeling second-rate: 'My eldest sister always wanted to learn; she really liked the stuffy schoolroom and the hateful books, and in consequence she received all the teaching . . .'[104] Certainly in 1876 Edith Gates found that it took very little to bring out the rivalry between Mary and Harry Wiggett:

> The children are all fond of arithmetic, particularly mental, and Friday, on which we have it, is called by them *'screaming day'*, and is looked forward to with joy all through the week. I examine them in all sorts of things which has to be done mentally, and he who finds it out first is allowed to answer. The excitement is universal, and I am sorry to say the noise sometimes great, in fact I am often obliged to threaten to give it up to keep them within bounds. Mary and Harry are the two great competitors, and the look of triumph when one answers before the other is quite amusing.[105]

In the end a curious position was reached whereby written tests were considered to be acceptable as long as no extra work had been done for them. Sybil Lubbock and her sister were so anxious to win a prize from Miss Cutting (they had their eye on a particular book which they could not afford themselves) that they swotted up the night before. On achieving full marks in their paper, they were obliged to confess what they had done, whereupon Miss Cutting refused to award them any prize at all: their conduct, she explained, 'was not quite conscientious'.[106]

This lack of an examination element in home schooling did not mean that the governess was free from anxieties about her own performance. As Mrs Murray, employer of Anne Brontë's fictional Agnes Grey remarked pointedly, 'while . . . [the governess] lives in obscurity herself, the pupils' virtues and defects will be open to every eye . . .'[107] The increasing obsession of parents that their daughters should be accomplished musicians and linguists put a burden of expectation on the women charged with teaching them. When a child failed to sing in tune or chatter fast enough in French, the governess could not fail to sense that her own competence was open to question. Employers as a class seem to have been reluctant to accept that their offspring lacked talent or application, preferring instead to lay the blame at their governess' door. Throughout the century article after article in the periodical press condemned the low levels of achievement attained by governesses – a fact which cannot have failed to create feelings of personal inadequacy in particularly conscientious women. For instance, Edith Gates remembered how, on starting work at the age of eighteen in 1875, 'I had very little experience of teaching, so that it was perhaps natural that I looked forwards with some dread and misgiving as to my future success'.[108] Even after she had been in her post a year she still experienced waves of guilt at what she perceived to be her own inadequacy, 'I only wish I were a "savante", or at least possessed of an infinitely larger store of knowledge than is the present Edith Gates'.[109] Yet whether Gates was justified in feeling so uncertain about her abilities is far from clear. According to Charlotte Brontë, writing several years after she had quit the schoolroom for good:

> The young teacher's chief anxiety, when she sets out in life, always is to know a great deal; her chief fear that she should not know enough. Brief experience will, in most instances, show her that this anxiety has been misdirected. She will rarely be found too ignorant for her pupils.[110]

Denied any other means of measuring their proficiency, it was inevitable that governesses should become oversensitive on the subject of their pupils' performance. Some, like Cynthia Asquith's Fraulein von Moskovicz, displayed an embarrassing vanity at second hand as a way of shoring up her own shaky self-esteem:

It was a wonder I wasn't lynched by exasperated contemporaries and their affronted governesses, for whenever we went out to tea with other children, she would maddeningly edit her own pupil by extolling the swiftness with which she ran and the agility with which she jumped. Worse still, she would expatiate on the retentiveness of her memory and the quickness of her mind. Worst of all, while I sat dumb as a stone, or merely mumbling of the weather, was the irony of overhearing the stage-whispered words, *'tellement originale'*, or *'si spirituelle'*.[111]

Other examples of one-upmanship were likely to occur when an aunt or family friend dropped in on the schoolroom only to boast about the superior achievements of her own children. Finding herself in just this situation, Mary Carbery's Miss Moll gave as good as she got, explaining away her pupils failure to speak French by insisting that she always believed in teaching the more difficult German first (in fact Miss Moll's knowledge of French was rudimentary). When it seemed as if, under strict questioning from their aunt, her pupils were about to reveal their backwardness, Miss Moll swiftly dismissed them for break, half an hour earlier than usual.[112]

Towards the end of the century, the possibilities widened for those girls who showed real intellectual ability, but whose parents still looked with suspicion on the new generation of public and high schools for girls. With governess still in tow, a girl might attend a course of 'lectures for ladies', or she might spend afternoons in the British Library.[113] In 1870, for example, Catherine Paget went to lectures at the Royal Institute in London and heard a series of talks on subjects as varied as 'The Nervous System' and 'The Migration of Fable'.[114] There was even a possibility of participating at one of the public schools on an *ad hoc* basis: once a week Cynthia Asquith and Fraulein von Moskovicz set off on the twelve-mile trip to Cheltenham Ladies College.[115] All the same, when intellectual enthusiasm threatened to outrun social propriety, the forces of convention were quick to make themselves felt. When London University lecturer Dr Heath suggested to Miss Cutting that a girl of Sybil Lubbock's ability should be tutored in Middle English, Sybil's parents refused point blank on the grounds that they had no desire for her to turn into a 'blue-stocking'. It was a decision which still rankled fifty years later.[116]

One effect of the professionalisation of all branches of school-teaching during the second half of the century was to make the able and conscientious governess more self-conscious about the theory and practice of her work. By 1876 Edith Gates' uncle was sending her clippings from an article outlining a new method of teaching geography,[117] while under the influence of her employers, the Kay-Shuttleworths, May Pinhorn developed a keen interest in educational issues. In her memoir written at the end of her life she bore witness to the impact that her time with this most famous of reforming dynasties had had upon her (her employer was the son of Sir James Kay-Shuttleworth):

> I . . . saw and heard much of educational people and ideas and had gained quite a different conception of the aim and object of my profession. At one time I went through a severe course of study in Psychology, Pedagogy, etc. with the intention of going in for the Cambridge Training of Teachers Diploma . . .[118]

May Pinhorn, however, was in an unusual position. Although Margaret Thornley, writing a manual for governesses in 1846, could advise her readers that: 'Public examinations of schools or individuals, the routine of school occupations of every class, public or private, are scenes to which you should never lose an opportunity of introducing yourself',[119] in general governesses remained aloof from the vocational qualifications that from 1870 onwards were becoming increasingly necessary for the independent schoolmistress. Even at the end of the century the governess was understood to have received only the same education as that of any middle-class woman: if her academic standards had improved from the nadir of the 1840s and 50s, this was simply because she had been keeping pace with her non-working sisters.

The fact that a child educated privately received the consistent attention of one teacher – albeit shared with a trio of siblings – does suggest that, at its best, home education offered an opportunity for swift academic progress that was simply not available in the school classroom. While there were many omissions to the home syllabus, there was also a real chance of following one or two subjects in depth. Most governess-educated girls advanced way beyond basic literacy and many became accomplished linguists and musicians. In the days before examinations, qualifications and certificates became available to women, there were plenty of governesses whose combination of wide reading and interest in children made the home schoolroom an inspiring place to be.[120] Some girls absorbed from it the habits of regular study and disciplined reading which they were able to carry with them into their adult lives.[121] Others, such as clergyman's daughter Mary Paley Marshall, only discovered how much they owed the governess once she had gone: 'It was after she left . . .

and we had no regular occupation that we began to feel bored, especially in winter ... visiting the poor, practising the singing for the church services and teaching in the Sunday School were hardly adequate occupation.'[122] While there is no doubt that home education lacked overall coherence, this was also true of the tuition on offer to those men who attended the country's most prestigious public schools and universities. When giving evidence to the Schools Inquiry Commission of 1867-68, Frances Buss, founder and headmistress of the academic London Collegiate School, revealed that those pupils who had received their early education at home were academically better prepared than their classmates who had been sent to preparatory schools.[123] Of the first generation to attend the new women's colleges at Oxford and Cambridge, a 'significant proportion' had been educated at home.[124] For every Miss Edgworth – the sheepish and incompetent woman who taught the Garrett girls[125] – there was a Mlle Germain, governess to Lady Georgina Peel, whose intellectual conversation so enchanted the French King Louis Philippe during his exile in Twickenham.[126]

As her pupils grew into their mid teens the governess gradually relinquished her role of teacher for that of guide and friend. Schoolroom life no longer centred upon slate and globe, but increasingly encompassed lessons from outside masters, visits to the local poor, and even a number of afternoon social engagements (evening parties remained the preserve of those who had officially Come Out). As her pupils made more and more forays into the world beyond the front door, the governess' presence was necessary to guard against contamination from vulgar persons or compromising situations. This was also the time, as confirmation and first communion approached, that questions of ethical and moral conduct presented themselves more strongly than ever. Although 'Religious instruction should in *every* case be given by one of the parents, preferably the mother',[127] it was the governess' job to ensure that these formal precepts were integrated into the conduct of everyday life. One woman who took her task seriously was Miss Pearson, governess to the ten-year-old Lady Frederick Cavendish:

> She was a woman of stern and upright mind, with a high and stern standard of duty, and little pity for those who did not reach it. Truth and openness were the first of human virtues with her. She had no mercy upon the equivocating habits that had grown upon us, and

punished them relentlessly. She quickly won our affection, though it was ever greatly mixed with fear, and her influence over me was such that, though I knew her hatred of what was sly, I confessed many things to her, choosing rather to face her bitter indignation – for she would not allow that confession palliated the fault – than to have anything on my mind in the presence of her clear and unshrinking openness.[128]

Paid to embody the bourgeois-Christian virtues of sobriety, honesty and order, it was a small step for the governess' behaviour to slip over into generalised smugness. Popular novels of the period often depended on a running contrast between the near saintly behaviour of the governess heroine and the dissolute carryings-on of her employers.[129] Perhaps with the fate of the fictional governess in mind – all too often she is threatened with dismissal for her 'impertinence' in daring to point out the failings of her betters – advice books warned her real-life counterpart against making too much show of her own moral superiority: it was her task to 'carefully, but not ostentatiously endeavour to become the model, which the mother ought herself to be'.[130] Rather than point out that the rest of the household was late for a particular event, it would be better to wait quietly until everyone else was ready, improving the shining hour with some knitting or a book.[131] Unfortunately, not every governess managed to be so unobtrusive in her virtue. Mary Smith's disapproval of her employer's taste in expensive jewels, on the grounds that it was not compatible with her Baptist faith, went a long way to explaining why she left her position after only a week.[132] One of the many causes of friction between Mary Bazlinton and the Bradshaws during 1854-55 was over her one-woman crusade to convert the Catholic natives of Pau, including her employers' domestic staff, to her stern and enthusiastic brand of Protestantism.[133]

Although probably not the case with Bazlinton, there was always a danger that a charismatic governess might be able to influence her pupils on the doctrinal issues of the day. Cynthia Asquith's parents, for instance, were horrified to find that their daughter had taken up the ritualism of her Anglo-Catholic governess, Miss Jourdain.[134] The scrupulous care that Sybil Lubbock's Miss Cutting took not to abuse her position only reinforced the sense of potential conflict and embarrassment:

She thought, I now believe, our religious training to have been both lax and ritualistic, but was far too conscientious to force her own doctrinal views upon us. 'You will be guided by your dear mother at present', she would say, 'and later you will judge for yourselves.'[135]

It was to avoid these tensions that employers were urged to employ a governess who shared their doctrinal believes: 'You must, for the sake of domestic harmony in that most vital of interests, have the assurance that her [the governess'] opinions are in accordance with your own; her convictions as fixed – as sincere'.[136] In some cases such words of warning were superfluous. A governess as socially and financially vulnerable as Edmund Gosse's Miss Marks was far more likely to develop a sudden and convenient commitment to the doctrinal beliefs of her employers:

> I believe I do her rather limited intelligence no injury when I say that it was prepared to swallow, at one mouthful, whatever my Father presented to it, so delighted was its way-worn possessor to find herself in a comfortable, or at least, independent position.[137]

Yet in taking to religion so passionately, Miss Marks may have discovered more than a way of keeping a roof over her head. Advice writers were fond of advising their readers that 'in the Middle Ages the education of the young was a *religious* vocation on the part of women as of the men',[138] and many went on to suggest that the contemporary governess should continue to consider herself as a member of a holy order:

> The governess who teaches history and geography, and hears scales practised, with the conscientious care of one who has the fear of God before her eyes, is just as much a handmaid of the Church, as if she were a nursing or teaching Sister in a community.[139]

There were certainly many experiences that were common to both nun and governess, not least chastity, poverty, self-restraint and a concentration on book learning. Just as the idea of teaching as a quasi-religious vocation sustained many of the women who entered the classrooms of the new generation of girls schools after 1870,[140] so too it offered a way of easing some of the tensions which the resident governess faced in her employers' household. For instance, by telling themselves that their daughters' teacher had her mind on Higher Things, employers were able to go on paying her little and working her hard without too much trouble to their consciences. By mentally removing her from the material to the spiritual world, they also had to worry less about fitting her in to the household structure or including her in their own social activities. Moreover, by assigning the governess the role of celibate, it was possible to emphasise the contrast with the 'fruitful' mother, at the same time neutralising an association with the sexualised 'working woman'. For her part the governess could blank out the financial motivation which had brought her into this work and substitute the more flattering impression that she had been 'called' to her vocation. By concentrating on that day when the meek and poor were certain to inherit the earth, she could insulate herself against the emotional, social and financial snubs which marked her daily life. So seductive did some governesses, including the redoutable Miss Jourdain, find this version of themselves as God's holy daughters that they took things to their logical conclusion by becoming deaconesses, the nearest thing the Church of England could offer to religious sisterhood.[141]

Whether she was loved or loathed, the departure of the governess frequently set off a reaction as violent as those which follow bereavement. Having experienced such discontinuity herself, Eleanor Farjeon was perceptive about what effect such a series of losses might have on small children:

> The departure of the First Governess, like the departure of the First Nurse, creates a Nursery cataclysm. They are *The* Nurse, *The* Governess, as our parents are *The* Parents. Could there be others? These were the life we knew. Was there another? (What if *The* Parents one day departed too?)[142]

A fear of abandonment, grounded in the first traumatic parting from nanny could permeate the child's subsequent relationship with her governess, even when there was no real chance of her leaving. Edith Gates recorded in her diary that

> Mary assured me today that if I were to go away she should cry every day till I came back, so that they would have to send for me again, as she was sure she could never like anybody else as much as me . . . .[143]

Meanwhile Fanny Monday began to be extremely nice to her governess Mary Bazlinton during their last month together in October 1859, perhaps because she had some guilty notion that she was in some way responsible for her teacher being sent away.

In return, Bazlinton found her mind wistfully running on what-might-have-been: 'had she [Fanny] always acted as she did during this last month what a happy home I might have had with her'.[144]

When fears became reality and the time came for the governess to pack her trunk, the effect on her pupils could be devastating. The motherless Marchioness of Londonderry found herself particularly distraught, 'This was a very real grief to my sister and myself for she had mothered us for seven years'.[145] Likewise, Cynthia Asquith became unconsolable on hearing that her beloved Miss Jourdain was to be sent away:

> I neither ate nor slept. Still less would I speak. Before long, I had cried myself into such a state of hysteria that my unfortunate mother had to be telegraphed for and doctors called in.[146]

On the other hand, while Mary Bazlinton was moved to tears when the time finally came to say goodbye to an earlier pupil, Toddy Bradshaw whom she taught during 1854-55, the girl herself 'bid me farewell with a perfectly unmoved manner'.[147] Toddy Bradshaw's behaviour confirms a feeling born out by the autobiographies of the period that, with the superb arrogance of their age and class, few girls seem to have given much thought to what such a parting would mean to their governess. While for the girls themselves this represented a personal loss, for the governess it might well spell the beginning of a period of insecurity and unemployment. It was the perceptive Miss Cutting who reminded Sybil Lubbock which one of them had most to lose by the ending of their association.

> I turned to Scutty. 'Oh, dear, I am going to miss you so', I said, and clutched her hand.
>   But she disengaged it gently. 'My dear, don't distress yourself,' she said with her usual composure, 'I don't think you will miss me very much, though it is natural for you to think so. Your life is beginning. You will find new friends and new interests. You will have little time to miss anyone. But I shall miss you, for my life is not opening but closing in, as is natural at my age, and I shall be very glad whenever you find time to write to me.[148]

5

They Dwell Alone

It is only the governess, and a certain class of private tutors, who must
hear the echoes from the drawing-room . . . feeling that, in a house
full of people, they dwell alone.

Anon., *Fraser's Magazine* (1844)

Insolence to a governess is an old stock complaint. In real life, I
never heard of it from anyone by birth and breeding a lady; the only
instances I can recollect were in one case from a thoroughly vulgar
employer, in the other from a servant, who was sharply rebuked, and
I think, dismissed for it.

Charlotte Mary Yonge, *Womankind* (1876)

On 1 July 1839, during her short stint as governess to the Sidgwick
family, Charlotte Brontë dashed off one of many notes to her best
friend Ellen Nussey, apologising for the fact that it was in pencil
by explaining: 'I cannot just now procure ink without going into
the drawing-room, where I do not wish to go'.[1] It was not because
her employers' drawing-room was utterly out of bounds that Brontë
did not wish to go there but precisely because the situation was
ambiguous. If she suddenly appeared in the doorway the Sidgwicks
might insist that she join them for the whole evening; there again,
they might make it quite clear that they considered her presence
an intrusive nuisance. Rather than confront either of these painful
possibilities, Brontë decided to sacrifice her search for the ink-pot
in favour of a tranquil evening spent alone in her own room.

The problems which Brontë faced in her pursuit of writing
materials went far beyond her own lack of social skills or the
uncertain hospitality of her employers. Her dilemma, which every
governess faced in some form or other, struck at the very heart of
her incongruent position, both within the household and in society

at large.[2] The problem was this: to uphold her claims to ladyhood it was imperative that the governess should be treated as one of the family, mixing freely with its members on equal terms as far as her schoolroom duties allowed. Only by thus insisting upon her surrogate cousinhood could the fact of her paid employment be neutralised and her similarity to the working-class maidservant obscured. However, it was just at this time, during the first half of the nineteenth century, that the middle-class family was rationalising its personnel and organising itself around an increasingly firm distinction between kith and kin, family and friends, masters and servants. Shorn of the tangle of sisters, cousins and aunts which had lent it its sprawling character in previous centuries, the bourgeois household began to take on a more compact shape, similar to today's nuclear family but built on a more generous scale. At the same time, the employment of a growing number of servants to perform exclusively domestic tasks – as opposed to the more general duties that were required of them in the eighteenth century – meant that the activities and personnel associated with 'below stairs' were increasingly differentiated from those 'above'. By the 1850s the upper middle-class household was beginning to see itself as a microcosm of society at large, a self-sufficient kingdom, complete with ruler, consort, subjects and lower orders.

What was missing from this model of the household/kingdom was a middle class to which the governess might be assigned, an intermediary station which would ratify her position as neither family member nor servant. It was, ironically, the upper-class household with its elaborate hierachy of domestics including, at the top, such important personages as the butler and housekeeper, that was most able to provide its resident staff with the appropriate social and physical space. If Charlotte Brontë had been employed by aristocrats, the chances are that she would have found herself provided with the sort of furnished sitting-room that would have allowed her to side-step the dilemma of the ink-pot. Codes of conduct, evolved over centuries, enabled households such as these to acknowledge the governess' unusual position within the household, although, as former governess and manual writer Anna Jameson pointed out, the consequence of that recognition might be a fair degree of isolation:

> In general, the higher the rank the greater will be the *courtesy* with which you are treated; such courtesy being ever in proportion to the wideness and impassability of the distance which society has placed

THF FAMILY GOVERNESS.

She only said, "My life is dreary."

TENNYSON

A sad-looking governess finds the *cri de coeur* of Tennyson's Lady of Shalott particularly pertinent to her own situation (*c. 1840*).

(*Mary Evans Picture Library*).

between you and your employer. In a family of high rank and place, you will have more solitude, but more independence: you will be shielded even by your state of proscription from petty affronts; but you will have neither companionship nor sympathy. In a family of the middle classes, even where the people are well-bred, you will be in a more ambiguous and a more difficult position. You will have more comforts and companionship than in a family of higher rank, but the discomforts inseparable from your position will come nearer to you, and in a form more disagreeable.[3]

Those 'discomforts' which Jameson identified as part and parcel of a post in a middle-class home arose out of employers' simultaneous need to uphold the governess' membership of their family, yet at the same time resist its full implications. On the one hand, employers had a great interest in acknowledging their governess' ladyhood, since here was confirmation of their own gentility and, more specifically, their daughters'. On the other, they knew that to acknowledge the governess as a full family member, a surrogate sister or daughter, would be to drag down the social status of *all* the women of the family and, by extension, of the household as a whole. While the upper classes had little reason to fear that their daughters' governess might somehow be mistaken for one of them, a wealthy business family was likely to experience such a confusion as a challenge to its dignity. It was for this reason that some employers felt the need to mark their social distance from the governess by means of a hundred little snubs and petty slights of the type that passed so quickly into governess mythology. It was in these households, where space was cramped and social roles still in the making, that domestic staff were also likely to challenge the governess' right to claim the respect and attention due to a lady. If middle-class employers were anxious to stress their governess' unlikeness to themselves, their servants were equally keen to point out how little separated her situation from their own.

The reluctance of some employers to welcome the governess as a full family member could not fail to alarm the manual writers. Treating the governess in a way that hinted at her similarity to a servant suggested that ladyhood was not an absolute state apart, but rather was open to constant challenge and revision. If the governess was not automatically treated with the consideration due to a lady, it followed that no lady in the land, no matter how leisured, could assume that her own claims on the respect and deference of others were necessarily secure. Insensitive behaviour to the governess comprised a challenge to those codes of gentility around which the wealthier sections of the middle class had been organising itself since the beginning of the century. By 1850 the question of the governess' domestic comfort had become a litmus test which measured the gentility and morality both of the family which employed her and that of society at large. A contented governess, treated with the respect and consideration due to a gentlewoman, was a sign that all was right with the world. The sight of an unhappy or slighted governess, by contrast, suggested that the ethos of bourgeois gentility was not only unstable but possibly bankrupt. Rather than face such an alarming proposition, the manual writers worked hard to demonstrate that those employers who failed to treat their governess properly were betraying, above all, their own lack of breeding. Any matron looking for help in Mrs Valentine's *The Amenities of Home* would be left in no doubt that her failure to catch and keep a governess was a sure indication that she herself was 'not quite a lady':

> Neglect or rudeness to a lady thus circumstanced – for we suppose that only a gentlewoman would be received into the family – is inexcusable, from the side of good-feeling and generosity of character, as well as from good-breeding; and it is rather remarkable that governesses always prefer going into comparatively poor aristo-cratic families (because they will there be sure of being treated with consideration) rather than into the houses of rich middle-class people, where they always risk encountering vulgar superiority or patronage, or perhaps meet with (half-unconcious) rudeness.[4]

Once this correlation between the governess' happiness and the moral and social health of the community at large had been established, the manual writers went on to offer advice on how the former might be achieved. To this end they scrutinised the governess' relationships with every person who passed through the household, since it was only by assessing and, if necessary, normalising the behaviour of others towards her that they could be satisfied that the governess was indeed regarded as a gentlewoman. The following account sets out to give a sense of the breadth of social relationships on offer to governesses, both within their employers' households and in the wider world beyond the front door. Some employers turned out to be considerate, some did not; some governesses were cheerful, some were proud. People change constantly and so do the connections that they make with others. The point in this case is not simply to describe the paradigm of the governess' life so carefully mapped out by the manual writers, but rather to search for the actual experiences of some of the many thousands of women who entered the schoolroom during the period.

No one was more anxious to uphold the governess' claims to ladyhood than the governess herself. Severely compromised by the fact that she had left her family home and taken up paid employment, it was inevitable that she should wish to remind the people around her that she had been born and raised a gentlewoman. The most obvious way to do this was to adopt what Frances Power Cobbe, recalling her own governess of the 1830s, dubbed an 'I-have-seen-better-days' air.[5] Fraulein von Moskovicz, for instance, who was governess to Cynthia Asquith during the 1880s would declaim dramatically to whoever happened to be listening, 'I did not sink I vould ever be having to earn my own livings . . . I vas never brought up to be doing my own mendings',[6] while Jane Panton recalled how, during the 1840s, she had been taught by

> one of the primmest and most particular governesses that could be procured, with claims to gentility that we never disputed but that she waved before anyone who would listen to her . . .[7]

Implicit in this concern, that her own gentility should not be overlooked by those around her, went the governess' highly developed respect for the claims and privileges of good birth. Cynthia Asquith recalled how: 'My governess loved walks in the Park, especially on Sunday mornings between Church and luncheon when a dazzling parade of fashion was always to be seen',[8] while Lady Frederick Cavendish remembered how, on their first meeting in 1855, her new governess 'was merry as a grig, and chattered away about the Queen, the French Emperor, William 1V, George 1V, Bonaparte, Lord Palmerston, Uncle William [Gladstone], and what not'.[9] For this reason, posts which allowed the governess the opportunity to rub shoulders with the rich and famous were particularly sought after. Despite the careful distinction that commentators liked to make between material wealth and social class, it was still overwhelmingly the case in nineteenth-century Britain that the most socially elevated families were also the richest, enjoying a lifestyle crammed with the tangible trappings of wealth. A well-to-do family like that of Mary Carbery was able to provide Miss Moll with the chance to pick up her relatives from the station in a smart landau complete with male servants – something which evidently gave the German governess enormous pleasure.[10] Inevitably this pride in an employer's status could at times degenerate into the crudest sort of snobbery. Governesses who worked in grand households were warned against identifying too closely with their employers,[11] a tendency savagely satirised by Thackeray in the figure of the snobbish Miss Wirt:

> we only live with the country families. The Duke is abroad: we are at feud with the Carabases: the Ringwoods don't come down till Christmas: in fact nobody's here till the hunting season – positively nobody.[12]

For a young governess, brought up in relative poverty but with a large stock of family reminiscences about 'the good old days' ringing in her ears, working for smart, sociable people proved very tempting. Yet it also brought its own stresses and strains in its wake: Mary Cowden-Clarke remembered that during her time with the Purcell family in 1826, 'how odd it seemed to me to be followed in the street by a footman'.[13] Little had changed by the end of the century: in her first job in a grand house in 1889, May Pinhorn found herself 'almost afraid to use my knives and forks at first in case I should make a mistake'.[14] Moreover, as Charlotte Brontë discovered during her time with the Sidgwicks in 1839, the opportunities to participate in the glamorous goings-on were so few that they served only to emphasise the distance between the governess and her employer: 'I used to think I should like to be in the stir of grand folks' society; but I have had enough of it – it is dreary work to look on and listen'.[15]

This yearning to have one's genteel status buttressed through association with a highly-placed family could swiftly turn into the deep scorn of disappointment when an employer's social origins turned out to be less than impeccable. May Pinhorn, who throughout her working life placed great importance on having some contact with her employers' social set, felt let down during her time with the businessman Mr Fletcher in 1889 because 'hardly anybody called ... partly because the country squires etc looked down upon him ...'[16] Memoirs and letters from governesses drip with contempt for the mistress with flat vowels, florid dress sense and vulgar manners. Much of this sarcasm was nothing more than a defence mechanism, a displacing of the resentment that the governess felt at her own lowly status in relation to people whom she felt to be her social equals or even inferiors. Writing at the end of her life, Elizabeth Ham still burnt with scorn for the unfortunate Nias family in whose schoolroom she had worked during 1818:

Mrs N. was always talking of her mother and sister living in London, as if they were somebodies, and her great anxiety to extend and improve her acquaintance made me suspect that their connexions were nothing to boast of. This was confirmed by a visit from a brother of Mr N., a bigoted, vulgar-minded puritan; from whose conversation I discovered that he kept an Ironmonger's shop at Newbury. One day when the children were about some fancy-work they produced a number of pieces of silk and prints of various patterns. 'Wherever did you get such a variety of pieces?', said I. 'Oh, they came out of the shop when papa left off business' was the answer, followed by a blush, and a conscious look in the sisters that said plainly enough 'There, you have let the cat out of the bag'. Of course, I took no notice, and then, as now, thought no less of them for the fact, but only for the foolish vanity of concealment.[17]

Luckily, Ham did not have to wait long before she found the consideration that she felt was her due; her next employers, the Eltons, turned out to be exactly the sort of people of whom she approved (Mr Elton was the eldest son of a baronet):

No one could imagine the relief it was to me to find myself a *valued* inmate in a family of 'real gentlefolks', well informed and bred. Intellectual conversation was such a treat to me, and I was treated with so much consideration that I cared nothing for my somewhat onerous duties.[18]

Significantly, Ham discovered that her own status was also boosted by her association with the well-placed Eltons. Returning with them to Bath, where she had previously worked for the Nias family, she found herself being made a great fuss of both by her own family and even by local shopkeepers, 'who had looked superciliously on the Niases, and, of course, quite ignored such a person as their Governess'.[19]

This phenomenon of gentility-by-association could also work the other way round. Rich, unpwardly-mobile families frequently employed a governess to provide their daughters with that whole baggage of attitudes, manners and attainments which went under the heading of 'ladyhood'. A captain of industry like Sir John Barran could purchase gentility for his girls by providing them with a clergyman's daughter, May Pinhorn, as guide and mentor. For her part Pinhorn, acutely aware of the tiniest nuance of social class, analysed her employers' aspirations with the cool detachment of a social anthropologist:

> The money of the family came and comes from the manufacture of ready-made clothing.

> They evidently had natural good taste and a wish for education, for all of them are well educated and refined, even in the generation previous to Sir John's.'[20]

This evident hunger of vulgar employers to capitalise on the gentility or accomplishments of their governess (the two, of course, were intimately bound up) could sometimes reach outrageous proportions. In Thackeray's *Book of Snobs*, Miss Wirt's employers clearly felt no embarrassment about annexing their governess' musical skills as a way of bolstering their own social prestige:

> What a finger! Glorious creature, isn't she? Squirtz's favourite pupil – inestimable to have such a creature. Lady Carabas would give her eyes for her! A prodigy of accomplishments'.[21]

Not surprisingly, some governesses felt embarrassed, offended even, by their employers' attempts to cash in on their social or intellectual pedigree. During her employment with the White family in 1841, on whose social origins she looked down with scorn, Charlotte Brontë recorded with resentment that Mr White had written to her clergyman father, inviting him to feel free to make an extended visit. Far from earning him the gratitude of his young governess, Brontë burnt with resentment at what she perceived to be the patronage of her father by a lesser man: 'I don't at all wish papa to come, it would be like incurring an obligation'.[22]

Running through their letters and diaries there are hints that some governesses found this constant obligation to shore up their claims to gentility a wearisome burden that they would gladly have exchanged for what they perceived to be the unselfconsciousness enjoyed by working-class women. Charlotte Bronte declared that 'I could like to work in a mill. I could feel mental liberty',[23] echoing the increasing number of female industrial workers who were choosing the freedom of factory work over the close personal supervision of the servants' hall. Elizabeth Ham, meanwhile, maintained that: 'necessity had made me a Governess, neither education nor inclination had anything to do with it, and but for the loss of *Caste*, and the necessity of mixing with inferior and often coarse associates, I often thought I should have been less miserable as a Milliner, or even a Lady's maid.'[24]

Yet as Ham realised, such desires had to remain at the level of fantasy. The moment there was any real danger of being mistaken for a lady's maid, the defences went up abruptly. In 1810, while working as governess to the Pedder family in the Lake District, Ellen Weeton mentioned in a letter to her brother Tom how her cousin had been spreading strange rumours in her home town as to the precise nature of her employment:

> I have just received a letter from Miss Winkley. She says my cousin Latham called there a week or two ago, and gives a curious and laughable account of the various enquiries she made respecting me. Do go over to Holland, Tom, if you have not been, and hear what my aunt says. My cousin asked if I were gone to be a lady's maid. Waiting maids don't visit with their mistresses. I visit with Mrs P., and have been noticed in a pleasing manner by those who visit here.[25]

Being mistaken for a lady's maid was a particularly highly-charged insult for the governess, since the whole point of emphasising her ladyhood was to make clear the difference between her own situation and that of an upper female servant. For that reason her dealings with her employers' own domestic staff were a very real test of whether she was regarded as a lady. Over the previous two centuries, definitions of respectability had become increasingly concerned with the keeping of servants. By the beginning of the nineteenth century the employment of at least one maid was a signal to the world at large that the women of the house were no longer required to engage in the rougher sort of housework and could therefore be considered, if not ladies, then at least ladylike. To a large extent being considered genteel depended on being able to count on other, working-class, women to carry out menial chores on one's behalf. In the large upper-class household serviced by a team of specialist domestics, there was, in theory at least, every chance that the governess would receive the respect and attention that were her due. In the modest middle-class home, however, where three or four domestics strained under a heavy burden of labour, a battleground was frequently drawn up in which the governess tried to assert her claims to service, while the servants, in turn, resisted what they saw as her pretensions: 'The servants invariably detest her, for she is a dependent like themselves, and yet, for all that, as much their superior in other respects as the family they both serve'.[26]

This detestation most commonly took the form that 'every thing relating to the schoolroom is carelessly done':[27] fires went out, meals were allowed to get cold, bedding was left unaired. Clara Mordaunt, the heroine of Lady Blessington's 1839 novel, *The Governess*, was obliged to descend to the servants' hall to ask for her dinner when the parlourmaid refused to answer the schoolroom bell. Betsey, for her part, justified her negligence by arguing that, since Clara was not really a lady at all, she was not obliged to offer her the service due to a gentlewoman – 'I never seed no ladies as went out to service as governesses, and took wages the same as us servants'.[28] It was a sentiment which echoed around the servants' halls of the period, as governesses found their requests for the most basic services snubbed and ridiculed by their employers' domestic staff. In this their situation compared poorly with that of the nanny who was frequently provided with a nursemaid to clean and sew for her. Moreover, the nanny, as a servant herself, was more likely to be able to count on the allegiance of the cook and housemaids in catering for her basic needs. One of her greatest weapons in the battle with the schoolroom was the fact that she entered the fray well-fed, watered and warm.

Although manual writers remained convinced that it was in the three- or four-servant household that the governess encountered most difficulties, there is plenty of evidence that the specialist upper servants of the wealthier establishments also resented the governess' claim to service. Footmen particularly disliked having to show deference to a woman whom they considered to be no better than themselves: more than one gave notice muttering that 'he would not live, indeed, where he had to open the door to the governess'.[29] Lady's maids, too, seem to have resented the governess' demand to be recognised as a gentlewoman, perhaps because they felt that their own claims were no less great: concealing her employer's jewellery in the governess' bedroom was just one of the ways in which a jealous lady's maid had been known to avenge herself on her unfortunate rival.[30] As an expert in dress, hairstyling and fashionable manners, the lady's maid prided herself on being the next best thing to a gentlewoman. Although her social origins were frequently obscure – and, more often than not, foreign – her access to the mistress' confidences and cast-offs allowed her to assume the patina of ladyhood. Novels of the period frequently use a comparison with the sharp, sophisticated but ever-so-slightly-vulgar lady's maid as a means of emphasising that the governess' gentility (and, by implication, the gentility of all 'real' ladies) rests on much more than the external props of dress and appearance.[31]

The sight and sound of servants ridiculing the governess' claims to gentility could not fail to influence the younger members of the household. Small children, just beginning to become aware of the complexities of social class, found it hard to grasp how a woman who led a life so different from that of their mother's and so similar to that of their nurse's could still count as a lady. Snide remarks from the nursery and the servants' hall about the governess' social ambiguity reinforced her pupils' sense that something was not quite as it seemed – a sense which they were only too happy to express as often and as loudly as possible. In 1855 the fourteen-year-old Lady Frederick Cavendish noted sarcastically in her diary every little nuance of her new Mademoiselle's vulgarity of speech and dress, rejoicing when she was soon replaced by another more 'ladylike' governess;[32] young Edmund Gosse recovered from the shock of being presented with Miss Marks to note that she was 'not quite, I imagine, what is called "a lady"'.[33] If the governess had particular pretensions towards being 'high class' then the children's reaction to her exposure could be all the more savage. One man, born in the late 1870s, recalled 'our unkind delight when we discovered that her father was only the gardener at the Hall . . . She had described him to us as "a horticulturalist"'.[34]

On the other hand, by the time they reached adulthood and came to write their memoirs, very few former pupils recalled their governess as anything other than a perfect lady. The reason for this may not have been so much nostalgia as vanity: to admit that one's upbringing had been superintended by a woman who was less than genteel was to put a question mark over one's own breeding as well that of one's mother. One of the more unpleasant insults that could be thrown at a young Victorian gentlewoman was the suggestion that her governess was not quite a lady:

Eleanor proceeded to the school-room in no very amiable mood. A milliner's daughter for a companion and governess! Unbearable![35]

Eleanor Clereton's determination to rid herself of the reputedly plebeian Miss Smyth provides much of the plot and driving power of *The Young Governess*, an 1872 novel by Henry Courtney Selons. Spurned by her employers, the governess is eventually taken up by some of their friends who, recognising her to be a 'real lady', bestow the social recognition which has previously been denied the obviously refined young woman. The discrepancy in the way that the governess is treated by different households allows the author to mount a discussion about the nature of ladyhood and, most importantly, the social obligations and responsibilities attached to it. In the following exchange it is not simply Miss Smyth's gentility which is confirmed, but also that of her gracious hostess, Lady Laura Douglas:

'Aunt', said Marion, stopping short and turning round, . . . 'what is to be done about [Miss Smyth] dining? Greaves wanted to know'.
'With us, certainly,' said Lady Laura.
'Adelaide says she does not appear at Clereton at all in the evening,' said Marion.
'She is a lady, my dear,' said Lady Laura quietly, 'and my guest; and I wish it'.[36]

The high church novelist Elizabeth Sewell used the figure of the governess as a starting point for an exploration of female gentility in action. According to Sewell, or rather according to the eponymous heroine of her 1844 novel, *Amy Herbert*, being a lady had as much to do with morals as manners. Impressed by her kindness and gentle ways, the ten-year-old Amy tries hard to define just what it is that makes her cousins' governess – or, indeed, anyone – a lady. While her cousin Dora continues to wrestle with a distinction between status at birth and acquired gentility, Amy gets straight to the heart of the matter by maintaining that Miss Morton's greatest claim to gentility lies in her virtue.

'Not all the rank in the world will make persons ladies and gentlmen without manners' [said Dora].
'But I mean something besides manners', said Amy; 'because what I like in Miss Morton is not quite manner; it is her being good that helps to make her a lady, I think'.[37]

Both *The Young Governess* and *Amy Herbert* resolve the problem of the governess' disputed gentility in different though not dissimilar ways. Eleanor's failure to recognise Miss Smyth as a lady is made to appear doubly ironic when it turns out that the governess is none other than the thoroughly well-born Dorothea Stanhope in disguise. Eleanor's reliance on fashionable manners as a way of deciding who is a lady and who is not have clearly let her down, and she is obliged to relearn those codes which should have been familiar from birth. Similarly Emily Morton is rejected by her employers when, as a result of (highly unladylike) deceit by her pupils, she is forced out of employment. Recognised as truly moral, and thus genteel, by the neighbouring Herberts, she is taken into their home and gradually became 'dear to them as their eldest child', although not before being vindicated of the charges which led to her dismissal.[38] In both cases the governess' social rehabilitation is inseparable from her success in clinging to those standards of moral conduct to which all ladies should adhere. At the end of the day Emily Morton and Martha Smyth find themselves welcomed into the heart of the genteel Christian household not because they are graceful but because they are good.

In their wild ideas about becoming maidservants and mill girls, Elizabeth Ham and Charlotte Brontë had grasped that, para-doxically, it was the very fact of their ladyhood which caused the difficulties and isolation that they experienced within their employers' home. Every gentlewoman, unless she had enough money to live independently, was assumed to exist as part of a family group whose head was responsible for her financial and moral welfare. It was by making use of this assumption to obscure the economic bond which tied the governess to her employers that her claims to ladyhood could be upheld. Yet while the governess placed herself under the discipline and authority of the family group, the inescapable facts of her daily existence made it impossible for her to become a fully participating member. Her schoolroom duties automatically excluded her from activites which took place during the day and, as far as the evening was concerned, there was no agreement at all on how she should spend it.

The question of whether the governess should dine with the rest of the family was debated with such intensity by her contemporaries precisely because the rituals surrounding the serving and eating of food had for centuries been a means of confirming and displaying social hierarchy. Even if she was expected to accompany her pupils to the dining-room for lunch, it was quite likely that the schoolroom party might be made to sit at a different table and eat plainer food than the rest of the company.[39] In the evening, the situation became even more ambiguous. Some employers welcomed the governess and children to dinner – but only once the main course had been cleared away.[40] Others expected the governess to spend the whole meal with them but still had ways of making her inferior status abundantly clear to the assembled company. Looking back from the vantage-point of 1893, one governess recalled:

> Well do I remember arriving, tired from a long journey, at a London house, where I was for the first time to act in the capacity of

governess, and on sitting down to dinner how keen a sense of friendlessness and isolation it gave me to find myself pointedly helped after the ladies of the house.[41]

Dinner over, a fresh set of quandaries presented themselves. Only very occasionally would an employer like Elizabeth Ham's Mrs Elton have the foresight and the courage to spell out exactly what was to happen next:

> She spoke with perfect frankness of all that would be required, said that I should take my dinner with them, and that they should be happy with my company in the drawing room till after tea, when I might like to be alone myself, and Mr Elton would prefer having his elder daughters left without any restraint in their parents' company, that they should always be happy to have me with them when they had other company.[42]

More typical was the situation where the governess was left without guidelines about what to do after dinner. In these circumstances, suggested the advice writers, she should fall back on ladylike intuition and tact to decide whether or not her presence was required in the drawing room. Thus, the perfect governess

> recognizes her exact place in the home circle, and keeps it; she does not expect more consideration or attention than any other member of it. If she is much with the family her ready tact enables her to perceive in a moment when the presence of one not exactly *of it* may be intrusive and disagreeable, and she glides away with some smiling excuse.[43]

Imperatives such as these were hardly conducive to spontaneous and relaxed behaviour. Being constantly on one's guard, having continually to judge whether one's presence was really desired, put enormous strain on the most robust constitution, as Charlotte Brontë tried to explain in a letter to her friend Ellen Nussey: 'If teaching only were requisite, it would be smooth and easy; but it is the living in other peoples' houses – the estrangement from one's real character – the adoption of a cold, frigid, apathetic exterior, that is painful.'[44]

The situation became doubly difficult whenever the governess was obliged to accompany her employers into society. Relationships which had been established and worked well within the context of the household could break down in the wider social arena. Once again the governess was left with the dilemma of whether she was to behave towards her employers' friends with the easy approachability of a family member, or whether she should rather keep the respectful distance of a mere domestic. So excruciating was the problem to all concerned that many employers and their friends adopted the cowardly, though effective, tactic of simply pretending not to 'notice' the governess on those occasions when she was obliged to be in their company.[45] As a result, governesses often found themselves squeezed out of conversations and even ignored altogether. Such was the experience of Anne Brontë's Agnes Grey as she walked to church with her pupils and their friends:

> when I did walk, this first half of the journey was generally a great nuisance to me. As none of the before-mentioned ladies and gentlemen ever noticed me, it was disagreeable to walk beside them, as if listening to what they said, or wishing to be thought one of them, while they talked over me or across, and if their eyes, in speaking, chanced to fall on me, it seemed as if they looked on vacancy – as if they either did not see me, or were very desirous to make it appear so.

> It was disagreeable, too, to walk behind, and thus appear to acknowledge my own inferiority; for, in truth, I considered myself pretty nearly as good as the best of them, and wished them to know that I did so, and not to imagine that I looked upon myself as a mere domestic, who knew her own place too well to walk beside such fine ladies and gentlemen as they were . . .[46]

Social gatherings which took place within the household were just as likely to prove uncomfortable, and once again the governess frequently found herself disappearing from view:

> If . . . [the governess] is to be present at an evening party, or to occupy the place of tea-maker, she is not introduced to the visitors, and often one who has formerly moved in the best society, is only just noticed by a formal bow, which is strangely contrasted with the cordial greeting, received by her pupils, and perhaps, during the whole evening, no word of courtesy is addressed to her . . .[47]

One of the very few circumstances in which the governess was treated with some attention by the assembled company was when she was required to start off the after-dinner entertainment with a song or a piano piece. Even here, however, it was made clear that her status was that of a stop-gap whose superior technical skills were useful insofar as they filled those awkward moments 'when the party was dull, or when no-one else would begin'.[48]

Treated as if they were invisible, many governesses responded by removing themselves quite literally from the sight of their employers, retreating to the schoolroom during off-duty hours. After the strain of being 'always in the way',[49] not to mention the fatigue that came from coping with children all day long, solitude must initially have come as a welcome relief.[50] For an experienced woman, such as Sybil Lubbock's Miss Cutting, keeping one's distance was an important way of maintaining an identity beyond that of 'governess':

> Her life, she made it quite clear, outside lesson hours was her own. It had been the same always, I fancy. In the large and well-to-do family of children of various ages where she had lived before she came to us, she had always refused, she said, to dine downstairs except on Christmas Day or other festive occasions. 'If you want me, my dears', she would say to her pupils, 'you will always find me in the schoolroom, and I shall be delighted to see you. But I am not one of the family and it is idle to pretend I am. Besides we are all the better for a little time to ourselves'.[51]

Nonetheless, evening after evening spent in the schoolroom with only, as Edith Gates put it, 'the chairs as audience standing around me in respectful silence' must have proved dismal, especially for a young girl who had been used to the companionship of her own family.[52] Returning to her employers after spending Christmas with her aunts, Gates recorded how 'I certainly felt my first evenings alone in the school-room rather lonely ones, and it was with difficulty I supressed the continually returning longing to be where my thoughts so often lingered'.[53]

Edith Gates' loneliness would have been eased by the chance to carry on some sort of independent social life – visiting friends, and in turn receiving them in the schoolroom. However, many employers, including the Wiggetts for whom she worked, were reluctant to extend this privilege. In many households domestics were not allowed to socialise outside the servants' hall, although many found a way around this ban. With the governess the situation was more ambiguous. As a family member she ought, in theory, to have been granted the same privileges and subject to the same restrictions as a grown-up daughter. One of the reasons why employers did not like employing a governess the same age or older than themselves was that it upset the authority structure of the household. As long as the governess was to be perceived as a family member, it made life easier for everyone if she was of an age to play elder daughter rather than aging aunt. In general, governesses *do* seem to have been allowed to visit locally and to receive their family and friends in their employers' homes, but such events, when they come to be written about in memoirs and diaries, are always characterised as acts of kindness,[54] or indulgence,[55] on the part of the employer. Although she might be treated with every 'consideration', the governess was obliged to negotiate and renegotiate what should have been the most spontaneous and pleasurable part of her life. Like any unmarried girl, she was expected to ask permission every time she wanted to leave the house, even during off-duty hours.[56] Even greater difficulties were encountered when it came to returning hospitality. Charlotte Brontë agonised for days before begging Ellen Nussey to come to tea at the Whites:

> Now can you tell me whether it is considered improper for gover-
> nesses to ask their friends to come and see them. I do not mean,
> of course, to stay, but just for a call of an hour or two? If it is
> not absolute treason, I do fervently request that you will contrive,
> in some way or other, to let me have a sight of your face.[57]

Even once these hurdles were satisfactorily cleared, the circum-stances of the governess' working life made it difficult for her to form and maintain friendships. While women who entered nursing or schoolteaching from the 1870s discovered that one of the pleasures of paid employment was the companionship of other women,[58] the governess found herself even more isolated than she had been at home in her parents' drawing-room. According to one anonymous essayist:

> factory-girls, shop-women, teachers of accomplishments, return to
> their homes at night. The servants gather round the work-table
> or the hall-fire ... It is only the governess, and a certain class of
> private tutors, who must hear the echoes from the drawing-room
> and the offices, feeling that, in a house full of people, they dwell
> alone.[59]

If the governess worked far away from her native county she was unlikely to know anyone locally, while her daily duties brought her into contact with virtually no one outside her employers' family.[60]

Even Sunday morning worship provided few opportunities to mix
with the local residents:

> We happen to know of a gentleman who would not sit in the same
> pew as the governess! We have heard of one law for the rich, and
> another for the poor, but we never heard of two gospels.[61]

In a letter to a magazine at the end of the century, one governess
described how her attempts to form friendships had foundered on
the aloofness of professional families who wanted nothing to do
with her:

> It seems, indeed, to require some such explanation as a very deep-
> rooted prejudice against the genus 'governess', particularly in county
> towns, in order to account for the social isolation in which cultivated
> women engaged in the teaching profession seem condemned to pass
> their lives in them.[62]

Snobbery alone, however, could not account for this social ostra-
cism. One of the chief reasons why people hung back from making
friends with governesses was that, as a group, they had a terrible
reputation as gossips:

> There are few who have not heard it said of a governess: 'I should
> much like to see more of Miss –, but I feel a delicacy in encouraging
> any personal acquaintance with my girls, or inviting her often, because
> she is so apt to talk of the failings and private affairs of the people
> she has lived with.'[63]

In fairness, the governess' choice of topic sprung less from a
chronic lack of discretion and more from the fact that she really
had nothing else to talk about. Closeted with children for 80 per
cent of the time – Edith Gates recorded how she had 'had nobody
to speak to since Friday except the children and now and then Mrs
Wiggett' – it was easy to lose the knack of making conversation
with other adults,[64] especially since she was unlikely to know the
people and places who might naturally form the subject. For this
reason, friendship with another governess was the most natural
relationship available to her. Governesses might meet and cement
their acquaintance while accompanying pupils out to tea or on the
daily walk. As their charges chattered and played, the two women
could gradually get to know each other and exchange confidences.
Not that envy and competition were unknown: a favourite ploy

amongst governesses was to converse in a language other than one's own in order to demonstrate a superior linguistic talent.[65]

Nonetheless, warm and sustaining friendships were struck up between governesses. During the spring of 1876 Edith Gates relied on Madame Sulkowska, who worked for a neighbouring family, for both intellectual stimulation and emotional support: 'now and then we have had such glorious conversations, I felt she could understand me, and never minded giving my opinion'.[66] The fact of their age difference – Edith was nineteen, Madame Sulkowska middle-aged – meant that inevitably there was something of the mother-daughter about their relationship. Meeting every couple of days while out on a walk with their pupils, the two women were able to talk frankly about their day-to-day experiences in a way that would have had them labelled them as indiscreet in any other context: 'This afternoon Grace and I went out, met Madame and Rose. Had a long talk with the former, who told me things scarcely credible which showed me how thankful I ought to be in having such a nice situation.'[67] When Madame finally quitted her post (on the grounds that she was not paid enough), Gates felt abandoned and isolated: 'I cannot think how it is I do not get a letter from Madame, it almost seems as if she had forgotten me.'[68] The replacement Mademoiselle turned out to be haughty and, despite Edith's best efforts to get her to open up, remained an unrewarding companion. Within days of her departure, Edith found herself longing for Madame's company: 'There is not a day passes but what I wish dear Madame were here, I used to look forward quite to meeting her out; I wonder how she is getting on in London, how I should like to take a peep at her in her lodgings!'[69]

Deprived of personal friendship, Edith Gates turned to written correspondence as a way of forging emotional connections with others: 'in the evening I wrote to Auntie Maud . . . I should like to have squeezed myself in the letter . . . and a sweet crushed flower I should have made no doubt, but I refrained out of respect to the envelope and postman'.[70] Nearly one third of the entries in Gates' diary mention either writing or receiving letters and she was also obsessed by the mechanics of the mail – a new post box in the village had her rushing to inspect it, while the only person of whom she gave a physical description in her diary was 'the dear old postman'.[71] By the time she was working in the mid seventies the Penny Post had been established for thirty-five years and the ability to write almost daily to her family and friends went a long way to making the social and emotional isolation of her life tolerable.

For Mary Cowden-Clarke, working in 1826, the cost of staying in touch was far greater: a letter from her family in Shacklewell to her employers' house in Montague Square cost 3d. and she marvelled that her parents were able to afford to write so regularly.[72]

Yet this reliance on letters to maintain contacts with friends and family produced all sorts of resentments when correspondents did not write often enough, or failed to express the desired sentiment. Edith Gates, for instance, was gripped by the fear that her absence was not sufficiently mourned by everyone back home: 'All is going on well at home, for although they *say* they miss me, yet my departure does not seem to have had bad effects on any of them'.[73] Behind her fears that her family were getting on very well without her lay a larger anxiety. Rarely venturing outside her employers' house, talking freely only to another governess, Edith Gates had, in a sense, become hidden from view. Deprived of the human contacts that would have given her a sense of mattering in the world, she began to wonder whether she had become invisible, whether, indeed, she existed at all.

One way of by-passing the circle of confusion and embarrassment which the governess set in play in the Victorian household was to employ a foreigner. Aside from offering the opportunity of acquiring fluency in a foreign language, the attraction of a French or German governess was that she was difficult to place socially. Her accent, her clothes, her references to her family could not be used so easily as evidence for or against her gentility. The novelty of her foreignness obliterated those subtle pointers which defined a British governess as a lady – or not, as the case might be – and made the fact of her paid employment an embarrassment. The political unrest experienced by France as well as the Italian and German states at the end of the 1840s produced a stream of middle-class refugees to Britain, the majority of them in need of employment: according to the national census, there were 1,408 foreign governesses living in Britain in 1861, 58 per cent of them originally from Prussia, France and Switzerland.[74] The fact that these young women had received an education which was not only academically sound but gave them instruction in how to teach others only added to their attraction.[75]

While employing a foreign governess by-passed the problem of social difference, it brought with it a fresh set of tensions. It would be hard to overestimate the depth of anti-Catholic feeling at all levels of society. For instance, the talented Jane Harrison was denied a foreign governess to help her learn languages by her father on the grounds that 'all foreigners were Papists, all Papists were liars, and he wouldn't have one in the house'.[76] While it was fairly easy to find a Protestant German or Swiss governess to teach one's children, there were simply not enough French Huguenots to go round. Nonetheless, acquiring a Parisian accent for one's children was worth putting up with the inconvenience that came with employing a French Catholic governess. Worry that she might try to win her pupils to her own faith was only one of many fears about letting her into the house. Protestant doubt about the moral probity and sexual chastity of priests, monks and nuns spilled over into a more general perception that all who followed Rome were sensuous liars and vain idolators. A whole cluster of prejudices, fears and misapprehensions focused on the threat posed by a French Catholic governess to the smooth-running of the British Protestant household. Charlotte Yonge advised against employing one on the grounds that 'it is notorious that the French standard of truth is very unlike the English, especially in Roman Catholics',[77] while Mary Maurice suggested that to allow a French governess to cross the threshold was to open 'a wide flood-gate to frivolity, vanity, and sin'.[78] There was a general perception that the French governess was likely to be sexually aggressive in her dealings with the men of the house, to initiate her pupils into all sorts of unspecified 'sin', to dress too well, to lie and possibly to steal. Much of this was left at the level of implication, yet nonetheless a stock caricature soon emerged. In her novel of 1844, *Amy Herbert*, Elizabeth Sewell described the French governess as:

> a tall, thin, inelegant-looking person, with a good-natured merry face, a dress made in the newest Parisian fashion, and a cap which seemed formed rather for the purpose of receiving a certain quantity of ribbon and artificial flowers, than as any covering to the black wig which it only half concealed.[79]

It was to counteract this sort of vicious stereotype that the more perceptive advice writers suggested that mothers should make use of the foreign governess' presence in the house to teach its inhabitants a practical lesson in toleration.[80] However, even if parents managed to suppress their xenophobic sentiments for the sake of household harmony, the servants could almost certainly be guaranteed to mutter something unfavourable about the foreign governess within earshot of her pupils. Daphne Fielding may have been unusual in having a Jewish governess to supervise her Edwardian childhood, but there was nothing unique in the racial taunts which she soon learnt to throw at the unfortunate Miss Solomons:

> In the nursery there was some jealousy, as there usually is, between nurse and governess, and aspersions were cast on the Jews so as to reflect on Solly. Hearing these, Tony and I took it into our heads to start baiting poor Solly ourselves. The next time we went to Hyde Park, we refused to walk with her but followed a few yards behind pointing at her and chanting: 'Who crucified Je-sus? Who crucified Je-sus?' to a horrible little tune. Solly paid not the slightest attention and kept on walking, ignoring our taunts and the attention which they attracted from the onlookers ... [She] remained calm and indifferent. We tried the same performance for several days but, getting no rise out of her, gave it up.[81]

In their attempts to address the problem of low standards amongst governesses in the 1860s, commentators made much of the superior education and training available to European home teachers, especially those from Prussia.[82] Certainly the idea, peddled by some of the manual writers that foreign governesses were over-excitable and lacked sticking power,[83] is not born out by the evidence of the autobiographies which contain examples of French and German women who stayed many years in one position. There was the remarkable Miss Cutting from Cologne who worked for Sybil Lubbock's family for almost ten years, Miss Haas who stayed with Jane Panton and her siblings until her eldest pupil married, Fraulein von Moskovicz who taught Cynthia Asquith for six years, and the hated Miss Moll who stayed far too long in the view of her long-suffering pupil, Mary Carbery. Some European governesses married British men and settled for good in this country, while even as committed a patriot as Sonia Keppel's Moiselle, who bore a grudge against the British, could give herself over to the spirit of international co-operation when appropriate: during the First War she and her pupil were decorated by the Belgians for the sterling work they had done in dishing out tea in the London Bridge canteen.[84]

While contemporary commentators acknowledged that the peculiarities of the governess' position might give rise to a degree of isolation, they remained quite clear about where responsibility for her loneliness must lie:

Touchiness, jealousy, self-assertion, are the faults most often created by the governess's peculiar position; a morbid fear of any invasion of her dignity, and a looking out for offence, which are extremely foolish and disagreeable and which in any situation would make her unhappy.[85]

In reality the infinite combination of social circumstance and human personality make it impossible to be so certain about who was to blame: there were sensitive and insensitive employers, secure and insecure governesses. Doubtless the situation looked quite different depending on where one was standing. For instance, Charlotte Brontë was eloquent in her descriptions of the cold and snobbish manner in which she had been treated by the Sidgwicks during 1839. Yet a cousin of the family later recalled that the Sidgwicks had done everything in their power to make the young governess feel at home. It was *her* prickliness, not that of her employers, he maintained, which had made her stay such an unhappy one: 'if she was invited to walk to church with them, she thought she was being ordered about like a slave; if she was not invited, she imagined she was excluded from the family circle'.[86]

One woman who was unfortunate enough to find herself in a situation where everything seemed to conspire against her was Mary Bazlinton, who worked for the Bradshaw family during 1854 and 1855. The Bradshaw household, which consisted of Mr and Mrs Bradshaw, their two daughters, two small sons, a string of both British and local servants and Bazlinton herself, left Britain in April 1854 for Pau, a popular spa town in the French Pyrenees. With its large British population and its relentless gentility, life continued here much as it might have done in Bazlinton's near-native Buxton. Yet her diaries make unhappy reading. Whether her employers were especially unpleasant or she particularly touchy is hard to determine. All the same, there can be no doubting her experience of hurt, loneliness and longing.

The main stumbling block was religion. For the devoutly noncon- formist Bazlinton, the Sabbath had always been a day of solitary prayer and introspection. For the Bradshaws, caught up in the gaiety of French-Catholic culture, it was a time for social recreation. No sooner had she arrived in Pau than Bazlinton announced to her astonished employers that she would not able to accompany her pupils on the Sunday family walk along the promenade since, 'I cannot consent to go to a public promenade and parade up and down amid a number of fashionably dressed idle people'.[87] A few

months later it was clear that Bazlinton's strict approach to Sundays
– and indeed, to every day of the week – was beginning to irritate
her employers. On 15 July 1855 she recorded that:

> My habit of spending my Sabbath evenings alone I can see continues
> to excite much bitterness of feeling towards me. The remarks Mrs
> Bradshaw made about pride were I well know indirectly levelled at
> me. They consider that to be my motive and that because I absent
> myself from them I wish to appear better than they.[88]

In fairness, Mrs Bradshaw may have had good reason to feel
annoyed with Bazlinton: the previous entry in the latter's diary
hints at more than a dash of self-righteousness:

> Though cast down to-day in mind and not well in body I can
> still feeling [sic] adoringly grateful that my lot is I trust *infinitely*
> preferable to that of any one of the giddy multitude thus eagerly
> pursuing the unsatisfying vanities and pleasures of this fleeting,
> passing world.[89]

Matters came to a head, however, when Bazlinton decided to commence a one-woman conversion mission amongst the Catholic natives
of Pau. Her technique was to start up a conversation with a complete
stranger before steering the subject around to God, and handing
out one of her ultra-Protestant tracts. Particularly unacceptable, as
far as the Bradshaws were concerned, was Bazlinton's attempt to
convert Marian, the local girl who came in to do the household's
ironing.[90] Furious at what she considered the governess' unwarranted
interference in the running of her household, Mrs Bradshaw extracted
a promise from Bazlinton that she would in future leave the domestic
staff well alone.

While Bazlinton's behaviour was doubtless sometimes irritating,
there can be no doubting that she was unfortunate in her chief
protagonist. Mrs Bradshaw seems to have displayed just that in-
sensitivity of which the manual writers so frequently complained,
subjecting the thirty-eight-year-old governess' behaviour to the sort
of scrutiny that would have been more appropriate in dealing with
a woman twenty years younger. In the following typical exchange
between the two women, noted in Bazlinton's diary for 29 July
1855, Mrs Bradshaw seems cynically to have played upon the
governess' insecurities about whether or not she really was 'a
lady':

After dinner as I was seated on the balcony Mrs Bradshaw came to me and expressed her regret that I yielded so much to the habit of borrowing. I had the night previous borrowed a reel of cotton of Tiney having been unable to procure any strong enough for my dress. I had too for some little time past used a pair of small scissors of Tiney's because Mr Bradshaw had found mine and in joke would not restore them to me. One or two other little things I had borrowed – but that I am habitually in the habit of doing so I cannot admit to be a just accusation. She however 'hoped I would refrain from it in future' and said that 'no-one with ladylike or *refined* feelings would ever think of doing so'. Oh I cannot help thinking this is part of the feeling that leads them to seek occasions against me. But I will endeavour to abstain while here from borrowing the most trifling thing in future.[91]

Mrs Bradshaw seems to have been distinctly grudging in her granting of free time to Bazlinton. In the Summer of 1855 the latter started to take drawing lessons with a certain Mme Mornard and, within a few weeks, was spending nearly all her leisure time sketching. Perhaps annoyed that the governess' interest was no longer focused solely on her professional duties, or maybe simply out of spite, Mrs Bradshaw seems to have deliberately taken steps to stop Bazlinton pursuing the one activity which brought her pleasure in the material world. No amount of ladylike tact or 'consideration' could conceal the brutal reality of the governess' powerlessness in the face of an inconsiderate or downright malevolent employer. In her diary for 12 June Bazlinton described how she

> went to Mme Mornard's for an hour and settled to go sketching in the afternoon as the Montebellos were coming to tea and I concluded I should have the time to myself. Sketched a drawing after dinner. As I was finishing Toddy came in to say that her Mama would want me to return at half past 5 to be in readiness to walk with the Montebellos if they felt inclined. I was extremely disappointed as this at once put an end to my sketching plans. I could not help feeling it was done purposely to thwart me.[92]

Bazlinton's growing obsession with sketching may have had less to do with artistic ambitions than the fact that the woman who taught her was her only friend in Pau. Her earlier attempts to make acquaintances, both within her employers' circle or independently in the community, came to nothing, with the result that she found herself increasingly emotionally isolated. In her diary for 1 March she recorded an incident while out walking with friends of her employers which echoes the unhappy experience of Agnes Grey while walking to and from church:

> I walked with Toddy, Miss Cust and the two Miss Robbins . . . it was a lovely afternoon but my spirits did not feel in unison with the bright sun shine. They treat me so coldly and indifferently – but I try as much as possible not to notice it, and though I cannot but be silent when I perceive that I am not wanted to join in the conversation, I have not in any way resented it.'[93]

To make matters worse, Bazlinton's own family failed to provide the emotional support which might have sustained her through her troubles. For while they continued to write to her regularly from Lincolnshire, their letters failed to provide any reassurance that her absence was missed or, indeed, noticed at all:

> 28 July 1855 . . . About half past 7 Guillon brought me in a letter which I found to be from Uncle and Aunt written from Skegness. I was so much disappointed on reading this letter as I had been at first rejoiced to see it. Tho' it contained much news relating to dear old Sleaford and tidings of dear friends there which interested me, there was not a single sentence which might not have been addressed to another equally well with myself. I had written to Aunt almost three months before giving her every particular relating to myself, and also a short time previous to their going to Skegness to Charlotte, but not a single word of allusion was there to any thing those letters contained, not one word of sympathy for me in my trials, no word expressive of pleasure at the prospect of my speedy return to England . . . I did not expect or desire the letter to be filled with allusions to my circumstances or situation or with expressions of sympathy towards me – Two or three kind words such as 'we know you meet with much that is trying dear Mary, and we often think and pray for you' would have sounded cheering – but there were none such at least from Aunt, dear Uncle did say he prayed for me and I believe he does.[94]

Although quite possibly she felt as though she were the only person on earth to suffer such misery, Mary Bazlinton's situation represented nothing more than the governess' 'plight' taken to its ultimate extremes. The unlucky combination of an uncongenial employer, an over-sensitive governess, and the isolation of a foreign country could not fail to produce dissatisfaction if not downright despair. Bazlinton tried every way she could think of to ease her anguish – attempting to form friendships, throwing herself into creative hobbies and, of course, praying ceaselessly to God for deliverance. Unfortunately for Bazlinton, her only real option was to grit her teeth and resolve that, next time, she would handle things differently. By the time they came to part, on 20 November 1855, it was clear that both employer and governess felt nothing but relief:

> Mrs Bradshaw simply shook hands with me. I can not but doubt the prevailing feeling in her mind was pleasure at being rid of a presence evidently disagreeable to her.'[95]

Isolating the governess from the rest of the household did nothing to resolve her incongruent status. No solution would be forthcoming for as long as her position was defined exclusively in terms of the place she occupied within the family structure. It was not until the turn of the century that writers like Mrs Devonshire could substitute the idea of the governess as an autonomous professional as a way of normalising her position:

> A governess who 'knows her place' is not one who considers herself a social inferior, a sort of humble menial, but one who understands that she has entered upon a contract to give her time in exchange for a reasonable salary . . .[96]

Even so, Mrs Devonshire was by no means consistent in her approach. Later in the same article she railed against governesses who read their letters at breakfast without asking permission, consigning them once more to the role of junior family member.

Yet this continued attachment to the familial model did not necessarily bring bad feeling in its wake: in practice it could open the way towards warm and sustaining relationships. As well as playing mother to her small pupils, and aunt to the older ones, the governess might become a sister, daughter or best friend to her employer. It was not only the governess whose isolation made her hungry for friendship. Married women frequently found themselves living far away from their own families and childhood communities. Acquaintance with other women in the neighbourhood was hedged around with an etiquette which contained and distanced any spontaneous displays of affection or exchange of confidence. According to Mrs Beeton's redoutable *Book of Household Management* of 1861:

> The courtesies of society should ever be maintained, even in the domestic circle, and amongst the nearest friends. During these

visits, the manners should be easy and cheerful, and the subjects of conversation such as may be readily terminated. Serious discussions or arguments are to be altogether avoided . . .[97]

With the governess no such barrier to intimacy existed. In a middle-class home she could hardly be avoided: she was there every day at the breakfast table, on the stairs, in the garden. Relationships with husbands were often far from close: men in the capital were increasingly spending their evenings at the new gentlemen's clubs of Pall Mall, where business and social activity blended in an atmosphere of masculine bonhommie. Friendship between a mistress and servant was out of the question, in theory at least. The governess, often the same age as her employer to within ten years, was an obvious and natural confidante. Far from her own family, and with few opportunities to make new acquaintances, she was only too happy to find a friend.

Yet whether these relationships were ever balanced must remain doubtful. May Pinhorn was probably not alone in feeling that her employer only bothered to come and talk to her when there was no one else more interesting on the scene, 'my place was only in the schoolroom unless Lady Barran was alone and had no other society, when she sought my companionship'.[98] In her diary for 1855, the fourteen-year-old Lady Frederick Cavendish recorded that: 'It was not long before Miss Pearson clung to Mama with the whole affection of her earnest mind, and there is no one who so appreciates the exceeding beauty and perfection of Mama's character as she does'.[99] In some instances the atmosphere became so intense that steps had to be taken to end a situation that had begun to unsettle the whole household. Writing thirty years after the event, Cynthia Asquith's over-casual tone seems to hint at the pain she still felt over the sending away of the remarkable Miss Jourdain:

> Though devoted to Miss Jourdain, my mother may well have found both the force of her personality and the strength of her devotion to herself too much for continuous proximity. Whatever the reasons, it was decided that the time was come to put an end to a situation that had somehow become over-charged.[100]

It was situations such as these which prompted the advice writers into issuing the sternest warnings:

> It may happen that if the lady is an attractive, amiable and kind-hearted woman, this sympathy may become a kind of idolatry on the

113

part of the governess, a sort of sentimental exaggeration to which many girls are subject. It would be very regrettable that this should lead to long conversations, usually introspective, wasteful of the time of both women and more harmful than useful.[101]

What commentators seem to have feared most in this closing up of the emotional distance between the governess and her employer was that the governess would become indistinguishable from a family member. Once the emotional discipline of the household had broken down, social disorder would result. Men were seen to be particularly likely to draw the governess into the intimate affairs of the household – 'the gentleman may choose to make you the umpire in a conjugal dispute'[102] – perhaps because they were thought to be less concerned than their wives with the erecting and maintaining of social distinctions. The solution, as far as the advice writers were concerned, was to take the governess right outside the family and shore up her identity as a visitor or guest, in front of whom all the proprieties needed to be observed:

> Many husbands who have thoughtlessly acquired the detestable habit of discourtesy to their wives, and who give no attention to their language or appearance, when alone with their family, will be ashamed to utter 'swear-words' before a well-bred young lady, or to come down to breakfast unshaven, or in slippers.[103]

Yet the single most complex relationship facing the governess was with the elder sisters of her pupils. These were the young women, often in their twenties, who represented the what-might-have-been in the governess' own life. In previous centuries they might even have carried out the work which she now did, taking responsibility for the education and supervision of their younger sisters. Yet by the 1830s the ban on any sort of useful labour women meant that this task had now to be performed by a surrogate, the governess, leaving the young ladies of the household free to devote themselves to leisure and material display. What made the situation so highly charged was that this was the life for which the governess had herself been educated, yet from which she was now excluded. To witness at first hand other women enjoying the pleasures that should by rights have been hers must have provoked a tangle of resentment and envy. What is more, the strategies suggested by the manual writers to deal with the situation seem designed to exacerbate its painfulness. Charlotte Yonge suggested, for instance, that:

The grown-up girls in the house can do much for the governess's happiness. Often she can be made a very delightful sympathizing friend, and the audience for all their experiences; and even if she be not suited to this happy *role*, she can be made much happier by their considerateness in bringing her flowers, books, music, etc., and telling her bits of news.[104]

One family in which this was quite definitely not how things were done was that of the Liberal parliamentarians, the Kay-Shuttleworths. Here philanthropy and self-improvement rather than social and material display were the order of the day, so that the differences between the governess and the young ladies of the house were less marked than they might otherwise have been. In this context it was easy for May Pinhorn, who went to work for the Kay-Shuttleworths in 1895, to develop a close relationship with Angela, the elder sister of her pupils who, at twenty-two, was only four years her junior. In her unpublished memoir May Pinhorn paid tribute to the profound effect which her friendship with Angela had had on her own emotional and intellectual development:

I soon became very much attached to her and she a great influence on me, she broadened my views and helped me to form ideals, so that I was soon far more interested in my work than I had been before and began to grow opinions of my own. She also made a definite attack upon my reserve with considerable success; when once the barriers were partially broken down, I began to see that there was no merit in entrenching oneself in such a stronghold and that life was far better and happier when one gave one's personality more freely. She took care that I should not hide myself in my shyness, she sought me out, threw me with other people, and took me with her to lectures, educational meetings, etc.[105]

May Pinhorn and Angela Kay-Shuttleworth became very good friends, at least to the extent that the former's schoolroom duties allowed. Together they tramped the East End of London in the name of philanthropy, made close studies of the newest educational theories, and even toured Europe together on the £50 which had been given to each of them by Angela's father. Yet in 1899, at the age of thirty-two, Pinhorn was obliged to come to terms with the fact that she and her dear friend had diverging destinies. Angela had become engaged to a certain Captain James, brother to one of Pinhorn's former employers. In her description of the courtship and subsequent wedding Pinhorn both relished her power as Angela's best friend – she has the influence to make or break the relationship, she is the first one to hear the good news – yet expressed profound surprise at being given a central place in the public celebrations:

> I had only been at 39 Princes Gardens a few days when the news came that Angela Kay-Shuttleworth was engaged to Mrs Ashton's brother, Captain James, which was a great surprise to her but not to me as Angela had confided all her doubts and fears to me and I had helped her to decide in his favour. To my great pleasure and astonishment, she asked me at once to be one of her bridesmaids. At Christmas I went up to Barbon for the wedding and helped with the preparations. The dresses of the six bridesmaids were of white bengaline with turquoise-blue sashes and soft lacy fischus, the hats trimmed with a litte blue and white ostrich tips.[106]

Within this passage can be found all the untidiness, confusion and ambiguity which characterised the governess' relationship with her employers' family. For while Pinhorn does not seem to have doubted the strength and importance of her personal bond with Kay-Shuttleworth, she had no expectation of playing any but the most minor role in the forthcoming festivities. On those occasions when the genteel Victorian family celebrated – dressed up in fine clothes and put itself on display – the governess anticipated no more than an obscure position on the very edge of the family group. That Pinhorn was asked to move centre stage in a white dress with a blue sash stands as a testimony both to the strength of her friendship with the bride, and to the way in which the governess' status both within the family and in society at large was beginning to change by the turn of the century.

6

A Tabooed Woman

[The governess] is a bore to almost any gentleman, as a tabooed
woman, to whom he is interdicted from granting the usual privileges
of the sex, and yet who is perpetually crossing his path.

Lady Eastlake, *Quarterly Review* (1848)

After lessons this evening we had a game of 'old maid' and strange
to say I was it twice running, so that we all declared that if it came
to me once more it would certainly come true, it did not however, so
there may still be some hope left for me perhaps.

Edith Gates, Diary (10 February 1876)

The spinster was regarded with particular scorn and pity by the
Victorians. Unable to fulfil the highest female goals of marriage
and motherhood, any woman who was unmarried at thirty-five
was judged to have failed at life. Commentators were convinced
that a disproportionate number of the fifty-three women in every
thousand who in 1861 were 'surplus' to the male population were
to be found in the middle and upper classes.[1] Although this was
probably not the case,[2] there can be no doubt that the genteel
spinster found herself in an increasingly vulnerable and conspicuous
position as her economic opportunities dwindled to almost nothing
by the middle decades of the century.

From the 1780s, as we have seen, the only option for a respectable
single woman without means was to find a place under a relative's
roof where, depending on the circumstances, she might act as unpaid
housekeeper, companion or nurse. In large families the youngest
daughter was frequently expected to remain single in order that
she might look after her parents in old age. The problem with this
arrangement was that it left the unmarried woman at risk from a
change in her family's circumstances. When a brother married or a

father died the spinster was obliged to take up her search again for a home amongst her remaining relatives. As she herself grew older, and her usefulness to the family declined, the aging single woman found herself the object of grudging charity.

While the spinster's contribution to the household could be invaluable in replacing costly domestic help, her situation was characterised by commentators as that of the 'redundant' woman who was nothing but a drain on the emotional and financial resources of the middle-class family. Doctors stepped in to reinforce the negative associations of spinsterhood by characterising it as an unnatural state of affairs for any woman over thirty and one which gave rise to a range of physical and emotional ailments.[3] Although many of these doctors were adamant that there was no such thing as female sexual desire, they were equally clear that celibacy in women led to a state of frustration which manifested itself in hypochondria, hysteria and nervous irritability (all conditions which were linked causally with the 'solitary sin' of masturbation). In time, a stereotype of the 'old maid' emerged. She was sour, ugly and aging – characteristics which were supposed to be the result of her disappointment in love but which were also invoked to explain why she had been left on the shelf. For the thousands of Victorian women who had no hope of marrying, it was a hard identity to bear.

Those middle-class women whose families were not able to offer them a home were left with no alternative but to earn their living in the schoolroom, with the result that governesses emerged as one of the most conspicuous group of spinsters in Victorian England. While a proportion of daily governesses were married, those women who lived with their employers were expected, along with domestic servants, to remain single. Some women did not take up governessing until it became apparent, in their late twenties, that they were unlikely to marry. It was this association with the figure of the spinster which laid the basis for the popular image of the Victorian governess as dry, old and ugly, an embodiment of frustrated emotional and sexual desire.

Yet this characterisation of the governess as an archetypal 'old maid' could not hold firm in the face of evidence which suggested that many governesses were neither old nor committed to a life of celibacy. In 1861 two thirds of all governesses were under thirty, some were as young as eighteen,[4] and there is no reason to believe that they had all given up hope of marrying one day (even if, as we shall see, they faced considerable difficulties in realising this ambition). Moreover, if 'experts' insisted that the governess, as a spinster, must necessarily be plain and sexless, there is little evidence that this was actually the case.

The frequency with which contemporaries insisted that the governess was ugly does suggest that at some level they feared that the opposite was the case. As a woman who worked for her living, the governess was associated with the working-class woman,[5] whose sexual aggressiveness was seen as inseparable from her economic independence and consequent liberation from her father's or husband's home. But while, with the exception of the maidservant, the working-class woman remained outside the front door of the wealthy middle-class household, the governess took up her position at its very heart, bringing with her the explosive threat of un-regulated sexuality. Middle-class men tended to live at home until marrying around the age of thirty, with the result that the governess was almost bound to find herself the daily object of scrutiny by men of roughly her own age. Unprotected by her own family network, she was vulnerable to sexual approaches in a way that marked her out from the majority of single middle-class women who were chaperoned in the presence of men to whom they were not connected by blood. In the circumstances, it is hardly surprising that some commentators felt a strong need to insist upon the governess' spinsterish qualities.

It was this sense of sexual vulnerability which linked the governess to the figure of another woman whose services allowed the Victorian household to run smoothly – the prostitute. While prostitution was seen as a vice, an agent of moral and physical contamination, contemporaries also acknowledged the function it performed in containing those male desires which were unable to find an outlet within respectable society, either because a man was unmarried or because his wife had no interest in sexual relations.[6] The practice of buying sex from a working-class woman, it was argued by some, protected the middle-class family from the greater disruption that adultery with a woman of the same social class might bring. The role which the prostitute performed as surrogate wife preserved the tranquillity and good order of the bourgeois Christian household, just as the presence of the governess as surrogate mother ensured its status and social standing. Like the prostitute, the governess was propelled into the domestic heart of the upper and upper middle class from the world of the streets, the world of financial desperation. Both categories of women were defined in terms of their distance from the ideal role of wife and mother: prostitutes and spinsters alike were believed to be barren and repulsive to decent men. The figure of the governess threatened to combine the most disturbing aspects of these two archetypes, so that the spinster's desire for social and economic security became fused with the prostitute's sexual aggressiveness to create a figure whose one ambition was to snare a son of the house and leave the schoolroom behind for ever. Fuelled by the fear that lower middle-class women were now entering the schoolroom with this very goal in mind, even the normally sympathetic Harriet Martineau spoke smartly of 'adventuresses who hope to catch a husband and an establishment of one or another degree of value'.[7]

Yet at the same time as the governess was identified with the sexually and economically aggressive prostitute, she was also linked with the more ambiguous figure of the fallen woman. Such a woman was defined by social investigators as a person of respectable birth who had been seduced by a man with the promise of marriage before being 'betrayed' or abandoned by him. Although the fallen woman might be obliged to make her living subsequently by selling her body, the implication was always that she derived nothing but shame and remorse from the experience. When Edinburgh surgeon William Tait conducted an investigation into prostitution in the city, he insisted that all the governesses he had located had embarked upon this way of life following seduction, in contrast to their working-class counter-parts in whom he identified 'a looseness in their characters which would lead to the belief that no deception was necessary to decoy them from the path of rectitude'.[8] The distinction was an important one to Tait and his contemporaries. As Lynda Nead has pointed out, the victimised fallen woman invoked none of the connotations of power and independence which made the prostitute such a threatening figure, and the way was left open for the former's rescue and rehabilitation into respectable society.[9]

Although the vast majority of governesses had not been the victims of actual seduction, the paradigm of the fallen woman seemed a particularly appropriate way to understand the situation of those women who had been brought up to expect a life of leisure before being obliged to 'descend' to the schoolroom. They too had 'fallen' from an absolute state of gentility, while still managing to cling to the outward forms of behaviour which marked their former state. Moreover, just like the fallen woman, the governess' degradation could be seen as the result of one man's folly – in this case her father's – rather than her own wilfulness or desire. The following passage from a periodical article of 1844 suggests how easily the language conventionally used to portray the respectable girl's descent into vice could be appropriated to describe the 'plight' of the governess.

> [Governesses] spring up suddenly in premature development, like plants in a hot-house, – old in heart, aged in appearance, before the bloom of youth is brushed from their years, drawn upwards by the insufferable light, from which, in their glass-houses, there is no shelter. It is no exaggeration to say that hundreds snap yearly from the stalk, or prolong a withered, sickly life, till they, too, sink, and are carried out to die miserably in the by-ways of the world.[10]

As the competing and even contradictory nature of these various associations suggests, the governess' sexuality was the subject of intense scrutiny, idealisation and attempted regulation throughout the first part of the Victorian period. As a result it sometimes becomes difficult to find a way of uncovering the governess' own sense of herself as a sexual being, not least because, in the midst of all this debate, she herself was often unclear about where her true feelings lay. Another problem is that governesses, like all Victorians, remained shy about naming their experience of sexual desire within the pages of their diaries and memoirs. Loneliness and joy are frequently noted without embarrassment, but such emotions are seldom cast in terms of physical desire or emotional longing. In the end what we tend to be left with is a sense not of the governess' experience of her own sexuality, but rather of the fantasies and fears that it provoked in her contemporaries.

Whether the household in which she worked was modest or large, there could be no doubting the disruptive impact of the arrival of a young governess on the lives of its inhabitants. Expected to live as one of the family, she was nonetheless unprotected either by an incest taboo or the watchful eye of her parents. As a result, in homes where accommodation was cramped, the opportunities for both illicit sex and its detection ran high. During the 1840s Samuel Kent, a factory inspector from Sidmouth, took every opportunity to creep out of the marital chamber and into the bedroom of his daughters' governess, Mary Pratt.[11] Even in more spacious homes, suspicion and resentment could flare up at any point. Aristocratic Loelia Ponsonby remembered how, during her Edwardian childhood: 'My mother sometimes accused my father of flirting with the governesses, because he addressed a few civil words to them'.[12]

Nor was this inevitably a situation where a middle-aged man lusted after a young girl. As the distance between the domestic and the public sphere continued to widen, the opportunity for men and women to mix freely with one another diminished. Within the confines of the middle-class home, however, the way was clear for a governess and her male employer to meet daily to discuss matters of common interest without too great a fear of impropriety. Thirty-seven year old Elizabeth Ham found in her employer, the writer Mr Elton for whom she worked during 1820, the cultured conversational partner she had dreamt of for so many years: every night after supper she would sit with him in the drawing-room discussing Poetry, Art and Life. Not surprisingly, Mrs Elton was less than sanguine about the amount of time that her husband was spending with the governess and insisted the latter should be treated with less 'consideration' in the future.[13] Decades later Ham was still trying to mediate between her affectionate feelings for Elton, her moral sense that these were wrong, and her need to justify herself to the readers of her autobiography:

> . . . Mr E. often sat so long as to bring Mrs E. down to see what was become of him. This annoyed me, but I now confess with shame that I felt more annoyed with her than with him. For though there was not a word said but what all the world might hear, yet it was not right that the servants might have to say that Mr. E spent the greater part of his evenings with 'the governess'. I have nothing worse with which to reproach myself than that of liking his company.[14]

Yet while adulterous relationships between a married man and his children's governess caused personal pain and social embarrassment, it was the chance of a love affair with a bachelor brother or uncle which posed the greater threat of social disruption. Unlike the parlourmaid, the governess could not easily be bedded and then abandoned by the young men of the house: as a lady she retained the right to a wedding ring in return for her sexual favours. In theory there was no reason why a family should not be entirely delighted that one of its sons was marrying a governess; in practice, nothing could be further from the case:

> Just let a remote idea be entertained of marriage between a son, or any other member of the family, and the governess; why another siege of Troy would scarcely occasion more commotion – the anger, the scorn, the vituperation lavished on the *artful* creature.[15]

Although evidence about the sort of men governesses eventually married is extremely limited, there is no reason to suggest that they were particularly likely to carry off a member of their employers' household. Yet the fact that so much was thought, said and written about just such a possibility, suggests that a highly sensitive nerve had been touched. As long as middle-class women were responsible for displaying the social position of their household, being obliged to acknowledge a governess as a sister- or daughter-in-law was to compromise not only one's own gentility, but the standing of the whole family. It was for precisely this reason that George Osborne in *Vanity Fair* was filled with foreboding at the prospect of his future brother-in-law proposing to the governess Becky Sharp:

> He had been revolving in his mind the marriage-question pending between Jos and Rebecca, and was not over well pleased that a member of a family into which he, George Osborne, of the –th, was going to marry, should make a *mésalliance* with a little nobody – a little upstart governess.[16]

While commentators had considerable investment in this picture of the governess as a social and sexual climber, what empirical evidence there is suggests that something quite different may have been happening. For a particular set of men, the socially and economically ambiguous figure of the governess became an object of erotic fascination. Such a man was Augustus Hare's Uncle Julius 'who had always a passion for governesses'[17] and ended up by marrying one – Esther Maurice, sister of the theologian F.D. Maurice who did so much to raise the educational standards of the profession through his work at Queen's College.[18] The obsession that some men had with governesses as a sexual type must be explained to a large extent in terms of accessibility. For a shy bachelor the hurdles involved in courting a girl of the same social class could be daunting. Chaperoned by her mother or married sister, she could be approached only through a minefield of etiquette and social convention. The governess, by contrast, could be approached simply and directly: nothing could be more natural than a father, uncle or brother slipping into the schoolroom to check on the progress of the younger members of the family and finding himself in conversation with their teacher. Yet the appeal of the governess may have gone even deeper. Just as respectable men mounted missions to save the fallen women of London's back streets,[19] so others such as Uncle Julius were driven by a barely-conscious drive to 'rescue' governesses from the 'degradation' into which they had fallen and to bring them back within the fold of genteel society via the legitimacy of marriage.

There were even stronger currents to be navigated in those cases where a governess worked for a widower. Here she was often required to step into the gap left by her employer's dead wife, assuming total responsibility for the physical and emotional well-being of her pupils. In these cases an irresistible force seems to have been at work propelling the governess from her position of surrogate mother to that of step-mother. Such an arrangement suited both parties. For the man it dealt with the dilemma of how to provide for the practical and emotional needs of a young family; for the woman it supplied the financial and social security which she so conspicuously lacked. Given the apparent naturalness of the arrangement, embarrassing situations frequently occurred in those households where either a governess or an employer presumed too much. In his autobiography Edmund Gosse described how his middle-aged governess, Miss Marks, collapsed in hysterics on hearing that her employer was to marry again – clearly she had harboured hopes of becoming the second Mrs Gosse herself.[20] May Pinhorn, in her unpublished memoir, described what happened in 1890 when, at the age of twenty-two, she took a job as governess to the children of Mr Fletcher, a wealthy widower of Norwich:

> I was still very young for my age in some ways, and I had no suspicions when Mr Fletcher began to be particularly attentive and affectionate. I only thought it was kind but rather boring of him to be so *fatherly*. He took me to a shop and gave me a dress which embarrassed me much, and I received his advances with much brusqueness. At this juncture Miss Bradley [the housekeeper] fell ill and had to go away for a rest, leaving Mr Fletcher's niece, Ethel Massey, a girl a little older than myself, in charge. Things went on apace, and she and I amused ourselves by thwarting and teasing poor Mr Fletcher, who made elephantine attempts to be young and active. If he took my hand on coming to a breakwater, I cruelly made him leap from the top and otherwise treated him with scant consideration. Still, I hardly foresaw the end till one Sunday afternoon when he got me into a summer-house and told me he hoped I would be his wife, an offer I very promptly and brutally refused. I was now in an awkward position with Miss Bradley away and it being impossible for me to leave suddenly. I wrote to Mother and she came to Norwich for a day or two and saw Mr Fletcher and me and put things on a calm footing. It was a very funny experience and she and I both laughed over it and Mr Fletcher's ponderous seriousness.[21]

More ambiguous altogether was the sexual tension between male servants and the governess. This was a problem only for the grandest households – during the 1860s footmen were an unaffordable luxury for anyone with an income of less than £800. What is more, despite the celebrated end-of-century example of Miss Jessel in Henry James' *The Turn of the Screw*,[22] there is little evidence to suggest that many governesses actually did form a sexual relationship with a male domestic. Nonetheless, their social and sexual ambiguity lent a certain edge to even the most fleeting of encounters. One young woman described what happened when she arrived at a Mayfair address for an interview for a post as governess:

> On asking for Lady G., the footman said he would see if her ladyship was disengaged, and he left me standing in the hall; three more men servants presently made their appearance, they each stared, and the one out of livery asked me what I wanted. I said I had an appointment with Lady G. He said I might wait, but in so rough a manner, that my courage began to fail me.[23]

What gave such tension to this little scene was the fact that both social and sexual self-images were being challenged. While a footman could accept that he had to adopt the position of an inferior towards the female members of the family, to have to do the same for a woman of the same social class as himself (in his estimation) was an affront to his manhood and made him appear servile and even effeminate. Likewise, what was so humiliating for the young governess was the way in which the footmen felt that they were clearly within their rights to appraise her face and figure as if she were a girl of their own class.

To defuse these various situations, the manual writers did not, as logic might have dictated, direct a stream of advice at sons, husbands and footmen on how to restrain themselves in the presence of the governess. Instead they set about stripping the latter of every last shred of sex appeal, drawing on stock images associated with the spinster and the surplus woman, until the point was reached where the commentator Lady Eastlake could insist that the governess had become 'a bore to almost any gentleman, as a tabooed woman, to whom he is interdicted from granting the usual privileges of the sex, and yet who is perpetually crossing his path'.[24] Yet even this was not enough. Unable to admit the simple fact that governesses were no less or more attractive than any random sample of women, writers like Mary Maurice (sister to Esther who married Augustus Hare's Uncle Julius) were forced to explain away men's continuing alliances

with these supposedly ugly women by assigning to them [...]
sexual predator. Thus the circle of guilt was completed: u[...]
were obliged to become governesses because they were [...]
find a husband; and, because they were sexually frustr[...]ed
developed a manic appetite which ran wild in a house fu[...]

> Frightful instances have been discovered in which she, to whom the
> care of the young has been entrusted, instead of guarding their minds
> in innocence and purity, has become their corrupter – she has been
> the first to lead and to initiate into sin, to suggest and carry on
> intrigues, and finally to be the instrument of destroying the peace
> of families . . .

> These are the grosser forms of sin which have been generally
> concealed from public notice . . . but none of the cases are imaginary
> ones, and they are but too well known in the circles amongst which
> they occurred. In some instances again, the love of admiration has
> led the governess to try and make herself necessary to the comfort
> of the father of the family in which she resided, and by delicate and
> unnoticed flattery gradually to gain her point, to the disparagement
> of the mother, and the destruction of mutual happiness. When the
> latter was homely, or occupied with domestic cares, opportunity was
> found to bring forward attractive accomplishments, or by sedulous
> attentions to supply her lack of them; or the sons were in some
> instances objects of notice and flirtation, or when occasion offered,
> visitors at the house.[25]

It followed that any advice directed to a governess about how to
avoid compromising situations developing with male employers
always involved a modification of her behaviour, rather than any
challenging of his:

> to force conversation, or to take the lead in it, or to show off what
> little is known, cannot fail to disgust. To keep in the background is
> the safest plan, and wait to be brought forward, rather than to force
> yourself into a place, which it may be necessary hereafter to quit.[26]

What is more, the governess was sternly informed, it was precisely
because she refused to adopt a suitably retiring demeanour towards
her pupils' male relatives that female employers were left with no
option but to hire plain women. When recommending one of her
pupils for a post as governess in a private house, the redoutable
Miss Pinkerton of *Vanity Fair* felt obliged to point out that 'as she
is only eighteen years of age, and of exceedingly pleasing personal
appearance, perhaps this young lady may be objectionable . . .'[27]

In contradiction of that earlier connection between ugliness and sexual aggressiveness, appeal was now made to the principles of physiognomy to link plainness with moral worth. In 1836 when Mme Bureaud Riofrey was interviewing for a governess, she worked on the assumption that a good-looking candidate must also be a stupid one. As for Miss R., the woman whom she eventually picked for the job, 'had it not been for her intelligent countenance, she must have been decidedly termed ugly'.[28]

Underlying this preference for plain governesses there was a sense that a woman who had known grief and hardship, to the degree that she was obliged to go to work, ought to look sufficiently chastened by the experience. High spirits and energy were all to the good (weeping governesses were no use to anyone), but personal attractiveness seemed not only inappropriate but somehow mutely impertinent. For that reason the question of how a governess was to dress became a subject for intense debate, a battleground of conflicting desires and prohibitions. While clothing had always been used to fix and display social status, from the beginning of the nineteenth century the wealthy began to pay particular attention to elaborate dress codes as a way of confirming their gentility. Different types of clothing were increasingly required for specific activities or times of the day, so that an upper- or upper middle-class woman might find herself changing several times as she proceeded through her schedule of morning calls, riding, afternoon tea and dinner. Following fashion was a way of announcing to the world that one could afford to discard clothes long before they had worn out, while the increasingly elaborate trends in luxury female clothing both reflected and displayed its wearers' distance from all forms of practical labour.

As a lady, the governess was expected to look like one, and pay for it out of her own pocket too: unlike the nurse or the lady's maid she was not provided with a uniform or her employer's cast-offs. If she was employed by a particularly grand family, as May Pinhorn discovered when she went to the Wolfe Barries in 1894, she would need a wardrobe that would not make her look conspicuous as she hovered at the edge of the drawing-room or the conservatory: 'I felt very shy and lost in London life . . . I did not know how to take my part in a house where there was much cheerful young society, and I soon found that my clothes were not suitable, which did not add to my comfort.'[29] Even in the most unshowy of households, a special outfit for Sundays – something which had not been seen on any other day of the week – was an essential part of genteel Christian observance. The problem was that such clothes were delicate and expensive. Gloves, for instance, could not be made oneself and had to be replaced at the shop counter every time they spoiled, which was often. Saving money by scrimping on clothes could be counter-productive – looking shabby compromised one's status as a lady and diminished the chances of finding a job with a well-placed family. In 1819 Elizabeth Ham put her failure to secure a particular position down to the three-year-old pelisse she wore to her interview,[30] while in the 1840s Mary Smith's career as a governess was punctuated by fears that her clothes were on the point of falling to pieces.[31] According to one well-informed source of 1844, the governess was obliged to spend almost half of her annual salary on dress.[32] So important did the GBI consider the matter that it made small grants to governesses to update their wardrobes, with the result that many 'have been enabled to take situations which they are now filling with credit, which they must otherwise have lost for the want of suitable apparel . . .'[33]

Despite an awareness of the need to maintain an appropriate appearance, few governesses in the first half of the Victorian period were able to do more than keep themselves clean and decent. When the GBI opened its offices in Harley Street in the 1840s, governesses were said to be easily spotted amongst the other West End pedestrians by virtue of their unfashionable dress. Likewise, when that most celebrated of fictional governesses, Jane Eyre, first encountered her employer Mr Rochester she was dressed in the governess' 'uniform' of 'a black merino cloak, a black beaver bonnet; neither of them half fine enough for a lady's maid'.[34] Moreover, without the help of just such a lady's maid, the governess was unlikely to have much time free to tong her hair into the elaborate styles that were so popular throughout the Victorian period. When the seventeen-year-old governess Mary Cowden-Clarke was invited by her employers, the Purcells, to attend a ball in 1826, she was obliged to rely upon Mrs Purcell to help her with her clothes and hair in order that she might not look out of place in the assembled company.[35]

Confirmation of the way in which the governess was marked out by her sober appearance comes in the form of 'The Governess', a painting by celebrated artist Richard Redgrave which was displayed at the Royal Academy in 1844.[36] Redgrave, at least two of whose sisters were governesses, painted a series of pictures in the 1840s describing the plight of the respectable woman obliged to work for her living. One of his most popular, 'The Governess', shows a young woman sitting in a sombre schoolroom gazing sadly at the floor. In her lap she holds a black-bordered letter, while on the piano the piece of music she has been playing – 'Home Sweet Home' – suggests that her thoughts are with the bereaved family that she has left behind. In the middle distance, amidst a haze of natural light, we can make out three young women, presumably her pupils, who are occupying themselves with what appears to be light-hearted conversation. Most striking of all, however, is the difference in the way in which the four women in the picture are dressed. While the governess wears the plain black dress of mourning, her charges wear frocks of light, bright colours. In the place of the governess' deep white collar, the girls reveal the bare flesh of their shoulders and upper chest. The governess may allow herself a couple of modest ringlets, but her pupils' hair is styled in an abundance of curls which fall luxuriously over their neck and shoulders – always a coded symbol of female eroticism.

Yet woe betide the governess who dressed too well. The fondness of servants for wearing clothes in their off-duty hours which made them indistinguishable from their employers excited a stream of disapproving comment throughout the century.[37] In the case of the well-dressed governess, the fear may have had as much to do with the sexual as the social pretensions of her wardrobe. To look like a lady was all very well, but ladies had instinctive good taste, knew which colours went with which, understood just how to tie a scarf or fix a shawl. These qualities were dangerous ones for a governess to possess because they threatened to make her look unnecessarily attractive. Moreover, starting work in the schoolroom often marked the first time that a girl was responsible for her own wardrobe, a fact which evidently worried the advice writers. While May Pinhorn continued to send her dress patterns home to Wolverhampton for approval,[38] young Miss K. brought down the wrath of Mme Bureaud Riofrey on her head when she confided to her that she was looking forward to starting work because it meant that she would be able to get away from her parents and buy lots of new clothes.[39] It was to guard against what they perceived to be the dangerous desires of a Miss K. that the advice writers expended much energy in maintaining that good taste and economy were not, in fact, mutually exclusive choices but actually one and the same thing. The tortuous prose that Anna Jameson was obliged to adopt in order to put across her point suggests that this synthesis remained both uneasy and unconvincing: 'perfect neatness, a simplicity, not without elegance, because dictated by the sense of propriety and natural good taste, will be found at once most lady-like and most economical'.[40]

This was how the governess was supposed to behave. Such were the codes which had been constructed to cope with the situation where men and women, unconnected by family ties, lived together in close proximity. The implications of such a model did not stop with the relations between the adult members of the house. For her younger pupils the governess completed the triad of female archetypes which populated their nursery-tale world. Mothers who never scolded and were seen only for an hour after tea soon became princesses – beautiful but incorporeal creatures whose mysteriousness was underpinned by their remoteness: 'The word "Mother" conveyed absolutely nothing to me but a name for the beautifully scented and dressed lady, whose silk petticoats rustled as she walked and whose fingers glittered with jewels'.[41] Nanny, meanwhile, was a good witch, full of healing magic, who ruled over the comforting realm of the body. That left the governess, who smacked and snapped and was *always there* to be transformed into a hag – old, plain and sexually denying. Such, at least, was the way that Fanny Almedingen remembered her first sight of her new governess, Miss Jardine:

> In her pretty sunlit sitting-room my mother sat very upright as was her custom. She wore a pale-blue stuff gown with touches of lace at the throat and wrists. She sat facing a thin, middle-aged woman, pale and grey-eyed, in a plain dark-blue dress; two bony hands were folded in her lap.[42]

Even more graphic is the account from Eleanor Farjeon's *A Nursery in the Nineties*, which describes the act of self-mutilation necessary to transform princess into hag, mother into governess:

> One day a sinister figure mounted the stairs and came to the Nursery Door; a thin queer formless figure draped in black, with a shapeless hat swathed in a heavy veil that darkened the visitor's features, and black kid gloves protruding from a strange mantle. Visitor? Rather, a visitant wandered out of a bad dream. It stood in the doorway, announcing in a squeaky voice: 'Well, dear children! I'm the New Governess.'

> We stood appalled.

> The creature minced into the Nursery. A howl rent the air, and Bertie burst into tears.

Shaking with merriment the figure flew at him open-armed. Light flashed upon me; I darted at the horrid image, tore the veil from its face, and screamed, 'It's all right, Bertie! it's all right! It's Mama!'

The Nursery was loud with lamentations and laughter. Bertie, still yelling, shrank from and clung to the skirts of the New Governess, who cuddled and comforted him in Mama's voice, brimming with fun, brimming with self-reproach. Joe was overwhelmed with his concern for Bertie; while I was torn between appreciation of Mama's funny trick, sympathy for Bertie's terror, which I had for a moment shared, and a curious horror of the things Mama had done to her darling face. The cheek-bones, and even the tip of her nose were liberally reddened, and she had burnt-corked her eyebrows, which were naturally so fair as to be almost invisible.[43]

The intense scorn that the governess encountered when her be- haviour threatened to challenge this unflattering stereotype suggests just how great was her pupils' need to go on seeing her as old and ugly. Forty years after the event, Jane Panton described with a sneer how a surprise summons to the drawing-room had her governess rushing to the looking glass:

... Miss Wright had to unpin and shake herself out, to prune her feathers generally at the glass, and arrange her curls with an eye to conquest, of whom I don't quite know ... but at last she felt quite satisfied, gave a final smirk at herself in the mirror, and ordered us to descend ...[44]

Likewise any attempt by Panton's next governess, Mrs Port, to form a romantic relationship was greeted with sniggers and characterised as a pathetic craving for affection to which no decent man could possibly respond:

Her last offence was being perpetually found at the Brompton Oratory where she had a friend – a priest with very bright blue eyes, who disliked her, I think, as much as we did: for at last he communicated with Mama, and Mrs Port departed weeping aloud, and declaiming that ... she ... [was] now condemned to starve! I never could understand her affection for the Brompton Oratory Priest, for we never went inside the chapel, but always met him coming in or going out, and she was, moreover, a militant Protestant.[45]

Passionate friendships with other women were seen as an even more desperate version of this search for love by someone who was intrinsically unloveable. Thus, in a typically off-hand remark from her recollections of the 1830s, Georgiana Sitwell recalled how 'Governess Number Four . . . was romantic, worshipped the curate, and formed a passionate attachment to our newly imported French governess . . .'[46] Alternatively, if these alliances passed beyond the level of flirtation, then there was absolutely no doubt about who was to be cast into the role of aggressor. When recalling a story she had been told about her employer's own schoolroom days, it never crossed May Pinhorn's mind to question the received version of the role played by the governess:

> The german governess was a fiend who ill-treated the children & acquired such an uncanny influence over Lady K.-S. that she succeeded in separating her from her husband when his health broke down, and carried her off to the continent for the rest of her life. Lord S. could not speak of the woman without a shudder, even when a middle-aged man, his youth having been so poisoned by her influence.[47]

As children grew older and their interest in sexual matters increased, their reaction to the governess' romantic life became both more generous and more complex. In Edith Gates' diary entry for 6 February 1876, her own anxiety about her lack of marriage prospects contrasts sharply with her elder pupil's optimism on the subject, and the younger child's determination to continue denying that such a thing could ever happen:

> Mary made me promise her that when I married, Grace and she should be my bridesmaids, I did it all the more willingly as there is so very little chance of such an event ever taking place. I am on the right way now to become an old maid, in fact it has been settled a long time, that Grace (who also has a great objection to marriage) and I are to live together and keep a number of cats, over whom her dearly beloved black Sambo with the green eyes is to reign.[48]

The growing acknowledgement of the governess' sexuality by her adolescent pupils did not happen on any formal level: sex education was not frequently handed out to girls but, if it were, the mother, as a married woman, was considered a more knowledgeable source of information. Informally, though, a governess might represent an alternative viewpoint on such matters which her pupils could usefully set against the one provided by their parents. In 1858 thirteen-year-old Annie Rothschild had been visiting estate cottages with her mother, who had taken no pains to conceal her extreme disapproval of some of the inhabitants who were unmarried mothers. A few days later Annie recorded in her diary: 'I related to Mlle our little histories with the young women and their babies but the latter did not look very much shocked; she said that she had heard always the same complaint so that she had now got used to it'.[49]

If of marriageable age, the governess provided her pupils with a limitless source of speculation, fed by those highly commercial 'governess' novels of the period in which appeared 'the type of governess who ... either by her charms married into the ducal family which employed her, or died in a decline'.[50] Dukes were not much forthcoming in real life, but solid young men employed in teaching and the church did occasionally step forward to deprive a family of its governess. Even the most prosaic suitor could be turned into something more glamorous by the fervent imaginings of adolescent girls. In her diary, seventeen-year-old Florence Sitwell referred to the engagement of her governess Miss Dobelshoff to Mr Bacon in a tone that managed to mix high romance, sexual curiosity and a child-like matter-of-factness: 'they are in supreme happiness and I think they will be married next spring. He spends the whole of every afternoon with her . . .'[51]

In much the same way Annie and Connie Rothschild followed the engagement, wedding and early married life of their governess as if it were both a fabulous fairy tale and a taste of what was to come in their own lives. Connie recorded in her diary for November 26 1858:

> Mademoiselle came in radiant with delight, Monsieur Goldberg [her fiancé] had written to say that she could be married to-morrow if she wished it. I went to bed thinking of her and wondering whether I should ever be in the same happy position.[52]

Given her emotional investment in the situation, the actual meeting with Monsieur Goldberg was a highly-charged moment:

> She next introduced me to Monsieur Goldberg but I was trembling so violently that I could hardly look at him. He is decidedly good looking but not an Adonis, his complexion is olive, his eyes brown melting and soft, his mouth and teeth beautiful, his nose is too large and fat, his hair is black as ebony and his whiskers beard and moustache are auburn ... We slept wonderfully well and I dreamt all night of Monsieur and Madame Goldberg.[53]

As the wedding day approached, Connie's happiness for her former governess was overwhelmed by a sense of loss as she realised that from now on she was not to be the most important person in Mademoiselle's life (if, indeed, she ever had been):

> December 23rd 1858: I could think of nothing all day but that it was Mlle's wedding day. I should not see her again for a year and that when we did meet she would be a different person, married and altogether changed. The subject was too painful to be dwelt upon and I banished it as speedily as possible, but even My Novel could not take it quite out of my head.[54]

The discovery of the governess' sexuality by her older pupils was not enough to overcome the deepening ambiguities of their relationship. As adolescent girls prepared to leave the schoolroom, it fell to the governess to coach them in the intricate systems of etiquette and protocol that they would need to negotiate the social world. Her brief was to provide a model of genteel femininity which adolescent women could imitate as they took on their adult sexual identities. Yet as her pupils began to encounter the world beyond the front door, it became increasingly difficult to ignore the fact that, by virtue of her own spinsterhood, the governess had failed to practise what she preached. Once again doubts about her sexual attractiveness came to the fore, as the governess increasingly found herself pushed back once more into identification with the celibate spinster, leaving her employer to function as a more appropriate role model for the young ladies of the house. This time around, however, the governess was assigned the additional role of sexual policewoman, whose job it was to guard the boundaries between the chaste domestic world and the unregulated sexuality of the streets. In this new and final phase of their education, it was the governess' job to protect her pupils from sexual menace by accompanying them to their outside lessons, to the shops and even to parties. It was part of contemporaries' curiously confused thinking about young women that they were believed to be both sexually unawakened and inviolable, yet constantly in danger of being corrupted by contact with men. Rather than take the logical step of insisting that men were accompanied whenever they came into contact with the opposite sex, single women up until the age of thirty and frequently beyond were chaperoned wherever they went by their mother or another married woman. Any girl who chose to break this code by walking in public alone forfeited the sexual good name which was integral to being a lady. What made the contradiction in the governess' situation so humiliatingly apparent was the fact that in similar circumstances she was not considered to need a companion: the implication was not that she had no honour, simply that it was inconceivable that anyone should wish to deprive her of it.

The confusion which marked the Victorians' thinking about the sexual awareness of girls soon spilled over into the duties of those women set to chaperone them. Was the governess there to save her pupils from their own desires or from those of men? May Pinhorn had no doubt at all. Of her time as governess to the Evans family in 1887 she recalled how:

> The oldest girl, Gladys, was only three years younger than myself and was in a very difficult phase, unpleasant and stubborn in her home, though extremely bland to outsiders, and with the most undesirable tendency to flirt with low class Welshmen. I, therefore, had to be a responsible chaperon and keep on the look out for objectionable followers.[55]

As Pinhorn's attitude suggests, the focus of the governess' chaperoning activity frequently shifted from protecting innocent girls from the lustful advances of men to controlling any sign of sexual curiosity in the young women themselves. Using the governess to enforce sexual discipline like this could develop into something of an obsession with employers. In the Vienna of the 1880s one of Freud's earliest patients, a British governess called Miss Lucy R., was threatened with dismissal by her employer because she failed to prevent family guests from kissing her young pupils on the mouth.[56] Thirty years earlier an Anglo-French governess, Celestine Doudet, was charged by her employer Dr James Marsden with the task of rooting out the 'bad habit' of masturbation which he suspected in his five daughters.[57] So obsessed was Doudet with the subject of 'self-abuse', as well as with pleasing her employer with whom she was secretly in love, that she faked the tell-tale 'signs' of masturbation on the bodies of her pupils. Eventually, in 1855, she was charged with causing the death of Mary-Ann Marsden and with cruelty towards the remaining sisters. In the ensuing trials Dr Marsden, now remarried, anxiously distanced himself from Doudet, presenting himself to the court as a hapless widower who had naively assumed that the governess had the best interests of his daughters at heart.

Even though Lucy R. and Celestine Doudet were divided by forty years and half of Europe, their cases provide parallel insights into the tensions generated by the need of some employers to cast the governess into the role of sexual policewoman who must guard the boundary between the chaste middle-class household and the rampant sexuality of the streets. Both women had been appointed to take on the moral as well as the educational supervision of their motherless pupils. Both felt the irresistable urge to change their status from surrogate mother to step-mother via the marriage bed. Both, however, had the misfortune to fall in love with employers who did not return their feelings. These men not only denied them the opportunity to express their own desire, but then proceeded to charge them with the task of eliminating evidence of it in others. Lucy R. tried to resist the role, but found that the penalty was not only the knowledge that her employer did not love her, but also the possibility that he might send her far away from him. Doudet, by contrast, threw herself into her task and worked with the fury of a woman possessed: unfortunately it was not enough to win her the man she loved.

If the governess was an object of sexual curiosity for her female pupils, she provoked altogether more urgent feelings in their brothers. Edmund Gosse, for instance, recalled how his ten-year-old self became obsessed with Miss Marks' 'boudoir':

> Very properly, that she might have some sanctuary, Miss Marks forbade me to enter this virginal bower, which, of course, became to me an object of harrowing curiosity. Through the key-hole I could see practically nothing; one day I contrived to slip inside, and discovered that there was nothing to see but a plain bedstead and a toilet-table, void of all attraction.[58]

The effect that this fascination with the governess had on boys as they grew up is most clearly revealed in the pornography of the period, much of it marked by an obsession with flagellation or 'the English vice'.[59] The circulation of pornographic material concerned with spanking, flogging and whipping reached epidemic proportions during the Victorian period. While convents and servants' halls were popular locations for these repetitive essays, the largest sub-genre of all consisted of tales of schoolroom spankings. In this case the setting was either a girls' boarding school or a private classroom and the plot typically involved a governess whipping her pupil, who might be an adolescent girl or boy, for some petty misdemeanour such as sulleness or theft.

Aside from this material, which was quite obviously pornographic, and marketed as such, there was another category of flagellatory erotica which appeared in such respectable magazines as the *Englishwoman's Domestic Magazine*. Readers were invited to send in their thoughts on the subject of corporal punishment for girls. Many of the letters which found their way into print were clearly not written by long-standing readers at all, but were simply little pornographic essays lifted wholesale from more scurrilous sources. Because of the pretext under which the material was solicited – as part of a debate about the rights and wrongs of whipping girls – the setting of these tales was almost always a schoolroom and the principal players exclusively female. The following, extremely mild, example purported to be from 'a loving mother' and appeared in the *Englishwoman's Domestic Magazine* in December 1868:

> The eldest was first taken to her dressing room and prepared for the rod, and then conveyed to the boudoir by the governess, who at once administered the discipline. The younger one was then prepared, and received a wholesome flagellation. These whippings were administered *sopra* [sic] *dorsum nudam*, the delinquents being tightly strapped to an ottoman during the castigation, at the conclusion of which they had to kiss the rod and thank the governess, when they were permitted to retire.[60]

By and large Victorian middle-class girls were not ritualistically beaten in the way that this passage describes, either by their parents or their teachers (an exasperated slap was quite another matter). The same was not true for their brothers, many of whom seem to have derived a degree of erotic excitement from their experience of being flogged at public school. Yet the riddle remains of why these men should go to the trouble of dreaming up elaborate fantasies involving girls and governesses instead of simply drawing on their own boyhood experiences. That it was actually the girl being beaten with whom they identified (rather than the governess) is suggested by the large number of flogging brothels that flourished during this period run by 'governesses' who were paid to administer vigorous 'discipline' to their clients. The sex of the characters in so many of these stories was often remarkably fluid, so that behind the figure of the girl – often called 'Willie' or 'Georgie' – there lurked an unmistakably masculine presence. What is more, according to Steven Marcus, who made an extended study of Victorian pornography in the 1960s, the extremely aggressive figure of the governess wielding her ever upright 'rod' was nothing more than a screen for the teacher of the original public school scene. The appeal of governess pornography seems to have been that it enabled its readers to avoid any painful recognition of their own homosexual desires by allowing them to transpose the fantasy of a public school flogging on to a more acceptable female cast.[61] That the majority of these stories ostensibly involved a woman beating a girl only confirms that it was the same-sex relationship which gave the scene its appeal. It is a standard observation of the Victorian period that middle-class boys whose erotic feelings were first awakened by nannies and housemaids could often enjoy sex in later life only with working-class women.[62] For their homosexual peers it may well have been the governess who became the significant figure in their early sexual landscape. In this case it was not the discrepancy in class background which made her such a compelling figure (she was, in theory, at least, a member of the same class as the boy's family) but rather the ambiguity and malleability of her gender which determined her peculiar appeal.

Getting married – or failing to – became an obsession with Edith Gates while she was working as governess to the Wiggett family of Reading during 1876. Even though middle-class women did not marry much before twenty-five, Gates felt that, at only nineteen, hope was fading fast. In a sense she was quite right to worry: the social isolation that went with her job made it difficult to see how she would ever meet and court a man. Although one of the governess' chief qualifications for her work was the 'natural' love of children which all women were assumed to possess, she was also expected to suppress any desire for her own marriage and motherhood, even for the flirtation and flattery that might lead to them:

> February 14th St Valentine's Day. What a pity it is that people think me too old for Valentines as they evidently do, but I suppose I am, and that a young lady of nineteen, a governess too, ought to have more serious thoughts.[63]

Doubtless many a governess was only too happy to pass up Valentine cards for the opportunity of enjoying some of the pleasures of parenthood without the penalty of marriage: as we have seen, situations in motherless families were, for a variety of reasons, particularly popular. For the majority, however, enforced spinster-hood was an unwanted and unloved suitor; those like Edith Gates were forced to negotiate constantly between the demands of their occupational role and their private desires for a fully sexual identity. It was hard to accept and, in fact, Gates never quite did. She married finally, at the age of thirty-two: nine years and six pregnancies later she was dead.[64]

As Edith Gates was well aware, getting married represented the governess' only escape route from the schoolroom: while Victorian fathers had an unfortunate knack of losing money overnight, few of them seem to have been equally adept at winning it back again. How many disastrous and miserable marriages were contracted for the worst possible reasons it is impossible to tell, but Mrs Pryor from Charlotte Brontë's *Shirley* was probably not unique in her admission that 'if I had not been so miserable as a governess, I never should have married'.[65] One problem was, of course, that during the nineteenth century there were simply not enough men to go round. What is more, in the scramble for the altar the governess' chances were considerably lessened by the fact that she was both sexually and socially *declassée*. It took a strong man to disregard the penalties involved in marrying a governess. One who evidently did not have what it took was the fiancé of Blanche Borthwick, nursery governess to a Hampstead shipping family during the 1880s. Blanche and her young man were evidently much in love and planning to marry, but the determination of his mother, a formidable woman, that no son of hers was to wed a governess ultimately prevailed. The engagement was broken off and both Blanche and her young man remained single for the rest of their lives.[66] Perhaps in Blanche Borthwick's story lies the key to why there are so few references, even the most fleeting, to just what sort of men governesses married: those who managed to find husbands and start new lives as ladies of leisure were hardly likely to mention their former occupation when the wives of professional men came to call.

On a more practical level, the governess faced huge difficulties in her pursuit of a romantic and sexual life. Meetings with 'gentlemen followers' were usually forbidden and, in any case, the governess was required to ask permission every time she wished to leave the house. If she was living far away from her own home any existing engagement might well crumble under the strain of once or twice yearly meetings. For just that reason Mary Cowden-Clarke was delighted in 1826 when her employers decided to move back from Devon to London for the winter, since it gave her the opportunity to receive calls from Mr Cowden-Clarke, the clergyman whom she eventually married.[67] For less fortunate governesses the outlook remained bleak:

her prospects of marriage are almost blighted: even if her personal attractions and intellectual acquirements are considerable, she remains secluded and inaccessible; nor can she encourage the approach of an admirer, however equality of station and similarity of taste may justify it, without exposing herself to censure, and perhaps to unmerited suspicion. There is no impropriety in the female wish to cultivate an acquaintance that may lead to a matrimonial engagement; on the contrary, it is the common and the natural object of all parents to give their daughters every fair opportunity of thus 'establishing' themselves, as it is called: and it is difficult to say why the governess, who of all daughters has the most reason to covet such a change of her lot, should be expected to resign the wish with the resolution and the constancy of a nun. [68]

Precisely because fears about her sexual and social ambitions ran so high, the governess was under particular pressure to conform to the strictest codes of conventionally respectable behaviour. In the Countess of Blessington's *The Young Governess*, Clara Mordaunt is taken to task by her employer Mrs Williamson for daring to spend some time in conversation with a male family friend – behaviour which, as Mrs Williamson makes clear, would have been quite acceptable in a young lady of independent means:

You may well be ashamed of yourself – setting up, forsooth, for a fine lady, and running about the pleasure grounds all the morning with a gentleman, just as Miss Webster, or Miss Preston, or any of the other young ladies of large fortune that we ask down here, might do. What may not be wrong in them, is decidedly so in you. You are not on an equality with Mr Seymour, who is a young man of family, and heir to a good fortune. The young ladies I have named, know that they will meet here none but persons eligible to become their husbands, therefore they may meet in the pleasure-grounds of a morning, and indulge in a little love-making; but it is very different with you, who receive a salary to instruct and take care of my girls, and to whom no young young man of family or expectation can pay attention, except with dishonourable motives.[69]

Evidence about what proportion of governesses eventually married is unfortunately lacking, although it is possible to reach tentative conclusions about the sort of men they wed. Their situation was not unlike that of maidservants, who had a habit of marrying the shopkeepers who serviced their employers' household.[70] Popular myth paired off the governess with the curate precisely because he was one of the few men of similar social standing with whom she came into regular contact. While she might frequently be asked to forgo a trip to the village, a visit to some neighbours, or even dinner with some family friends, she could hardly be refused the right to go to church every Sunday, whether or not the rest of the household felt inclined to accompany her. Here was her one chance of mixing with the community on something like approaching equal terms. What is more a clergyman, by virtue of his profession, could call on a single woman without arousing fears of impropriety: the fact that Mary Cowden-Clarke was able to receive her suitor in her employers' home must be explained in part by the fact that Charles Cowden-Clarke was in the church.[71] If a governess was herself a vicar's daughter, the chances of her meeting a curate during her annual visit home were high, and the fact that so many clergymen were involved in some sort of teaching, whether tutoring upper-class boys or visiting the Sunday School, meant that they shared at least one interest in common with the governess. On the other hand, not all clergymen were considered, or would consider themselves, a suitable match. Ellen Weeton, who worked as a governess during the Regency period found herself greatly attracted to a certain Mr Saul, but 'the great difference between a governess and a clergyman of family and fortune made me cautious of being in his company more than I could help, lest my heart should be involuntarily forming an attachment that might cause me years of unhappiness'.[72]

Another group of men likely to marry governesses were those visiting masters who arrived once a week to provide specialist instruction in music or languages. If the family employed a male tutor for its sons, this too might be an almost inevitable pairing, although advice writers warned governesses against mistaking convenience for true love.[73] Employers were wary of such a relationship springing up – the dangers, according to the catty Blanche Ingram of *Jane Eyre*, were likely to include 'distractions and consequent neglect of duty on the part of the attached – mutual alliance and reliance; confidence thence resulting – insolence accompanying – mutiny and general blow-up'.[74] Like clergymen, tutors and masters had regular and unaccompanied access to the governess, and were perceived to enjoy a similar social standing, a perception reinforced by the fact that so many of these men were European, often political refugees, and were therefore hard to place socially.

Later in the century the tentative participation of governesses in organisations such as the Teachers' Guild provided increasing opportunities to meet men. It was at just such a gathering in 1902 that May Pinhorn first encountered F.J.M., the mysterious married man with whom she conducted a five-year sentimental friendship. Pinhorn's description of how she first met F.J.M. suggests how the governess needed to be able to retain a strong sense of her own sexual attractiveness if she were to avoid internalising other peoples' image of her as a drab neuter:

> On Shrove Tuesday the annual party for my section of the Teachers' Guild took place, and there I met a man who was destined to become a very intimate friend and to occupy a large place in the next five years of my life. His initials were F.J.M. I happened to have put on a dress of my favourite colour, bright scarlet, which no doubt marked one out among a very dowdy collection of worthy pedagogues.[75]

For the next five years Pinhorn dined frequently with F.J.M, an American publisher, corresponded with him constantly and even travelled abroad with him, all on strictly platonic terms. Although in her late thirties, she found herself battling against considerable pressure from her family to give up such an unsuitable association. Finally the time came for Pinhorn to bring her sentimental friendship with F.J.M. to an end. Despite the fact that she had never entertained any desire to marry him, she was obliged, as she turned forty, to confront the painful fact that she was no longer the object of a man's desire:

> After much thought I wrote my decision and, after a decent protest, it was loyally accepted. It meant much to me, but I have never regretted the step but have been thankful that I saw the right moment and used it. That summer life was very grey and dull after the close sympathy and mental companionship, not to mention the touch of uncertainty and excitement, that I had experienced for five years. I felt that the occasion was a milestone when Joan Ashton innocently remarked on the worst day of all that she had just noticed for the first time that I had a few grey hairs.[76]

There remains, finally, some mystery about those farmers' and tradesmen's daughters whom commentators were convinced were being sent into the schoolroom by ambitious parents in order to improve their prospects. Certainly the daughters of agricultural labourers used domestic service in the city as a 'bridging occupation' which allowed them to marry men, often shopkeepers, who occupied a higher station in life than their fathers. Whether housemaids married men they had met in the town, or instead returned to the country to find a husband locally, upwardly mobile marriage was facilitated by the savings they had accumulated over at least ten years of service, as well as the noticeably refined manners which they had learnt from studying their 'betters' at close quarters.[77] While governesses were not able to save dowries from their salaries, it may have been the case that those from lower middle-class backgrounds found that their exposure to the elegant ways of an urban professional family gave them an edge when it came to marrying well in their home communities.[78] On the other hand, there is some suggestion from the literary sources that governesses who had worked in aristocratic homes found themselves unable to cope with the banalities of provincial married life. In Elizabeth Gaskell's *Wives and Daughters*, Dr Gibson's new wife Hyacinth, former governess to Lord and Lady Cumnor, insists that Gibson should no longer eat with his students in the surgery, but should have his meals served to him formally in the dining-room.[79]

In real life governesses did not marry Mr Rochester and not just because there was something nasty in the attic. On the whole they chose their male equivalents, marginal men whose occupation as curate or teacher could offer them no fairy-tale ending. Life continued to be financially precarious and socially ambiguous: according to the summary reports of the Governesses' Benevolent Institution, many who left the profession to marry were forced to return to their former way of life following the death of their husbands.[80]

7

A Contract without Equality

The requisitions and stipulations are all on one side, all on the part of the employer . . . It is a contract without equality; a bargain in which, on one side, at least, there is no choice.

Anna Jameson, *The Relative Social Position of Mothers and Governesses* (1846)

Many ladies would not dare to treat their maids as they behave to the teacher of their children.

Anon., *Fraser's Magazine* (1844)

On 9 August 1846 Henrietta Stanley wrote a note to her husband, reminding him that their governess' salary was due:

Do you think you could give Miss White £20, we owe her a quarter. She did not ask for it, but I saw she was in distress & Alice told me that her brother wanted £20 & could not get it from some people that owed it to him. If you could send it her she would I am sure be thankful.[1]

Henrietta Stanley's carelessness about paying Miss White on time suggested both an aristocrat's relaxed attitude to credit and an unspoken assumption that, whether or not the governess received her cash, she would certainly continue to be fed, housed and kept warm. For her part, Miss White's demand for her £20 cut across the suggestion that she was connected to the Stanley family by ties of personal loyalty and insisted instead on her status as a salaried employee, bound by a contract, albeit implicit, which was being flouted. The fact that this was a silent plea only emphasised the governess' confusion about exactly how far she could go in claiming her dues.

The ambiguous situation in which Miss White found herself was the direct result of a shift in the social and economic function of the middle-class household which had been underway since the mid eighteenth century and would continue until at least the middle decades of the nineteenth. As industrial and agricultural production became centralised, those apprentices and farm workers who had previously received bed, board and financial support in their masters' homes now moved out into independent accommodation, binding themselves to their new bosses with a contract which, while informal, defined their duties in return for a fixed and regular payment. Domestic servants were required by the nature of their work to continue to live in, but ambiguities and strains thrown up by contractual expectations were becoming apparent in the servants' hall from the beginning of the Victorian period, even in households as traditionally paternalistic as that of the aristocratic Stanleys. Young men in particular were increasingly uncertain that the promise of a pension and a cottage in old age was enough to compensate for a lifetime of service and submission to the personal authority of their 'lord and master'. Mills and factories and, later on, offices and shops, offered the young of both sexes the chance to make an adequate wage without having to negotiate the petty constraints that came with living under an employer's roof.

On the other hand, those young people who did remain in the service of wealthy families found that the move towards market-orientated conditions of employment brought with it distinct advantages. Although the daily grind of domestic work remained punishing until the very end of the century, from the 1850s those servants who worked in the sort of well-heeled households which employed governesses began to experience a new kind of power as a consequence of their employers' increasingly urgent need to recruit and retain experienced specialist staff. In the impersonal city a twenty-seven-year-old cook or parlourmaid with at least ten years' work experience needed have no qualms about not sticking in one job for life. As long as she could produce an adequate 'character', she could move on to a new post every couple of years, bettering herself as she did so. Not only did her wages rise throughout the century at the same rate as those of her sisters who laboured in factories but, unlike them, she did not have to pay bed and board out of her own pocket.[2] Able to save for the dowry which allowed her, at the age of thirty or so, to make a good marriage to a shopkeeper or small farmer, there can be no doubt that the experienced specialist domestic benefited from the opening of the household's labour relations to the free market during the middle decades of the century.

The same cannot be said of the governess, who found herself a victim of the shift to a market-driven economy. Considerations of respectability kept her tied to the schoolroom just at the time when the vagaries of the youthful industrial economy were plunging thousands of middle-class men into bankruptcy, forcing their daughters to look for work. While an accomplished and, from the 1860s, well-qualified, governess could expect a higher salary than the woman who lacked these skills, the fact remains that most Victorian governesses received barely more than pocket money on top of their board and keep. Rather than embrace the logic of the market place and look for work elsewhere, distressed gentlewomen clung to the schoolroom as the only way of safeguarding their non-working status and hence their gentility. The result was what contemporaries perceived as a chronic over-supply of governesses, with demand for jobs far outstripping vacancies, creating conditions of fierce competition in the home schoolroom right through the century.[3]

At the same time this highly volatile economy threw up new, rich families eager to employ governesses while remaining intellectually and emotionally attached to the doctrines of economic liberalism from which they had benefited. People such as these saw no reason to pay the governess more than the vastly overcrowded market would bear. Nor did they feel any need to enter into a relationship with her that went beyond the strictly contractual. While an aristocrat like Henrietta Stanley may have continued to work on the assumption that Miss White was a semi-permanent responsibility, the professional family was more likely to dismiss their daughters' teacher after five years or so with nothing more solid than its good wishes for the future. As a result, the governess found herself falling between two stools and suffering some hard knocks in the process. She was neither a free economic agent who might take her labour into more profitable segments of the market, nor was she a valued family retainer who could rely on the open-ended financial, social and emotional support that characterised the passing order.

Yet none of this accounts for the prolonged and passionate public debate which the governess' 'plight' aroused between 1840 and 1860. Her low wages, long working-hours and poor employment prospects were discussed not only in the domestic literature of advice books and women's magazines, but in novels of varying artistic merit, as well as mainstream periodicals of all political complexions, including *Fraser's Magazine* and the *Saturday Review. Punch* even took up the governess' cause in a series of articles which appeared during the 1840s, poking vicious fun at those tight-fisted employers who refused to pay their daughters' teacher more than a pittance.[4] Yet in reality there were only 25,000 or so governesses in Britain around this time and, in comparison with other sections of the female population, their situation was really not so bad. Mill girls, milliners, prostitutes and even domestic servants were required to perform physically gruelling work for a standard of living that seldom came anywhere near that enjoyed by the governess. In addition they were, with the exception of domestic servants, required to find bed and, more significantly, board, at a time when food prices were reaching unprecedentedly high levels.

The governess' situation provoked a reaction in her contemporaries which cannot be accounted for by the material facts of her existence. What was shocking was not the conditions of her life *per se* but the contrast that these presented with the normal expectations of a woman of her class. Her presence in the household acted as a reminder that no woman, even the thoroughly genteel, could automatically assume the life for which she had been educated. The young woman who today received instruction from her governess might tomorrow be providing that same tuition in someone else's schoolroom. The governess gave the lie to the construction of the home as a place beyond and above the market place and suggested that it too might be touched, if not overwhelmed, by the social and material hungers so graphically expressed in the waves of industrial unrest which marked the first part of Victoria's reign. In this context, argues Mary Poovey, concern about the governess' poor working conditions signalled a displacement of a far greater terror about the grievances of those working-class men who, periodically throughout the middle decades of the century, smashed machinery, signed petitions and marched for bread.[5] Rather than ponder the disturbing implications of a hungry and disaffected workforce, contemporaries preferred to think about the more manageable problem of 25,000 unhappy middle-class women.

Yet for her contemporaries, the governess came to stand not only for working-class men, but also for those women who had displaced them in the factories and mills of industrial Britain. One of the biggest grievances during the Hungry Forties concerned the way in which manufacturers had substituted adult male workers with cheaper female and child labour. Not only did this mean that single adult men frequently found themselves without employment, but those who were married were frequently obliged to stay at home and look after children while their women went out to work. The commissioners who compiled the great investigations into industrial working conditions during the 1830s and 1840s were shocked at the social and sexual independence which working-class women now displayed.[6] In particular, they worried over the damage done to the domestic ideal which middle-class moralists and philanthropists had worked so hard to inculcate into the lower orders. In appalled detail they described the slovenly homes, neglected children and emasculated men they believed to be the direct consequence of the displacement of men as breadwinners by their wives and daughters.

In this context, the sight of middle-class women going out to work as governesses could not fail to mobilise a set of fears about the collapse of boundaries not only between civilised society and the mob, but between men and women and the separate spheres that they were supposed to occupy. These anxieties were fanned further from the 1850s by the beginnings of a sustained campaign for a series of social and legal reforms which, if realised, would free middle-class women from dependence upon their fathers and, more worrying still, their husbands. Although the governess' 'plight', and the need to end it, was used by reformers to justify demands that women should have access to sound education and interesting and rewarding employment, the long-term implications went deeper. For once middle-class women had established the right to train for professional work, there was no guarantee that they would continue to exercise it only as a last resort in case of failure to marry or family bankruptcy. The precedent of married working-class women displacing their men's labour evoked deep concern that, given the opportunity, middle-class women would flood the professional labour market and put their husbands and brothers out of a job.[7] Fears about the sort of revolution in social organisation that this might set in motion – with women living independently of the family unit and male control – only served to make the governess a more disturbing figure than ever.

Despite their insistence that the value of the governess' labour, like that of a mother, was beyond price, manual writers remained surprisingly keen to suggest to governesses that they should pin their employers down to a written contract specifying salary and working conditions. Mary Maurice, for instance, warned that:

In undertaking situations in families, a verbal arrangement is generally made, the particulars of which are soon forgotten. How much
more satisfactory to both parties would it be, if a written agreement
was drawn out, of which each had a copy, to which they could refer
in any difficulty. Not only should the salary be mentioned, but the
precise notice to be given on either side previous to a separation,
and any other particulars which may occur.

For want of such a document, many a poor governess, through
the versatility or want of consideration in her employers, has been
thrown out of a good situation; whilst they had no power to claim
their rights; and families have been inconvenienced in like manner
by the misconduct of their teachers. Cases are not unfrequent in
which the latter had adopted the dishonourable plan of engaging
herself to a situation she preferred, before she had expressed any
wish to quit that in which she was employed.[8]

Other commentators went even further, advising that the most
minute conditions of service – periods of rest, dining arrangements,
holiday times – should be thrashed out before accepting any post.
Only Anna Jameson seemed to grasp that the market conditions
in which such a contract would have to be drawn up rendered it
worthless since

the requisitions and the stipulations are all on one side, all on the
part of the employer . . . It is a contract without equality; a bargain
in which, on one side, at least, there is no choice.[9]

In practice the position was left flexible and exploitable, especially in middle-class homes where fewer servants were employed
and duties remained loosely defined: arriving at her new position
in a manufacturer's household in 1842, Mary Smith was baffled
to find that 'what I was wanted to do or teach, seemed somewhat
of a mystery'.[10] In this situation the governess could find herself
expected to help out wherever and however she was needed, much
in the manner of single middle-class women of the eighteenth
century. At times of illness or childbirth she might find herself
expected to double up as a sicknurse or midwife: in 1820 Elizabeth
Ham was obliged to shut up the schoolroom for several weeks
while she nursed the Elton girls and their mother through
whooping-cough.[11] Governesses who worked in church families
were often expected to take Sunday School, play the organ or
lead the choir on Sundays,[12] all skills which had presumably been
acquired when helping their fathers with their own parish work.

Less reasonable altogether was the permanent imposition of additional tasks, particularly sewing. The making and mending of her pupils' clothes had always been part of the duties of a nursery governess, but to ask a woman who was engaged to teach older children to do this was insulting, as it was clearly a job for the nurse, lady's maid or housemaid. Part of the problem about sewing was that it occupied an ambiguous place in the hierarchy of household chores: it was a clean job and even the most aristocratic of women were supposed to know how to do it. For that reason a canny employer could foist a basket of mending onto an obliging governess such as Mary Smith without anticipating outright revolt:

> I continued as usual all my duties in the nursery, neither asking nor taking any liberties of any kind; too proud for that; only taking care to do all that was required of me. Sitting closely at sewing, making all manner of things for the children, from frocks and tippets for common wear, to almost everything else that was needed, till nine o'clock in the evening.[13]

Charlotte Brontë, by contrast, was less phlegmatic about the imposition of 'oceans of needlework' and resolved to make it clear to her employer Mrs Sidgwick that the only condition under which she would stay in her post was if 'this burden of sewing' was lifted from her.[14]

The extra responsibilities assigned to the governess in a middle-class household were not necessarily menial or unwelcome: when the lady of the house was absent she might be asked to step into her shoes, giving rise to feelings of delight, embarrassment, or a mixture of the two. Miss Marks, who was employed in the 1850s by the widower Mr Gosse to carry out all the duties – administrative, maternal, pedagogic – formerly executed by his wife, clearly relished her role as a surrogate. Her dismay when she learnt that Mr Gosse was to marry again – to someone else – hinted not only at her sexual longing, but also at a desire to claim the social and financial status which went with the territory.[15] Conversely, in 1820 Elizabeth Ham found it uncomfortable to be seated at the head of the table opposite Mr Elton during his wife's absence because such a position gave her the sense of what it would be like to be his social and sexual consort, something for which she half-consciously longed.[16]

In a household where there was no butler or housekeeper, the governess was the most likely person to be left in charge when her employers went away: as a lady, she was a more suitable surrogate for the mistress than the cook. Mary Smith found, to her satisfaction, that 'I was trusted implicitly, the keys being left with me and the care of all in Mrs Sutton's absence'.[17] Whether or not the governess' time as head of the household went smoothly depended on the attitude of the servants towards her. If they took this opportunity to show the resentment that had been building up for months, this could be an uncomfortable period. Charlotte Brontë, however, was pleasantly surprised at the easy time she had, clearly relishing her new-found autonomy:

> I am again by myself – housekeeper and governess – for Mr and Mrs White are staying with a Mrs Dunce of Bleak Hall, near Tadcaster. To speak the truth, though I am solitary while they are away, it is still by far the happiest part of my time. The children are at least under decent control, the servants are very observant and attentive to me, and the occasional absence of the master and mistress relieves me from the duty of always endeavouring to seem cheerful and conversable.[18]

Nonetheless, without the protection of a formal agreement setting out the terms of her employment, the governess was dependent on her employers' good will. If this were lacking, she could find herself frustrated in her most basic expectations. When she took her holidays, for instance, could well be organised less around her own desires than her employers' timetable. The latter seems to have begrudged their governess' absence not because they were malign but because the prospect of having to supervise and occupy their own children filled them with alarm: in the grandest households a 'holiday governess' would be hired to fill this painful gap.[19] It was this anxiety which seems to have lain behind Mrs White's reluctance in 1841 to grant Charlotte Brontë permission to stay the weekend with her friend Ellen Nussey:

> ... I gathered up my spirits directly, walked on the impulse of the moment into Mrs White's presence, popped the question, and for two minutes received no answer. Will she refuse me when I work so hard for her? thought I. 'Ye-es-es', was said in a reluctant cold tone. 'Thank you, ma'am', said I, with extreme cordiality, and was marching from the room when she recalled me with: 'You'd better go on Saturday afternoon then, when the children have holiday, and if you return in time for them to have all their lessons on Monday morning, I don't see that much will be lost.'[20]

Who paid for the governess' travel home was another of those points which the manual writers urged their readers to sort out before they started work, precisely because it was the potential cause of so much embarrassment. If the governess was responsible for her own fares then she was unlikely to be able to afford to go home more than once a year. May Pinhorn, who earned only £25 in her first post in Wales, had to pass up the chance of an Easter holiday 'as the distance and expense of travelling was so great and the Edwards were glad to keep me'.[21] Likewise, in rural Northamptonshire during the pre-railway 1830s, the Sitwells found that 'our governesses [did not] desire any holidays, because of the difficulty and expense of travelling to their homes'.[22] Even when employers did undertake to pay the governess' travelling expenses they tried to find ways of cutting down the cost to themselves, inflicting considerable inconvenience in the process. Edith Gates, who was due to take a trip home to see her family in London over Easter 1876, had to wait to learn the precise date of departure until her employer Mrs Wiggett had decided when she herself would next be taking the carriage up to town. Only a week before Gates was due to depart did Mrs Wiggett finalise the arrangements, springing on her an earlier departure than either Gates or her family had anticipated.[23]

Even the most basic question of where the governess was to sleep could be the cause of disappointment. In a very large house, where it was possible to organise accommodation around the needs of its inhabitants, her bedroom was likely to be near that of her pupils and she might even have her own sitting-room for relaxing during off-duty hours. More typically the governess was expected to use the schoolroom as her sitting room, while her bedroom was often 'the very worst bed-room the house contains',[24] as Martha Smythe, the heroine of the 1872 novel, *The Young Governess* discovered on her arrival at Clereton Manor:

> 'Up here, Miss', said Annie; and Martha followed her wearily up a steep flight of corkscrew stairs to a little room at the top of the turret, – very dingy, very dreary-looking, with a small square window and sloping roof, and neither carpet nor curtains, and, to judge from the forlorn appearance of the half-whitewashed walls, rather damp. There was a little fire-place in one corner, plainly not intended to be used, for it was quite rusty, and there were neither fire-irons nor fender. The furniture was of the commonest description: indeed, as Annie privately noted to herself, the rooms of the upper servants at Clereton Manor were every way more comfortable.[25]

In cramped households the governess might even be deprived of her own space altogether. In this case she would be obliged to share with her pupils, a situation which caused emotional claustrophobia as governess and girls found themselves locked together around the clock. For a modest woman these sleeping arrangements brought a new set of problems. Miss Edgeworth, who was governess to young Elizabeth Garrett and her sisters during the 1840s, was obliged to creep 'fully dressed behind the curtains of the four-poster at night, to emerge next morning in the same genteel condition'.[26]

Even where a separate bedroom was provided, disappointment was not unknown, as Mary Bazlinton discovered during her sojourn with the Bradshaw family in south-west France during 1854-55:

> 18 June 1855. We arrived at Eaux Chaudes about 3. I could not help feeling dispirited and discontented at seeing my bedroom. The one I had occupied the previous year, a little room I was extremely fond of, was assigned to Graves and the little ones for a day nursery while I was put into a dismal damp dark room very dirty in appearance and with a most nauseous smell. I tried to overcome my discontent but without success tho' I gave no utterance to it – I felt bitterly disappointed as I wanted a comfortable bed-room, being accustomed to spend so much time in it and this Summer I had especially hoped for one because I expected to practise there my crayon drawing. It was bitterly cold.[27]

What added to Bazlinton's disappointment over her accommodation was the fact that the nurse had been given preferential treatment, something which, judging by comments in the periodical press, was by no means confined to the Bradshaw household. Good servants were in such short supply from the 1860s onwards that desperate employers frequently placed their parlourmaid's comfort and contentment above that of the two-a-penny governess.

There were other little economies which employers could inflict upon their children's teacher. Serving the schoolroom with less expensive food than that consumed in the dining-room (not to mention the servants' hall) was one of the most frequent: in some very grand households the cook would not even condescend to prepare schoolroom meals, leaving the task to the kitchenmaid instead.[28] Another economy was to supply the governess with tallow candles rather than the more expensive wax variety – a particularly hurtful slight since tallow candles, being considerably longer, made the snub obvious to the whole household, 'no one in serious folly can believe that any one's happiness is concerned in the matter of burning a wax or a tallow candle. But invidious distinctions do grate upon the heart'.[29]

For the governess who found herself in a position where wages were withheld, holidays denied, a bedroom non-existent, the outlook was, in theory, quite bright. According to Sir George Stephen's detailed manual *Guide to Service* of 1844, the governess was within her legal rights if she claimed a quarter's salary and walked out without giving notice.[30] In practice, however, to take this course of action would have entailed professional suicide. Going to court was out of the question, and even a polite request for salary in lieu of notice might ruin any chance of coming away with the good references that were essential in securing the next position. While very few employees were able to assert their rights against their employers in this way, the codes of behaviour to which the governess was committed as a lady, together with the market conditions under which she laboured, laid her open to the sort of exploitation that no self-respecting servant would have stood for a second:

> The maid has a broad field before her; she can afford to turn upon her mistress. The governess must endure all things, or perish.[31]

No other aspect of the governess' 'plight' disturbed contemporaries more profoundly than her poverty, thanks to scores of periodical articles during the 1840s and 50s which briefed readers on the gloomy cycle of low wages, early retirement and destitute old age that she was forced to endure.[32] Despite this apparent abundance of information, the financial facts of the governess' existence remain hard to determine, principally because writers shied away from making specific reference to salary levels. Newspaper advertisements are little help either, since gentility and desperation alike made governesses coy about naming their price in public. Gathering together the scattered references to schoolroom salaries from advice books, memoirs and diaries, it seems that between 1830 and 1890 nearly all governesses earned between £20 and £100, with the vast majority receiving between £35 and £80, although nursery governesses often worked for nothing beyond board and lodging. Within these broad limits there seems to have been ample room for some hard bargaining, particularly on the part of employers. In 1856 Mary Bazlinton's request for 60 guineas was several times rejected by prospective employers as being too high: so desperate was she to secure a position that she wrote back and offered her services for a lesser sum.[33]

There was a sensitive though unofficial market operating which ensured that those women who could offer particular accomplishments could expect to earn significantly more than their less polished sisters. Teaching music was the most highly rewarded skill in the governess' armoury, and those who were unequipped found themselves in the position of Miss Elizabeth Ann F. who, the GBI recorded in 1853, 'was resident Governess during 40 years; but not teaching music, her salaries were low'.[34] A finishing governess like Mary Carbery's Miss Teniel, who could offer a clutch of showy accomplishments such as dancing, the harp and Italian, might expect to get a great deal more than the Brontës who, although solidly grounded in the classics and English literature, were unable to offer fashionable French and singing. From the 1860s the possibility of gaining formal qualifications from Queen's College or the University Local Examiners meant that able women could look forward to the sort of salary progression which was not available to their gifted but unqualified counterparts of the earlier period. For instance, in 1826 Mary Cowden-Clarke earned £20 in her first post,[35] while in 1887 May Pinhorn was getting only £25 in hers.[36] Yet by the mid 1890s Pinhorn had raised her salary to £100 in recognition of her increased experience and clutch of Local University certificates. This sort of leap would not have been possible for Cowden-Clarke, had she continued to work in the schoolroom: in the 1830s and 1840s a governess of her calibre could expect to earn only £40.

In these earlier decades conditions were so crowded in the home schoolroom that even 'musical governesses' were scraping by on little more than £30. Unable to accept the brutal implications – that such a fate might befall any middle-class girls whose father died or failed in business – commentators insisted on reframing the governess' 'plight' in terms of the moral rather than the market economy. Thus they clung to their belief that, once upon a time, there had been a Golden Age when every schoolroom in the land was run by a true-born lady who received adequate reimbursement from her grateful and equally genteel employers. Salaries of between £100 and £200 were wistfully mentioned as being typical of this Eden, often unlocated in time, but generally taken to have existed at the end of the previous century.[37]

Commentators were equally emphatic about what had brought about the governess' fall to her state of mid-century wretchedness. It was one more example of pernicious 'fine-ladyism' – that desperate quest for gentility by those who had not been born to it. Now that every farmer's and shop-keeper's daughter was expected to learn singing and Italian instead of good honest butter-making and book-keeping, a whole new governess-employing class had come into being. Unable to transcend the crude utilitarianism of their trade backgrounds, these people felt no remorse about paying their governess the lowest wage the market would bear. What is more, this same hankering for social advancement had led many lower middle-class women into governessing as a way of bettering themselves – and it was precisely these ill-bred women who had forced down salaries by selling themselves for a pittance. As a result, suggested the commentators, even well-qualified ladies were cast at the mercy of a crude market economy which offered them the poorest wages and working conditions.[38]

This insistence on subsuming economic explanations into social and moral categories meant that proposals to relieve the governess' situation became correspondingly confused. On the one hand, female employers were charged with moral failure towards their less fortunate sisters, and urged to realise their 'mission' by paying their daughters' governess a decent wage and treating her with Christian kindness;[39] on the other hand, commentators such as former governes Sarah Lewis called for a system whereby salary was linked to training and skill, rather than financial need or genteel birth. In an article which appeared in the April 1848 edition of *Fraser's Magazine*, Lewis welcomed the recent initiative of the Governesses' Benevolent Insitution in setting up Queen's College with the intention of equipping governesses with the qualifications that would enable them to prove their competence and stake their claim to a reasonable wage.[40] Schemes such as these, however, completely undermined the careful and habitual construction of the governess as a moral rather than an economic agent. While commentators from across the political spectrum worked hard to suggest that genteel governesses were not only morally reliable but intellectually skilled, they also acknowledged that the reason why lower middle-class women had been able to find employment in the schoolroom was that many of them had been drilled in the required accomplishments from an early age. Bowing to the logic of the market place, by setting up a system of training and certification for governesses, threatened to benefit these women at the expense of the well-bred though untrained governess, and so reinforce the very social trend that it was designed to halt. These contradictions effectively paralysed early attempts to help governesses make the best of a hostile labour market: as far as the vast majority of commentators, reformers and governesses themselves were concerned, the governess remained a 'needy *lady*, whose services are of far too precious a kind to have any stated market value, and it is therefore left to the mercy, or what they call the *means*, of the family that engages her'.[41]

To emphasise how inadequate were the wages earned by the governess, an anonymous contributor to the November 1844 edition of *Fraser's Magazine* conducted a detailed comparison between her situation and that of the non-resident male tutor.[42] In a sense this was not an accurate exercise – the governess' nearest equivalent was the resident male tutor who was employed in a private household to teach those boys who, for whatever reason, had not been sent to public school. As it stood the study pointed up some interesting anomalies. While a tutor could make £84 a year teaching only one hour a day in the comfort of his own rooms,[43] the governess earned less than half this for a life spent permanently on duty in a stranger's house (although, of course, she did not have to find board and lodging). It was true that this young man would have a B.A. from one of the ancient universities, but given the uneven standards achieved by graduates of Oxford and Cambridge at this time, this was no guarantee of intellectual attainment. Even the provincial music master, to whom the governess might escort her pupils once a week, was getting 7s.6d. an hour.[44] What is more, both the male tutor and the specialist teacher enjoyed social identities which went beyond those provided by their teaching duties. The tutor was frequently an ordained clergyman, or on his way to becoming one, a fact which granted him a certain prestige. The specialist teacher of music or painting, meanwhile, could enjoy the role of artist whose genius transcended the petty constraints of social class and entitled him to respect and even reverence. In theory the governess' identity as a lady was supposed to remove her from the lowly reality of her everyday life; in practice she remained indelibly marked with chalk dust.

Commentators consistently exaggerated the lowness of the governess' wages, especially in comparison with those of the domestic servants who served her meals and cleaned her room. For instance, an anonymous contributor to *Eliza Cook's Journal* in 1849 declared that the governess' salary 'is generally below that of the cook and butler, and not above that of the housekeeper, footman, and lady's maid'.[45] Yet, according to the first edition of Mrs Beeton's *Book of Household Management* in 1861, footmen earned between £15 and £25, housekeepers between £18 and £40 and lady's maids between £10 and £20.[46] Compared with these figures, the £50 or so that the governess would have been earning by this date begins to look handsome. The point is, of course, that out of this £50 she was expected to supply the accoutrements essential to the appearance and habits of a lady: 'she must dress like a lady, travel like a lady, and in all her petty expenditure, pay like a lady: add to this, she requires an occasional replenishing of her library, her portfolio, or her music desk, beyond the need of most ladies'.[47]

Contemporary manual and magazine writers debated endlessly the absolute minimum income a man required to support his family in a genteel manner: estimates went as high as £500, but the figures most often mentioned was around £200.[48] In these cirumstances, the governess' salary, even with board and lodging taken into account, was clearly quite inadequate for her needs. On top of this there were other factors which made her situation compare poorly with that of the domestic servant. Cooks, parlourmaids and housemaids could all look forward to supplementing their wages with a variety of perks which ranged from selling off kitchen scraps to receiving a box at Christmas.[49] If the value of bed and board was taken into account, servants could be said to earn significantly more than their peers who laboured in shops and factories;[50] moreover their wages increased by 59 per cent throughout the century, at the same rate as those of industrial workers.[51] Working-class women chose service over a variety of other employments because they would be able to build up substantial savings; middle-class women had no choice but to enter the schoolroom in an attempt to keep body and soul together.

The governess' poverty had repercussions which went beyond her own material well-being, for the chances were that she went out to work not simply to keep herself but to contribute to the support of her family: there were sisters to be schooled, brothers to be articled, parents to be maintained in sickness and old age. In the annual reports of the GBI the catalogue of women who battled on working in order to support whole tribes of destitute relatives is lengthy: of the seventy-five governesses whose biographical details are given in the GBI's annual report of 1850, no less than forty-seven were specifically mentioned as having supported relatives out of their salary.[52] For instance, there was Miss Ann H. who during her long career spent £500 in educating five nieces so that they might also become governesses; or again, Miss Margaret T. who contributed 'from her salary for 27 years to the average amount of 60 guineas in support of her widowed parent'.[53] Yet far from feeling crushed by other peoples' need, many governesses, especially the younger ones, experienced real satisfaction in contributing to the well-being of loved-ones. Towards the end of her life Mary Cowden-Clarke remembered how, during her first job in 1826:

> an exceptionally proud gratification was mine when I earned my first five-pound note (my salary was twenty pounds a year), and I lay with the precious morsel of paper all night under my pillow. Next morning I was kindly allowed a holiday, when I asked leave to go and take the note to my mother myself.[54]

Those governesses who sent money home to educate a brother were probably tempering their generous impulses with a healthy dash of self-interest. Supporting a young man through university or articles could be construed as an investment for the future: the moment he started to earn a decent living, his sister, in theory, could give up the schoolroom. The fact that the GBI recorded the details of so many women who were left without support at the age of sixty suggests that, in practice, this particular insurance policy did not always pay dividends, preusmably because young men had a habit of marrying and starting families of their own. A more reliable way to guard against the poverty caused by sickness, old age or temporary unemployment was to save for the future. Yet out of a small salary already burdened with the support of a genteel wardrobe and a clutch of importunate relatives, it was virtually impossible to find extra money for this purpose. Unlike professional men – doctors, solicitors – the governess was unlikely to be working past the age of forty, the time when most men harvested the rewards of their youthful labour.[55] Not only were her promotion prospects nil but, if she did manage to keep on working into middle age, her salary, like those of domestic servants, would start to fall. In these circumstances, as the GBI pointed out in 1843, it was virtually impossible for the governess to save for the future:

> Working for twenty-five years at the utmost, at a salary commencing at £25 and seldom exceeding £80 per annum, if Domestic ties take part of her savings, or if ill health come, attended by the worst of all pains, *compulsory rest* – not only stopping the accumulation of her little fund, but instantly preying on it – how shall the Governess provide for herself in her old age?[56]

When it came to improving her financial situation, the governess did not have many options. Sir George Stephen advised her, no matter how painful, to turn her back on her needy relatives.[57] He also counselled against speculation with savings, despite the tempting thought of instant profits: the GBI was eloquent in its reports of women who had managed to save a couple of hundred pounds, only to lose it throgh someone else's incompetence or dishonesty. Finally, she was urged to provide for her old age by taking advantage of the GBI's help in purchasing an annuity at the National Debt Office.[58] Given the number of swindlers who lurked in solicitors' or estate agents' offices, finding a water-tight investment was by no means easy for a woman who had no father or brother to advise her:

> The lower classes have clubs, poor-laws, and unions – rough road-steads, surely, for that last anchorage. But the superannuated governess has not even these.[59]

Unfortunately Mary Cowden-Clarke's career did not continue as happily as it had begun on that day when she sped home to present her mother with the first instalment of her salary:

> As the season advanced, my health gave way so visibly that my parents resolved to withdraw me from my situation, where the noise and fatigue inevitable upon the daily presence of five young children had produced overwhelming headaches and almost total loss of appetite.[60]

Cowden-Clarke's failure of health was typical of the physical and mental breakdowns experienced by the hundreds of governesses who approached the GBI for financial help, as well as the thousands who did not. Cowden-Clarke's attribution of her headaches and nausea to the din made by her pupils was a link made by Elizabeth Ham to explain her own ill-health during 1819.[61] This classic cluster of symptoms was also experienced by nineteen-year-old May Pinhorn over sixty years later in her first post – symptoms doubtless made all the more severe by her overriding sense that she must carry on without complaint:

> I was not very well sometimes at Aberayron; the poor fare with very salt bacon affected me and perhaps the sea also, though I had not then found out that sea air did not suit me, as I have found to my cost many times since. My unruly charges sometimes worried me too, but when I ventured to suggest in writing to my aunt that a change might be pleasant I was given to understand that it was my

bounden duty to remain two years where I was for the sake of a good reference.[62]

What may have contributed to the loss of appetite of which so many young governesses complained was the ordeal of dining with employers: sheer nervousness often made it impossible to do more than pick at food. Powerful unconscious motives often underlie any refusal to eat: in the case of the governess, making oneself too weak to work may have been a useful strategy for getting out of a situation that had become unbearable. In Mary Cowden-Clarke's case, it was a tactic which paid off: during her convalescence at home she became engaged to the man she loved and never returned to the schoolroom.[63]

For older women the long years in the schoolroom were perceived to result most frequently in 'injured sight, and . . . loss of under-standing'.[64] Given the Victorians' understanding of the relationship between the mind and the body, it is hard to know whether the 'shaken nerves' to which the GBI Reports continually allude refer to a mental condition such as hysteria or some sort of breakdown in the nervous system – a stroke, for instance. Likewise, an ophtholmologist today would challenge the notion that eyesight can be permanently harmed through too much reading in poor light – an explanation frequently offered by the GBI. What is clear, however, is that the Victorians were under the impression that governesses were subject to a wearing down process which led, at the age of forty, to the disintegration of mind and body. This was one more reason why the governess' employment prospects diminished as she moved into middle age: even if she did not suffer from bouts of physical ill-health, it was thought unlikely that she would have the energy to keep up with rumbustuous children.

May Pinhorn's determination to carry on in her position for the sake of a reference despite her evident ill-health was, in the circumstances, extremely wise. Far from provoking concern on the part of her employers, the governess' discomfort often elicited nothing but the brisk advice to 'cultivate cheerfulness'.[65] Charlotte Brontë's experience with Mrs Sidgwick in 1839 seems to have been typical:

> I soon found that the constant demand on my stock of animal spirits reduced them to the lowest state of exhaustion; at times I felt and I suppose seemed depressed. To my astonishment I was taken to task on the subject by Mrs Sidgwick with a stress of manner and a harshness of language scarcely credible. Like a fool, I cried most

bitterly; I could not help it – my spirits quite failed me at first. I thought I had done my best – strained every nerve to please her – and to be treated in that way merely because I was shy and sometimes melancholy was too bad.[66]

Elizabeth Ham was even more unlucky. Her obvious exhaustion and misery earned her a swift dismissal in 1819: she later overheard a conversation in which it was suggested that she had 'gone stale'.[67] The fictional Maria Young of Harriet Martineau's *Deerbrook* had no illusions about the effect that her indifferent health would have on her prospects of finding another job: 'I cannot expect to be able to work always . . . and no strangers will take me if I do not get much better; which is, I believe, impossible.'[68] In such cases a governess might try and put off the moment when she had to resign for as long as possible, hiding her symptoms from her employers, though not from her sharp-eyed pupils: the young Lady Frederick Cavendish recorded in the early 1850s that Miss Pearson 'had wretched health and was often laid up' with the result that she and her siblings were often left to teach other as best they could.[69] Poor though the food might be and cold her bedroom, the governess knew that she had more chance of recovering in her present situation than she did in a lodging house. Employers, meanwhile, unburdened by any sense that they might have contributed in any way to their governess' ill-health, continued to select teachers for their children with all the detachment of a farmer buying livestock:

> 'You do not look very strong,' said one [employer], 'you look weighed down with trouble', glancing from head to foot at my slender figure. 'I am indeed', I said, injudiciously as it proved, for the reply appalled me. 'Ah, then I am sure you would not suit me, for I had a governess like that once before. First she lost her mother, and then her father, and then the little property that was left her. After this she really seemed so full of grief, that I was obliged to send her away.'[70]

Given the indifference of so many employers to their governess' emotional well-being, it was hardly surprising that, in the words of Lady Eastlake, 'the lunatic asylums of this country are supplied with a larger proportion of their inmates from the ranks of young governesses than from any other class of life'.[71] As Table 2 (p. 206 below) shows,[72] in 1861 the proportion of governess asylum inmates to total governess population, at 0.55 per cent, was higher than that of any other occupational group. Victorian thinking about mental illness – in particular a vagueness about whether it had a physical or 'moral' (that is, mental) cause – make it hard to determine just what was wrong with the 136 governesses whom the census enumerators found living in asylums in 1861. There was a feeling amongst contemporaries that governesses had a tendency towards alcoholism, as well as an addiction to proprietary medicines, both conditions which led to a state of melancholia.[73] The governess was also believed to be particularly prone to religious mania, the outcome, it was thought, of too much chastity, poverty and obedience. Dr J.A. Davey, head of the female department at Colney Hatch came near to explaining the preponderance of governesses amongst asylum inmates when he described how 'the unceasing, and in too many cases, the hopeless struggles of the poorer and middle classes for a bare existence necessarily predispose the brain to a diseased action . . . No wonder then that . . . some accidental addition to the bitter cup of sorrow . . . should wholly unbalance the tottering mind'.[74]

Most of the governesses to be found in lunatic asylums were not so much mad as senile, consumptive or simply homeless. At 8s. 6d. a week, the private asylum offered cheap and just about respectable accommodation.[75] When Florence Nightingale took over the Institute for the Care of Sick Gentlewomen in 1853 she had no illusions about why such a high proportion of her patients were governesses: 'it is the cheapest lodging they can find'.[76] From the middle of the century the private asylums took on an increasingly refined tone as they divested themselves of the pauper lunatics who were now catered for in the new public institutions. Run as profit-making concerns the private asylum wooed its inmates, or rather their families, by promising to provide the ambience and ethos of a genteel middle-class home.[77] Often located in a converted house or even stately home, the private asylum hid behind a resolutely genteel name such as Villa, Lodge or Grove. Organised on a family model, the superintendent and his wife took on a parental role, with the attendants playing that of elder siblings to their patients. A programme of lectures, outings, study programmes and lunatic balls were laid on for those able to benefit and, in return, female inmates were expected to contribute their time and labour in the asylum's sewing room. As far as the governess was concerned, it was almost a home from home.

While acknowledging the effect that the governess' rigorous working conditions could have on her emotional health, the manual writers made it clear where they considered the real responsibility for her wretchedness to lie. Anna Jameson, herself an ex-governess, admonished her readers in 1846 that 'many governesses ruin their health through their own neglect, ignorance, and weakness'.[78] Lady Eastlake, meanwhile, insisted that it was not the governess' actual conditions of employment which had sent her off her head, but her 'wounded vanity, [which] as all medical men will tell us, is the rock on which most minds go to pieces'.[79] 'Wounded vanity' is deliberately obscure, but it seems to refer to the frustration of the governess' wish to appear well in the eyes of others, to receive the social and perhaps financial recognition that she felt was her due. In the political and economic context of the century's middle decades, any such hunger for restitution had an alarming resonance, as Lady Eastlake went on to make clear in her 1848 review of *Jane Eyre*:

> There is throughout [*Jane Eyre*] a murmuring against the comforts of the rich and against the privations of the poor, which, as far as each individual is concerned, is a murmuring against God's appointment ... there is a proud and perpetual assertion of the rights of man ... [a] pervading tone of ungodly discontent which is at once the most prominent and the most subtle evil which the law and the pulpit, which all civilized society in fact has at the present day to contend with. We do not hesitate to say that the tone of mind and thought which has overthrown authority and violated every code human and divine abroad, and fostered Chartism and rebellion at home, is the same which has also written Jane Eyre.[80]

In this context the commentators' insistence that the governess' mental instability be understood not in terms of poor living conditions, but rather as a result of her inability to contain her own social and material desires, makes sense. For middle-class employers to accept responsibility for their governess' distress would be to collapse the distinction between the sanity of the household and the lunacy of the streets where 'Chartism and rebellion' fester. In the circumstances it was easier to extract the governess from the wider social and economic context and reframe her predicament in terms of individual moral failure.

For the governess who was planning her escape from the private classroom during the years 1830-70, the only occupation of comparable status open to her was schoolteaching. In fact, the two jobs were not even seen as distinct: a woman who had been employed in a family might take up a position as a mistress in a small girls' boarding school, then move back into a private appointment. Not to be confused with the public and high schools which appeared from

1870 onwards, these establishments were often tiny, taking as few as half a dozen girls, and employing a single assistant mistress. Working in this environment threw up many of the stresses and strains associated with home teaching. The deference and dependence which marked a private governess' relations with her employer also characterised her dealings with the headmistress who, as owner of the school, was also her paymistress. Working conditions could be just as bleak as those on offer in the private household: when Mary Smith went to work in a school run by her 'friends', the Osborns, she was given barely enough to eat.[81] During her period of duty in a Lincoln boarding school in the early 1850s, Mary Bazlinton found that the jealousy between the various assistant teachers was as intense as anything she subsequently encountered as a resident governess in the Bradshaw household.[82] The school building was very likely to be nothing more than the headmistress' own house, yet it was also the home of the assistant teacher. As a result, professional and personal roles were blurred, the schoolmistress was on duty twenty-four hours a day, her private life open to constant interference and supervision. As if to emphasise the similarities in the situation of a woman who taught in a school and one who worked in a private home, both were known by the title 'governess'.

Running one's own school, as opposed to working in someone else's, offered distinct advantages over resident governessing, as Anne Brontë's fictional Agnes Grey discovered: 'there was, indeed, a considerable difference between working with my mother in a school of our own, and working as a hireling among strangers'.[83] School-keeping preserved the genteel status of its practitioners by allowing them to present themselves as members of their employers' households. A woman who was lucky enough to have her own home could open up her front parlour to a handful of day pupils whom she might charge a few pence a week. Not only did she enjoy autonomy, she was also able to keep her own family together: younger sisters and daughters were frequently educated at the school with the expectation that they would join the teaching staff at the age of eighteen or even earlier. For those women who took the plunge and prospered the rewards could be great. Undeterred by her earlier exploitation in the Osborns' school, Mary Smith decided to leave her job with her much-loved employers, the Suttons, and set up on her own. The first few weeks were precarious. On the first Monday that her school was open she sat and waited for pupils to turn up, unsure that they would ever appear. By the end of the week she had six or seven pupils; three months later there were so many

The Misses Bronte's Establishment

FOR

THE BOARD AND EDUCATION

OF A LIMITED NUMBER OF

YOUNG LADIES,

THE PARSONAGE, HAWORTH,

NEAR BRADFORD.

Terms.

	£.	s.	d.
BOARD AND EDUCATION, including Writing, Arithmetic, History, Grammar, Geography, and Needle Work, per Annum, ...	35	0	0
French, .. German,.. .. .. each per Quarter, ... Latin ..	1	1	0
Music, .. Drawing,.. .. .. each per Quarter, ...	1	1	0
Use of Piano Forte, per Quarter, ...	0	5	0
Washing, per Quarter, ...	0	15	0

Each Young Lady to be provided with One Pair of Sheets, Pillow Cases, Four Towels, a Dessert and Tea-spoon.

A Quarter's Notice, or a Quarter's Board, is required previous to the Removal of a Pupil.

A Prospectus sent out by Charlotte Brontë and her sisters; it elicited no replies.

that she was obliged to rent bigger premises. At the age of forty, and twenty years after leaving home, Mary Smith found financial security and the respect of her community, for her establishment had become one of the main preparatory institutions for the local grammar school.[84]

Afraid that resident governesses might be tempted to try and emulate such success stories, advice writers appealed to them to stay put with the assurance that 'there is a strong feeling amongst those employed in education, that the teacher in a school is in a much lower position than that of a private Governess'.[85] In fact, according to Mary Porter's evidence to the Schools Inquiry Commission of 1867-68, there was no difference in the social status of the two occupations, although private governesses tended to earn more money than schoolmistresses.[86] This seems quite likely, given that many of these tiny establishments failed to bring in enough income to support the lady proprietress let alone her staff – some made as little as 3s. a week.[87] Finding pupils was a constant worry, especially in an area which already supported several establishments: the Brontës' long-cherished plans to give up private govenessing and open a school were foiled by the fact that few parents wanted to send their daughters to such an isolated spot as Haworth, especially when there were plenty of more accessible schools available.[88] If the local economy was going through a bad patch, it could have disastrous effects on the schoolmistress' chance of success: in 1853 the GBI reported the case of Miss Elizabeth C. who 'with a sister established a school, which they were obliged to relinquish after 16 years, chiefly owing to losses through the failure of parents of pupils'.[89]

The woman who had gone straight from her parents' home into that of an employer had never had the chance to cook, clean, shop or organise servants.[90] Her life as a resident governess may have been fraught with stress, but she was not, as commentators were fond of pointing out, obliged to deal with everyday practicalities. When a tile fell off the roof or the blackboard broke, it was not her financial responsibility to replace them. Just as factory girls were censured by middle-class commentators for being inadequate housewives and mothers, so the governess was seen as incapable of running a home. In these circumstances it is hardly surprising that the annual reports of the GBI list many cases of women who had been forced into resident governessing through the failure of their schools. Of the seventy-five governesses whose biographical details are given in the 1850 Annual Report, ten are specifically mentioned as at one time having run their own schools.[91] In nearly all cases these women lost everything they owned.

A governess' working life was frequently short: twenty-five to thirty was considered the ideal age, after which jobs became harder to find. Most women themselves facing retirement at the age of forty or even thirty-five.[92] Those who had absolutely no other means of support were obliged to continue working until they were almost falling apart. Mary Maurice's description of the ancient governess may be a piece of polemic, but it echoes the sad details of the case histories listed in the GBI's annual reports:

> At fifty, or fifty-five, she can do little more: the sight has failed, nervous diseases have shattered the frame, deafness, neuralgia, not unfrequently lameness or paralysis, have made her incapable of trying to support herself, except by taking a few daily pupils, or having recourse to the still scantier provision, arising from needlework.[93]

Even a woman in full possession of her youth and spirits could find herself facing dismissal without warning: an overstocked market allowed employers to indulge sudden fancies and dislikes without any inconvenience to themselves. Differences over religious observance were a common cause for a parting of the ways,[94] but the most frequent grounds of all were simply a falling out, a not fitting in. Worse than the actual news that one's services were no longer wanted were the weeks of hinting that might precede it. In a letter which she wrote to her mother in 1822 while working as a governess, Anna Jameson tried hard to convince herself that she had not been hurt by her employers' lack of candour:

> I have received a hint from Mr R. that Mrs R. wishes to have a French governess for Laura when we are at Paris; that sounds very inconsistent with all the professions Mrs R. has always made me, but, however I may feel it, I shall take it all as a thing of course, and we shall part very good friends.[95]

Mary Bazlinton's experience, typically, was even more traumatic:

> 19 June 1855. Mrs Bradshaw asked one of ... [the company] to read a letter which I afterwards discovered was concerning a lady whom they were recommending to Mrs Bradshaw for a governess. I had paid no attention to this letter while it was reading but towards the close I was roused by hearing something about

THE ASYLUM FOR AGED GOVERNESSES

WILL BE OPENED BY H.R.H. THE DUKE OF CAMBRIDGE IN PERSON,

ON THE 12TH JUNE, 1849;

And on that and the following day the FANCY SALE commenced at Chelsea, will be continued under the same Royal patronage.

THERE is something inexpressibly sweet in the idea of providing a haven for the storm-beaten mariner—a shelter for the weather-tried traveller—a place of rest for the wearied wayfarer.

The Committee have been repeatedly urged by some of their best and kindest friends to carry out the plan of a permanent Home for Aged Governesses; but they waited for the manifestation of a similar feeling on the part of the Public. In the form of donations for this especial purpose, and they have not waited in vain. Many liberal donors have come forward; and with the assistance of a highly-patronised Fancy Sale at Chelsea, a sufficient sum has been secured to commence the Asylum at once. It will be elected during the present year. A most kind friend is raising £1,000 towards the Endowment by a silver subscription, and has more than half achieved her self-imposed task; and there is every reason to expect the manifestation of a similar spirit by others. It is calculated by the Architect, that £200 will at any time secure the addition of room for two more occupants; the Endowment required is £500; or £15 per annum, legally and permanently secured; and a definite object is thus offered to donors.

As the Society is empowered to hold land, the assistance of liberal friends would be of great value at the present time to secure contiguous property, which will otherwise soon be built over.

In projecting the Asylum, the Committee are carrying out their professed principles of meeting the wishes of all classes of their Subscribers.

It has been a great desire of the Committee to facilitate all arrangements for the benefit of Governesses, without laying down dogmatic principles according with their own views. Any branch of the Society can thus be supported without committing its supporters to other details, their subscriptions being specially devoted to that peculiar fund. Thus the Provident Fund may be supported exclusively by those who consider assistance degrading to the class; the Annuity Fund by those who approve its system of inalienable security for its objects; *this Fund* by those who wish to see a tranquil home provided for the comfortless and aged Governess, and to give the largest amount possible *from income* to this good work. The Committees will be happy to spend upon this branch every shilling of subscription devoted to it; and an opportunity is thus afforded to test the number of those who are of opinion that the income of the Society should be thus employed.

The necessity of such a Home is more and more pressed upon them. It seems almost superfluous again to point out how impossible it is that Governesses in general should save sufficient to provide for their own old age: a reference to our Polling Paper will be the best course, as it will produce FACTS, which are always the soundest arguments. There were Eighty-four Candidates for Three Annuities of £15 each—EIGHTY-FOUR Ladies, many reduced to actual penury, and of this number seeking an annuity of £15! Of these, "seventy were married, and out of this number Seven had incomes above £20—two derived from Public Institutions: Sixteen had incomes varying from Twenty-six Shillings to £15." Thirty-six of this number seven had absolutely NOTHING! It will be recollected that all these Ladies are above Fifty Years of age; and of the utterly destitute eighteen were above Sixty. It is sometimes asked, could they not have averted this lamentable condition? The Committee would fain hope that all who have received a Polling Paper have read the cases to which they refer; to see that out of these Seventy Ladies, no less than Fifty-four had not provided for themselves, because they had derived their incomes from other sources, their sisters, or their families, from the support of "one or both parents for many years;" to the educating younger sisters—helping brothers in their onward path—and protecting and educating orphan nephews and nieces; to all who have benefited by the Governess' care (and who has not ?). It seems a duty and a privilege to provide a Home for the desolate old age of those whose high sense of private duty has thus deprived them of a self-provided home. We cannot give them the best blessing that are conveyed in that almost sacred word—we cannot surround them with the family ties and the sweet sympathies of Home: but we CAN take them from a cheerless lodging, and the anxieties of duty privation, and the miseries of petty creditors—the half-spread table—the *not half*-warmed room—the lonely hours of increasing helplessness; and give them warmth, and food, and care, and kindness—freedom from the cruel anxiety of rent—a hand to help, a voice to cheer—the blessed certainty that their weakness will be tended—their infirmities cared for—their last days allowed to pass undisturbed by the harassing anxieties of poverty.

The objects of this Society are all in operation.

TEMPORARY ASSISTANCE to Governesses in distress, afforded privately and delicately through the Ladies' Committee.

ANNUITY FUND. Elective Annuities to Aged Governesses, secured on invested capital, and thus independent on the prosperity of the Institution.

PROVIDENT FUND. Provident Annuities purchased by Ladies in any way connected with Education, upon Government security, agreeably to the Act of Parliament. This branch includes a Savings' Bank.

The Government have kindly consented to allow Foreign Governesses to contract for these Annuities.

A HOME for Governesses during the intervals between their engagements.

A SYSTEM OF REGISTRATION, entirely free of expense.

A COLLEGE for Governesses, with Classes and Certificates of Qualification: the Classes re-opened for the Lent Term, on the 22nd January, 1849.

THE ASYLUM.

(p. 170). Advertisement announcing the forthcoming opening of the Asylum for Aged Governesses on 12 June 1849. (*Mary Evans Picture Library*).

(p. 171). The opening of the Asylum: a high society event presided over by the Duke of Cambridge. (*Mary Evans Picture Library*).

the lady never having been accustomed to boys. My attention was unavoidably excited by this and another closing sentence relating to terms. But I afterwards found that Mrs Bradshaw was ignorant or at least alleged that she was of my being in the room when she requested the letter to be read. She professed to be extremely sorry for the occurrence, fearing I might think it was done purposely with the intention of wounding my feelings. I did think it strange indeed if the letter concerned a governess, but of that I had not previously felt at all sure. Having heard such an extremely short portion of it I intend asking Mrs B. her intentions respecting me on our return to England whether she wishes to part with me immediately or to ... [illegible] should remain until Christmas: the former I think it will probably be.[96]

A courageous woman like Elizabeth Ham, finding herself in just such a miserable situation, vowed not to let her employers see how they had succeeded in hurting her:

Miserable as I was, this misery was greatly increased one day on going to my room to dress for dinner, by finding on my Dressing Table a note from Mrs Nias containing a civil dismission as soon as my year should be completed. I was neither surprised nor mortified, but deeply grieved. I had no home, and I felt that any degree of suffering was better than living on sufferance with relations that could not well bear the burden, or that cordially wished you anywhere else. I felt that that unhappiness is not the worst that may befall where you have anything to do. Whatever I felt, my pride came to my aid, and I went down to dinner as if nothing had happened. Indeed, so very tranquil I seemed, that I believe Mrs N. thought I had missed the note; so directly after dinner she dismissed the children, and asked me if I had seen it.[97]

Even those women who were not dismissed, but whose services were no longer required because their pupils had either finished their education or were about to go off to school, faced a future that was far from bright. A few lucky ones like Eliza Redgrave might be asked to stay on as a companion to their pupils until they married,[98] while Quaker families were also likely to support an elderly governess in retirement, even though the salaries they offered during her working years were minimal.[99] Other retired governesses found themselves the recipients of small informal payments from former pupils or charitably-minded acquaintances.[100] In general middle-class families, accustomed to the strictly limited obligations of contractual relations, were unlikely to have the room, space or finances to take on support of the governess once she was of no use to them. Even upper-class families, who were more familiar with the idea of shouldering responsibility for former staff, felt less commitment to a governess they had known for only ten years, than the nanny who had given a lifetime of faithful service:

> when [the governess] . . . has lived in the family for perhaps fifteen years, and finished the sixth daughter . . . her employers [dismiss] her with every recommendation as 'a treasure', but without a fragment of help in the shape of a pension or provision to ease her further labours or approaching incapacity. In nine cases out of ten, the old servant is far more cared for than the old governess.[101]

For the majority of governesses the end of one job meant that the search for the next one had begun. On top of the anxiety this entailed, there was the worry about where to stay in between situations. From 1846 a few lucky women were able to make use of the GBI's Governess Home which had been set up for those who were in between situations;[102] others had to make use of lodging houses which not only provided them with less-than-genteel company, but ate into their savings.

As the social and economic turbulence of the early Victorian period gave way to the stability and prosperity of the later 1860s there is some evidence that employers began to develop relationships with their governesses which went beyond the strictly limited obligations of the 1840s. Contrasting this later period to the earlier Victorian period, Winifred Peck was quite certain that it was a mark of a genteel family that they were able to stay friends with their governess long after she left their employment.[103] Often these friendships spanned several generations: Sybil Lubbock recalled that one landmark of her own late Victorian childhood was

> the added excitement of tea with Mother's very ancient governess, 'Old Pussy', who lived in a semi-detached villa and made up for her rather forbidding appearance (she had a bearded chin, very prickly to kiss) by her tales of our mother's childish naughtiness . . . [104]

In much the same way, the family which employed Margaret Crockford as a governess during the 1880s kept in touch with her family after her death in 1929, even sending her great niece a twenty-first birthday present as late as 1940.[105]

These relationships were not simply a matter of charity or patronage. If a governess lived near her former employers, she could provide a useful extra pair of hands at times of particular strain. The Kay-Shuttleworths certainly called upon the services of May Pinhorn long after she had officially finished working for them. Their former governess could be asked to help with a new baby,[106] to go househunting,[107] to look after an invalid,[108] to escort children to the seaside,[109] and to act as a holiday companion.[110] Exactly what financial help she received in return for these services is unclear – thanks to a small inheritance from her uncle, Pinhorn was far from destitute – but it is clear that the Kay-Shuttleworths were generous with their financial help during her last illness.[111]

Towards the end of the century, some wealthier employers seem to have followed the arrangement which existed in France and Belgium of providing pensions for their governess.[112] However, this sort of support was forthcoming only to those women who had been employed in the same family for fifteen years or more: the governess who, for whatever reason, had worked for many different employers would be unlikely to benefit from this development. Also, changing economic fortunes meant that employers might find it hard to maintain their initial level of generosity: the Leveson Gower family who provided a small pension for their former governess, Miss Killick, were finding it somewhat of a strain by the time of her death in the 1920s.[113] Far more common than the commitment to a regular pension seems to have been the employers' habit of providing their former governesses with occasional help in the form of seasonal presents, offers of hospitality and contributions to the payment of medical bills.

For the governess of the earlier Victorian period retirement could be a very bleak period indeed. Unless she had taken advantage of the GBI saving scheme to purchase an annuity, her only way of living was through the kindness of friends who might manage to scrape together an allowance of a few pounds a year. The GBI annual reports contain many examples of elderly women being supported by the generosity of friends and former pupils although, in most instances, the amount raised was not sufficient to keep body and soul together and had to be supplemented by needlework,[114] letting out a pew,[115] or renting rooms.[116] Working-class spinsters and widows had long been accustomed to eking out their last years with such wretched activities; for the governess to end her days in the same manner only added insult to injury.

Perhaps the single greatest problem that the governess faced on her retirement was finding somewhere to lay her head – parents were long since dead, and brothers married with families of their own.

The extended family network of the late eighteenth century was no longer in existence to provide board and lodging. Sisters who had gone out to work as governesses often came together in middle age to set up home in retirement. Typical of this arrangement were the three separate governess households which the census enumerator found at 15 Victoria Grove Terrace, Paddington, in 1861. Here lived Fanny Kist, 67, and her sister Phebe, 71; Mary Stuart, 71, and her sister Julia, 68; and again Emily Sass, 63, all of whom gave their occupation as 'former', 'retired' or 'reduced' governess.[117] Although it is impossible to know just how prosperous these three little households were, it is significant that not one of them employed a resident maid, suggesting that in retirement the governess was unlikely to be able to satisfy even this most basic requirement of middle-class respectability. Even so, there was a group of retired governesses who were even worse off than the elderly women of Victoria Grove Terrace. Those souls who were not even able to afford their own accommodation were obliged to take refuge in lodging houses, either living there permanently in retirement or boarding temporarily between jobs. Given the centrality of the domestic ideal in the construction of genteel femininity, it was particularly humiliating to share a house with others on a commercial basis. As forty-year-old governess Caroline Davison discovered in 1861, the company one might be obliged to keep could turn out to be less than genteel: she shared her accommodation at 17 Star Street, Paddington, with a laundress, a carman, and a dress and mantle maker.[118]

A handful of unfortunate women found themselves facing an even worse fate. While, according to the 1861 census, only eleven governesses were to be found in the workhouse on the night that the enumerator came to call,[119] the *fear* of the workhouse seems to have hung over the schoolroom: the GBI frequently recorded cases where anxiety about destitution and penury caused an individual to suffer a breakdown in mental health.[120] What made the spectre of the workhouse so terrifying to the governess, beyond the loss of respectability and adult status which it represented, was the necessary abandonment of any aspirations towards a fixed class identity. Inside the workhouse seamstresses, prostitutes, servants and factory hands slept, ate and worked side by side with no distinction as to social background. The label of 'pauper' cut across any class identity that existed prior to entry into this grim regime and made a mockery of any definition of gentility as being independent of material circumstances.

The governess 'plight' was clearly concerned with a great deal more than the poverty and social ambiguity of 25,000 middle-class Victorian women. The discussion that her situation provoked in the periodical press during the middle decades of the century suggests that it touched on deeper fears about the threat posed by a hungry and destitute workforce to the country's social and political stability. The call by liberals to improve women's educational and employment opportunities in order to ensure that future generations of genteel women would be saved from the schoolroom also served to link governesses with the nascent campaign for female emancipation. Without her awareness, and certainly without her desire, the governess had been turned into a symbol of the potential radicalism and even socialism of working-class men and middle-class women. The conservatives' need to neutralise the governess' imaginative power by relieving her poverty through a series of charitable gestures clashed with the reformers' desire to capitalise on the contradictions in the construction of bourgeois feminity which her 'plight' so graphically exposed. It was this struggle, by no means as well-defined as this summary might suggest, which was to sabotage initiatives to improve the governess' working conditions in the second half of Victoria's reign.

8

A Lady With a Profession

[The governess] is a lady with a profession, just as much as a barrister
is a gentleman with a profession.

Charlotte Mary Yonge, *Womankind* (1876)

It is only the people who are inaccessible to public opinion by whom
the governess is still regarded as a cypher or a butt.

Alfred W. Pollard, *Murray's Magazine* (1889)

May Pinhorn[1] and Charlotte Brontë[2] never met, but a comparison
of their early lives reveals how little the preparation, training and
education of the governess changed between the 1830s and the
1880s. Both were daughters of clergymen without fortune and
had known from childhood that they would one day have to earn
their living by teaching. In the context of the 1820s, this meant
that Brontë had been sent to the spartan Cowan Bridge where,
along with other clergy daughters, she had been schooled in the
obedience and self-denial that were thought appropriate to her
future life. To add polish, as well as to save her health, she was
subsequently sent to the genteel Roe Head, a small proprietary
boarding school where she mixed with girls like her friend Ellen
Nussey who could look forward to a life of relative ease. After a
stint of keeping house for her father, Brontë returned to Roe Head
as an assistant teacher, earning a tiny salary but receiving free tuition
for one of her younger sisters – first Emily, and then Anne – both of
whom were also intended for the schoolroom. Brontë's subsequent
attempts to find a post as a resident governess were hampered by
a lack of musical ability at a time when the most valued skill for a
middle-class girl was the ability to bang out a waltz on the piano. Like
many a clergyman's daughter she was competent to teach Latin, but
early Victorian mothers were more concerned that their daughters

master the living languages. To plug this gap Brontë borrowed money from her aunt to pay for a year at a Brussels *pensionnat* where she could improve her French in the all-important native context.

In the early 1880s another clergyman's daughter was being prepared for her future life as a governess. May Pinhorn never seemed seriously to have considered any career other than teaching, although in adolescence she flirted with the idea of becoming a doctor.[3] Like Brontë she too gained the necessary academic grounding at an institution which put solid achievement before social frills:

> At the beginning of the year [1882] I started going daily to the High School; it was not considered at all desirable socially as there were very few children from similar families to my own there, most of them were from the lower middle-class, but there was no doubt that the education was more modern than at the more select 'ladies' schools.

> Some of our friends were rather shocked at such a step, but my people wisely realised that, as I had to earn my living by teaching later, I must have the best education obtainable.[4]

At the high school girls were prepared for the Junior and Senior 'Locals' and Pinhorn struggled through three hours of homework every night. Her diligence was rewarded at the end of the year with passes in the Junior exams, even in arithmetic which she was certain she had failed. Like Charlotte Brontë, Pinhorn was unusual in being able to offer Latin, yet remained hopelessly untalented at the far more valuable art of playing the piano: 'Every educated girl was supposed to learn music, so I spent many weary hours slaving at it and going in for examinations with no interest in it, and nothing but a small amount of technical and mechanical skill acquired in the end'.[5]

As with Brontë, Pinhorn's schooling experience changed decisively once she moved into mid adolescence. Now was the time for her to associate not with girls who would one day have to make their own living as clerks and shop assistants, but with young women who had more genteel expectations. In their preparation for the job of governess, both Brontë and Pinhorn were required to pull off the delicate balancing act of being academically competent while avoiding the tarnish which came with vocational training. In 1885, at the age of seventeen, Pinhorn was sent to Handsworth Ladies' College, a genteel boarding school run by 'two awful old hags' and characterised by 'harshness, petty tyranny, suspicion'.[6] This was followed, as it was in Brontë's case, by a period of apprenticeship as a governess-pupil at a small proprietary school. Pinhorn's account of Miss Longmore's establishment in Brentwood, Essex, is a valuable reminder of how these family-run insitutions remained an important part of the educational landscape until the end of the century and even beyond.

> The description, according to the Principal's letters and prospectus, was all that could be desired, and I started off expecting to find a pretty country house in its own grounds, instead of which I arrived at two new semi-detached villas, in one of which lived Miss Longmore with her mother and brothers, and in the other she housed the school. She was a very kind, pious little lady, extraordinarily like a frog in appearance. I think she probably had considerable difficulty in making both ends meet. Her staff consisted of a charming Dutch lady who acted as German governess, a succession of extraordinary French women, probably 'au pair', and one of her brothers, who on his return from business in London gave lessons in mathematics, Latin and Greek to any one who wished to learn those subjects. The boarders were nearly all on governess-student terms, even if they knew nothing, and there was a fair number of day pupils. I had had a more modern education than anybody else, and my examinations were so respected that nearly all the English teaching of the school fell into my hands, and I thoroughly enjoyed the importance of my position and the power to set examinations instead of writing them.[7]

Pinhorn followed in the footsteps of Brontë by rounding off her preparation with a period in a small girls' school in Luxembourg, receiving French and German lessons in return for providing conversation in English. Like Brontë before her, Pinhorn continued to study even once she had started work, returning home between engagements to be coached for the Senior Locals by one of her former high school teachers. It was perhaps this obvious commitment to her own intellectual self-development that landed her a job with the Kay-Shuttleworths in 1895. Her new employers displayed an evangelical relish for staying abreast of the latest developments in teaching practice, an enthusiasm which Pinhorn sometimes seems to have fallen in with for the sake of an easy life:

> . . . I was engaged to come to them after the holidays, but meanwhile they wished me to improve the shining hour by visiting the training colleges to see something of the most modern methods of teaching. I was not at all keen about it but felt obliged to comply as I was

lucky in getting such a promising post with a salary of £70 a year, raised later to £80 and £100.[8]

Brontë, by contrast, was earning only £20 in 1841, £4 of which was deducted for laundry expenses. Nonetheless, it is in the matter of training, preparation and qualification that one can best measure the point that a particular occupation has reached in its journey towards professionalisation, and it is in this respect that governessing made only the smallest progress between the 1840s and 1880s. Both Pinhorn and Brontë had acquired their skills through practice rather than by the cramming of a pre-ordained body of theoretical knowledge. Although both women were well-grounded academically, neither had undergone any special training for their job: in the last analysis, their chief qualification was not a particular piece of paper but simply the fact that they were ladies. Pinhorn, just like Brontë fifty years earlier, continued to understand and define herself as a member of her employer's household rather than as an autonomous specialist exchanging her expertise in return for a generally recognised rate of payment.

The similarity of these two women's careers may seem surprising, given that the campaigns of the 1860s and 1870s to reformulate the relationship between middle-class women and waged work were the result of a determination to alleviate the governess' 'plight'. Yet it was the very success of these reforms in preparing middle-class women for work other than that of governessing which effectively eased the pressure on the home schoolroom and so made the need for its reorganisation less acute. While the entry of middle-class women into new types of semi-skilled work from the 1870s appeared to herald a rethinking of the relationship between gender, class and the market economy, governessing continued to be defined as the natural preserve of the distressed gentlewoman whose chief qualification was her social and moral identity. The enduring nature of this definition, together with the continuing attachment of the privileged classes to home education for girls, does suggest that any wider shift in the understanding of women's relationship to paid labour during the last third of the nineteenth century was a pragmatic response to changing economic circumstances. Many of the new semi-professions followed overwhelmingly by women appeared as a result of the fortuitous expansion in the country's commercial and administrative sectors rather than as a direct consequence of any legal or ideological reform. This was at the time, too, when the older and exclusively male professions such as law and medicine were codifying their training and qualification requirements in such a way as to make the entry of women all but impossible. In these circumstances, the fact that governessing continued to organise itself in 1890 very much as it had done in 1850 begins to appear less puzzling. Far from being some relic of an earlier barbaric phase of female employment history, the late Victorian governess is a valuable reminder of how little the theory and even the practice of waged work for middle-class women had changed by the end of the century – and beyond.

Early charitable initiatives to improve the financial lot of the governess had spluttered out by the mid 1840s. The stumbling block for an organisation like the Governesses' Mutual Assurance Society, which had been set up in 1829, was that governesses did not earn enough to enable them to take advantage of saving schemes, no matter how well-intentioned.[9] It was not until 1843 and the setting up of the Governesses' Benevolent Institution (hereafter the GBI) that any consistent effort was made to intervene in the cycle of destitution-subsistence-destitution experienced by so many governesses in the middle decades of the century.

The Institution was just one of many charitable efforts associated with a group of Anglican clergy and laymen, the Christian Socialists, whose philanthropic activites reached into wide areas of mid Victorian life.[10] Their practical energy was powered by the teachings of their reluctant and unofficial leader, the theologian F.D. Maurice. Following Maurice's insistence that Christ's Kingdom was already in existence on earth, the Christian Socialists occupied themselves with a whole range of charitable activity designed to improve the life of the urban working class. As far as the second half of their label was concerned, never was a group so misleadingly named: men like Thomas Hughes and Charles Kingsley were motivated not so much by proto-socialist zeal as a snobbish abhorrence of bourgeois economic individualism and a hankering for an imagined rural past translated into the urban present. This is not to deny the radical nature of some aspects of the Christian Socialist enterprise: certainly the attempts of Ludlow to set up co-operative businesses owed much to the revolutionary ideas of French thinkers Fourier and Blanc. Yet while the support of Maurice and Kingsley for the Chartists during the 1848 crisis gave their enemies the opportunity to tag the whole group as seditious, these mild-mannered men were no more subversive in their intentions than many members of the evangelical and nonconformist communities whose charitable impulse they shared. Behind the philanthropic activities of the Christian Socialists lay an ideal of society composed of mutually dependent classes actively involved in working for each other's welfare. According to this analysis, the privileged classes relied on governesses to shape the minds and spirits of the next generation and that debt needed to be acknowledged in the form of higher salaries and a greater personal concern for their children's teachers. An abandoned and destitute governess was not simply an instance of individual bad luck but a sign that society as a whole was morally bankrupt:

> we appeal to *all*, for who has not, either individually or relatively, been indebted to governesses? We may say to each individually, Are you free from all further obligations to them? What would you have been without their care? What would you have known, if they had not laboured to teach you? . . . Then, if you admit this claim, how can it be discharged, but by helping the helpless, and aiding those who are willing to work in the cause? Have you yet done all that you can for it?[11]

Present at the inaugural dinner of the GBI on 20 April 1844 was a mix of high society, fashionable clergy and literary stars. The guest of honour was Charles Dickens, whose after-dinner speech set the governess' 'plight' and the Institute's attempts to alleviate it within the sentimental terms of his own prose. According to next day's report in the *Morning Post*, the novelist declared:

> From first to last he had a confidence that the society would do its duty; and he hoped by its means to see blotted out a national reproach, and that the profession of education would be placed on that honourable footing which in any civilised and Christian land, it ought to hold.[12]

Yet only a few years later Dickens had disassociated himself from the GBI when he discovered that the touching picture he had painted of red-eyed young women reaching out for a delicate helping-hand had been transformed by economic desperation into something far more savage. The handful of free anuities of £15 which the GBI had in its gift were competed for by old, sick women with all the determination of those fighting for their lives. Annuitants were elected by those who had sent a subscription of at least half a guinea to the GBI, so to stand any chance of success a governess was obliged to canvass individual subscribers in an attempt to secure their vote. The harrowing sight, which Dickens found so disasteful, of broken-down women petitioning the great and the good for their sympathy had at least one valuable by-product: the biographical details of the would-be annuitants which the GBI published in its annual reports alerted journalists and social reformers to the huge numbers of governesss living on the edge of destitution. Writers as unalike as Elizabeth Eastlake, Barbara Bodichon and Harriet Martineau quoted the life-histories of these women, littered with details of early bereavement, financial fraud and inevitable sickness and poverty, as evidence that something needed to be done to ensure that further generations of women were spared such misery.[13]

In common with much Victorian philanthropic practice, the GBI stressed that self-help was the best help. Most governesses, according to the annual reports, would much rather make provision for themselves than become an object of charity: what many of them were seeking was simply expert advice on how to stretch their meagre resources to cope with old age and accident. To this end the Institution undertook to invest the governess' savings in a secure bank, and to help her purchase an annuity from government stock which could be guaranteed not to disappear overnight. Fraudulent lawyers and insolvent banks need no longer destroy the possibility of a secure and peaceful retirement. The Institution also set up services designed to intervene in the governess' life just at those points where she was most likely to go under. A registry was set up to help her find work, a home was provided where she could stay in between engagements, and there was also an asylum for the sick and aged, together with *ad hoc* payments 'affording assistance privately and delicately to ladies in temporary distress'.[14] During 1850, the GBI calculated that it had helped no less than 2,460 governesses in various ways:

17	Annuitants at £15
25	Annuitants at £20
1	Annuitant at £22 10s
1	Annuitant at £30
16	Inmates in the asylum
640	Provident Annuitants
389	Assisted in difficulty
200	Received into the Home
951	Provided with engagements without charge
12	Free Pupils educated at Queen's College
75	Free Certificates granted at Queen's
133	Governesses attending the Free Lectures at Queen's College
2,460	Total number of governesses helped by the GBI in 1850[15]

The thoroughness and relevance of the progamme suggests that its originators had a first-hand understanding of the governess' needs and bears out Bessie Rayner Parkes' later assertion that there was no middle-class woman who did not have some friend or relative working in the schoolroom.[16] Certainly F.D. Maurice, who was Professor of History and English Literature at King's College and secretary to the GBI's Committee of Education, knew all about the difficulties faced by the unmarried middle-class woman without means: several of his seven sisters had worked variously as governesses, teachers and companions. It was one of these women, Mary, who was generally credited with focusing his attention on the work of the GBI: her two manuals, *Governess Life* and *Mothers and Governesses* went a long way to publicising the activities of the Institution.[17]

No amount of private and delicate assistance could tackle the underlying cause of the governess' poverty, which was simply that she was not paid enough. The way to higher wages, according to the GBI's Secretary, the Rev David Laing, was not simply to raise the academic standards of the governess, but to provide her with a means of proving those standards, so that no employer would be 'under the necessity of taking a Governess, without knowing whether she really has the proficiency, which she assumes to have'.[18] It was this argument which lay behind the efforts of a wide range of male middle-class occupations to win professional status during the middle decades of the century by tightening entrance and training practices. After several false starts, the first certificate to prove academic competence, in this case in Italian, was awarded to Miss Isabella Merritt in December 1847:

Miss Isabella Merritt having offered herself for Examination in Italian the Examiners are of opinion, that she reads that language fluently, and with a good pronunciation, that she is well instructed in the grammar, translating with facility, from one language into the other. The examiners think that Miss Isabella Merritt is quite competent to teach the Italian language.[19]

The certificate was issued under the auspices not of the GBI itself but of Queen's College, which had been set up by the Institution that same year in order to do something to improve the appalling level of education displayed by so many of the governesses who had applied for its loans and annuities. To this end the Committee of Education asked nine of Maurice's colleagues at King's College to provide a series of talks on their specialities which included Latin, maths, mechanics and theology as well as the more usual subjects.

After following a lecture series for a year a woman could gain a certificate in a single subject or a 'certificate of proficiency' if three subjects were offered. Later in the 1860s a certificate of associateship was introduced which could be won by attending the college over six terms and gaining an overall pass mark of at least 66 per cent.

Whether a series of lectures from university academics was really what was needed to fill the gaps in a patchy elementary education remained doubtful, at least according to one of the commissioners of the Schools Inquiry Commission of 1867-68.[20] On the other hand, a sufficient number of certificates were issued (118 in the first year of operation) to suggest that at least some of the women were following the gist of what they were taught. Moreover, the style and substance of the instruction was in self-conscious contradiction to the ornamental education of which governesses were held to be both the victims and the perpetrators. In one of his *Introductory Lectures* Maurice maintained that Queen's would aim to supply something very different:

> The teacher in every department, if he does his duty, will admonish his pupils, that they are not to make fashion, or public opinion, their rule; that they are not to draw or play, or to study arithmetic, or language, or literature, or history, in order to shine or be admired; that if these are their ends, they will not be sincere in their work or do it well.[21]

Only a year after its appearance the GBI was insisting in its ebullient annual reports that the Queen's certificate was fast becoming recognised as the basic qualification for governesses:

> The certificates granted by the Committee of Education are being more sought; and, as the public gradually insist upon them previous to engagement, will become nearly universal. The two classes, who stand aloof – they, who are conscious of a defective education and they, who rest upon an assumed high character for teaching – must eventually follow the crowd. The one class must seek improvement, or leave the profession: The other class will find the steady training of the College thrusting them aside to make way for powerful and scientific teachers, unless they descend from their dignity to *prove* their qualificaations.[22]

Yet the fact remained that 25,000 women were governesses in 1861, of whom only a handful held Queen's certificates. The college was accessible only to those who lived in central London and had the motivation and confidence to attend regularly and submit to the rigours of an examination – albeit a verbal one. Moreover, while the rhetoric of the GBI suggested that it aimed to put governessing on a professional footing with a recognised scheme of study leading to examination and certification, it was appalled by any implication that it might be setting up a special training scheme for governesses. The gentlemen of the GBI (no woman sat upon the governing body or taught in the college above assistant level), were quick to insist that:

> The Committee disclaim any idea of training governesses as a separate profession. They believe and hope, that the ranks of that profession will still be supplied from those, whose minds and tempers have been disciplined in the school of adversity, and who are thus best able to guide the minds and tempers of their pupils.[23]

The rhetoric and practice of the GBI reinforced the definition of the governess as a distressed gentlewoman whose chief qualifications were the moral qualities which were associated with her identity as a lady. She was, pre-eminently, an amateur. Along with every other educationalist, manual writer, and indeed anyone who voiced their opinions on the subject of home teaching, the GBI's Committee of Education was committed to the principle that the future governess should be educated alongside financially-secure girls on the grounds that 'many of her fellow-students might be connected with families to which hereafter she might be introduced, and they would early learn to respect and esteem their companion in study'.[24] As a result, Queen's College was open from the start to all women over the age of twelve, regardless of whether they planned to teach.

This shift of focus away from the immediate task of equipping governesses to demand better salaries to the broader aim of preparing genteel women for their civilising mission explains the way in which the college soon ceased to have much to do with the needs and concerns of those whom it had been set up to help. In the early days of Queen's College it was assumed that the certificates would be sought by 'any lady, desiring to prove her qualification for teaching any particular branch of knowledge',[25] yet after only a few years the Committee of Education declared that it would look 'rather to the expression of the knowledge of the subject evinced, than the capability of teaching it'.[26] In 1852 the lectures on pedagogy were dropped from the syllabus altogether. A two-tier system of instruction quickly developed consisting of day time lectures for fee-payers, who presumably did not have to work, with free lectures in the evenings for governesses: in its 1849 annual report the GBI proudly published a letter from a group of governesses humbly thanking the Institution for the chance of being able to attend the college *gratis*.[27] In 1853, when the college finally split from the Institution, the GBI retained the right to nominate four governesses for free places and a handful more to attend at half-price.

With each year that passed, the social tone at Queen's became more exclusive. The Schools Inquiry Commission of 1867-68 noted that those attending the college were drawn mainly from the upper and upper middle classes: this was hardly surprising since annual fees were £22-28 excluding extras (the City of London School for Boys charged only £9).[28] What is more, when it came to presenting governesses for free places, the GBI committee considered the background of the candidates carefully, limiting the scholarships to 'the daughters of professional men, that term including clergymen, barristers, solicitors, physicians, surgeons and apothecaries, or officers in the army or navy, or of such other persons in the same rank of society as the Board may deem eligible'.[29] In 1864 the Committee debated whether the college should exclude 'the children of retail tradesmen'.[30] They agreed that the occupation of the father should appear on all admission forms, and that 'in the case of publicans and others engaged in unsuitable callings, applicants should have a special recommendation from a member of the council, Committee of Education or Lady Visitors'.[32] The Lady Visitors – married women who took it in turns to chaperone at the lectures – even asked for a Lady Superintendent to be appointed at Queen's so that 'parents may feel secure against an indiscriminate association of different dispositions and ranks of society'.[33] And while the committee replied that 'it is a principle of the institution not to recognise any distinction of rank among the pupils',[34] it was still the case that lectures ran from 10 until 3 without a break, precisely to avoid girls meeting during the lunch hour. Later on the Lady Visitors vetoed a proposal for an evening *conversazione* of students and friends of the college by objecting that 'whilst casual association in a class by no means implied association elsewhere, the meeting together in an Evening party might lead to a more familiar acquaintance than parents could approve'.[34]

The attempts of the gentlemen of the GBI to professionalise home teaching were hampered by their own reluctance to move beyond an understanding of the governess as a lady and therefore an amateur. Inspired by the principles of Christian Socialism, their chief concern was the moral contamination which must follow the appearance of lower middle-class women in the home schoolroom. Locating virtue in the person of the genteel middle-class woman, they set about devising ways of ridding the governess body of anyone whose demeanour suggested that she did not fall into this category. In doing this the reformers were immediately confronted by a contradiction which had long-since worried social commentators. Any system of standardised training and qualification for the governess would operate as a sluice-gate for those clever but low-born women who were able to gain a fistful of certificates and so claim the right to teach in the home schoolroom. It soon became apparent, therefore, that the proposed reforms were likely to have the opposite effect from the one intended. In the circumstances, the gentlemen of the GBI retreated swiftly to a more orthodox understanding of the governess as a distressed gentlewoman who had received an education that was no different from the one that she was required to impart. Thus the first tentative attempts to professionalise the governess' position, to give her the status of a specialist which she needed in order to justify her claim to a decent wage and working conditions, were quickly aborted. Unfortunately, this capitulation turned out to be an omen for developments in the wider arena of middle-class female employment. Here, too, reforms which had as part of their impetus a desire to help the governess, ended by frustrating any chance she might have had of winning the salary and social status which her brothers had come to expect as part and parcel of their identity as professional men.

For the group of young feminists who became known as 'The Ladies of Langham Place', after the offices in which they gathered, the impoverished, ill-qualified governess was a symbolic figure. In her they saw a symptom of all that was wrong with the materialistic, snobbish and selfish culture of the middle class. For these financially-secure young women, the governess was a testament not only to the folly of professional men who failed to insure their own lives, but also to the limited educational and employment opportunities available to those of their daughters who were obliged to support themselves until marriage, if not for life. The scope of the Ladies' programme was ambitious, reaching as it did into virtually every aspect of contemporary social, political and economic life.[35] Organised partly in response to Parliament's rejection of the Married Women's Property Bill in favour of the Matrimonial Causes Bill during 1856-57,

Bessie Rayner Parkes, Barbara Bodichon and their associates set to work to publicise and, to a limited extent, create new legal and employment opportunities for women. They organised the first petition to Parliament for women's suffrage, set up the Society for the Promotion of the Employment of Women (hereafter S.P.E.W.), and allowed their rented offices to be used as an informal employment agency. Through the pages of their periodical the *English Woman's Journal* (hereafter *EWJ*) and its successor, the *Englishwoman's Review*, readers were alerted to the progress of various campaigns, including the efforts of Emily Davies to open public examinations to girls and found a women's college, and to the establishment of women's clubs and model housing.

Although the vigorous prose of so much of the *EWJ* suggested that the Ladies' chief concern was with finding a fast remedy to the oversupply of the home schoolroom and the poor working conditions that this engendered for the governess, the solutions that they proposed were on a time-scale that could benefit only those who were currently still receiving their education. It was a contradiction of which Parkes, Bodichon and their associates were aware, pondering openly whether their ambition should be 'to tide the female population of this country over a time of difficulty, or ... to develop a new state of social life?'[36] For there could be no doubt that behind the immediate intention of alleviating the misery of the governess lay the more ambitious desire of opening both the older professions as well as new types of semi-skilled work to women. Yet, these daughters of clergymen, squires and politicians remained very much a product of their time and class. While conservative contemporaries were quick to spot the revolutionary implications of their demands – if all middle-class women were to be prepared for work outside the home, then how could one be certain that some would not decide to live independently of men and the nuclear family?[37] – few of the Ladies were prepared to suggest that training middle-class women entailed anything more than the provision of a much-needed safety net. While they believed passionately that providing single middle-class women with the wherewithal to undertake rewarding work would put an end to unhappy or degrading marriages of convenience, they continued to see middle-class female employment as a solution to the problems faced by a woman who had no father or husband to support her.[38]

These highly orthodox notions about the relationship between class, gender and waged work shaped the way that the Ladies of

Langham Place approached the governess' plight. Following the lead of the conservative commentators of the 1840s, they assumed that most of her problems were caused by the crowding of the schoolroom with lower middle-class women. If only these daughters of clerks and tradesmen could be persuaded that there was no shame in earning one's living as a shop assistant or a clerical worker, the home schoolroom might be reclaimed as the exclusive territory of the distressed gentlewoman. According to Lincolnshire squire's daughter, Jessie Boucherett:

> If young women of the trading classes were thus enabled to become clerks and accountants, and to take part in commercial business, the number of candidates for places as governesses would be much diminished, and would consist principally of ladies who had known better days, and of daughters of the clergy and professional men left without fortunes; and as the competition would diminish with the numbers seeking engagements, these could ask sufficiently high salaries to enable them to live in tolerable comfort during their old age, without being beholden to charity; and being principally gentlewomen by birth and manners, the unfavourable impressions now existing against governesses would gradually fade away. The profession would rise in public estimation, and those following it would receive the respect and consideration due to them.[39]

As well as suggesting that lower middle-class women could seek work in offices, shops and hospitals, the Ladies of Langham Place came up with a seemingly endless list of ingenious employment suggestions including hairdressing, wood-engraving and jewellery-making.[40] Under the auspices of the S.P.E.W. Jessie Boucherett opened a business school which aimed to prepare lower middle-class girls for positions in the commercial world.[41] Such initiatives were designed to help women take advantage of the new range of white-collar jobs which had appeared as a result of the expansion in the service industries during the 1870s and 80s. The two most obvious categories were shop and office work: not only were these occupations clean and physically fairly undemanding, they could be organised to ensure that propriety was preserved by isolating young women workers from their male colleagues. Nursing, too, was gradually coming to be seen as respectable work for middle-class women, while teaching posts in a whole range of institutions from elementary to public schools provided employment for a broad swathe of single women.[42]

Important qualifications, however, need to be noted about the Ladies' work. None of these new occupations for women seriously challenged existing ideas about female nature, most particularly middle-class female nature, and the type of activities appropriate to it. While the sight of single middle-class women working outside the home was disturbing to conservative contemporaries, the style and content of the labour involved did much to allay fears about female independence. Nursing, teaching and office work all cast women in precisely the type of servicing or caring roles which had for so long been part of their domestic duties. Moreover, the appearance of new employment opportunities in these areas was not the result of any profound shift in women's political and social relationship to the labour market but rather of a coincidental expansion in the economy.[43] With a few exceptions, the Ladies did not create new types of work for middle-class women: rather, they drew their attention to its existence.

This reluctance to overhaul the relationship between gender, class and the market place meant that the Ladies left the dilemma of the distressed gentlewoman, the very person they had set out to help, quite untouched. New work opportunities were all very well, but many of them required numerical skills which not all distressed gentlewoman possessed since, according to the secretary of the S.P.E.W., 'sometimes the daughter of a small tradesman is rather better educated than those who have been in a higher position'.[44] What is more, many of these newer semi-professions and trades required the sort of costly training which the truly distressed gentlewoman was unable to afford – the appeal of governessing had always been that it required no preparation beyond the genteel education which every lady was presumed to have received. Even to teach in an elementary school – an option which was only just becoming respectable – one needed to be able to lay down £50 to attend a college such as Bishop Otter in Chichester;[45] likewise the minimum year's training required for nursing work set its probationers back by £30;[46] even lesser trades and crafts demanded a period of fee-paying quasi-apprenticeship so that, by the end of the century, commentators were reporting gloomily that 'the only openings nowadays are those involving special training and much hard work'.[47] While the new employment opportunities publicised by the Ladies of Langham Place did much to prepare the generation of lower middle-class women born after 1860 for work away from the home schoolroom, they did nothing for those who were already ensconced in it. Nor did the Ladies manage to rework ideas about gentility and paid labour to a sufficient degree to convince the daughters of the upper middle class that working in a department store was an appropriate way to earn a living, perhaps because, at heart, they did not believe it themselves. As a result, the second half of the nineteenth century produced no completely satisfactory alternative to the home schoolroom as a place of employment for the distressed gentlewoman.

One particular thread of the Ladies' programme has always been assumed to have had the most dramatic impact on late-Victorian governessing. Many modern accounts of female education imply, if they do not state, that the changes in middle-class girls' schooling, which were the result of the reforming activities of Langham Place associates Emily Davies, Emily Shireff and Maria Grey, rendered obsolete the governess and all she stood for. Yet closer examination suggests that, far from challenging the theory and practice of home education, the new generation of late Victorian girls' schools constructed themselves around similar principles. The paradoxical effect was to provide an alternative to the educational and employment possibilities that the home schoolroom offered without presenting any spur to its own re-organisation.

At the time when the infant service sector was beginning to provide alternatives to governessing for a younger generation of lower middle-class women, the new network of independent girls schools was doing the same for a slightly higher social group. These non-residential high schools and boarding public schools not only provided a sound education for daughters of professional and business families who could expect little financial support after their father's death but, for those who wanted it, a stable and respectable career as a schoolmistress. By the 1890s many of the high schools were drawing their younger staff from women who had first been pupils at the school before gaining a scholarship to one of the new women's colleges at Oxford and Cambridge. Even in smaller schools, an ambitious girl could start as a pupil-teacher while studying for an external degree from the University of London before taking up a lifelong position in her *alma mater*.[48] Teacher training colleges for middle-class women also began to make their appearance: Dorothea Beale of Cheltenham Ladies College started one of the first, enabling older students to study for a university degree while preparing for a career in the classroom.[49] From 1878 the Maria Grey Training College provided vocational training for those women who were unable to manage the intellectual or financial demands of a university degree course.[50] Most significantly, what distinguished the new independent schoolmistress was not just that she was academically competent but that she had also received formal training in how to teach others.[51] This more than anything allowed her to claim, although not necessarily to receive, the privileges and prestige associated with professional work.

In return for these three of four years of rigorous preparation the independent schoolmistress received a salary of between £100 and £120,[52] assistant teachers at the Girls' Public Day School Company earned £113.[53] Organisations such as the Teachers' Guild of Great Britain (1884) and the London Schoolmistresses' Association (1866) provided the schoolmistress with a means of contact with other women working in the field, as well as keeping a watching brief over her pay and working conditions. Moreover, the woman who worked in a high school was able to experience the personal autonomy that came with lodging in independent accommodation; even those who were obliged to live in at the residential public schools enjoyed a certain satisfaction at being associated so closely wih these increasingly prestigious establishments. Either way, the independent schoolmistress enjoyed the sort of freedom from petty restraint unknown to the resident governess:

> Lesson-hours being over, the public teacher mixes with the world, and is at liberty to enlarge her ideas and improve her faculties as she likes; the private teacher has, on the contrary, to take her charges for a walk, and to preside over them at meal-times, or else she goes for a lonely walk or sits in an empty schoolroom until lessons begin again.[54]

Within the walls of the new schools, strong and enduring friendships with other members of staff allowed many women to soften the emotional rigours of celibacy while side-stepping the demands of marriage and motherhood. Those women who succeeded in becoming headmistresses enjoyed an independence from the whims and demands of parents of which an earlier generation of lady proprietresses could only dream.[55] And while there may be an element of wishful thinking in her words, by the end of the century the headmistress of Manchester High School for Girls felt confident of her claim that 'the teacher is an expert professional and is entitled therefore to the deference shown to the skilled professional opinion of the doctor, lawyer, or architect'.[56]

Yet it is doubtful whether the ethos of these new schools represented a radical reassessment of genteel femininity, and whether, more specifically, the education they offered mounted a serious challenge to the principles and practice of home education.[57] In 1889 the periodical writer Alfred W. Pollard was declaring that, 'it is not likely, and certainly it is not to be desired, that the modern governess system should ever be wholly abolished, even if the constant supply of new schools for girls tends in some measure to supersede it'.[58] In fact the 'constant supply of new schools for girls' was little more than a trickle: even by the beginning of the twentieth century the G.P.D.S.C. could boast only thirty-six establishments catering for 7,000 girls.[59] Nor is it the case that the education on offer at these new institutions was so innovative that it rendered obsolete the resident governess and all she stood for. Although the prime movers in setting up the new institutions were outstanding women such as Davies, Shireff and Grey, the support of men remained crucial to the continuing success of women's educational reform. In the cicumstances, as the American historian Joyce Pedersen has suggested, the values espoused by these new institutions were highly unlikely to challenge the social status quo.[60] Funded by wealthy businessmen and patronised by clergymen, the high schools and public schools eschewed the worst excesses of ornamental education in favour of more solid cultural and intellectual achievement. Their goal was not so much to fit women for the workplace as to enable them to pursue the aesthetic and intellectual activities which would neutralise their male relatives' association with commercial life. According to its prospectus, the newly-formed Manchester High aimed to prepare girls

> for any future which may lie before them, so that they may become intelligent companions and associates for their brothers, meet helps and counsellors for their husbands, and wise guides and trainers for the minds of their children.[61]

Little, it seemed, had changed since the 1840s. While traditionally weak subjects like science and mathematics were better taught in the new schools, the tone of many of these institutions, whether day or boarding, resembled that of the genteel home schoolroom. Public examinations, as we have seen, were initially outlawed at the prestigious Cheltenham Ladies College since headmistress Dorothea Beale considered them socially *infra dig*.[62] Social homogeneity was maintained at boarding schools by scrutinising the background of prospective pupils, while day high schools guarded against any undesirable mixing by keeping the school day short and ensuring that girls who walked home together did so with the express permission of their parents.[63] Afternoon lessons were avoided at many of the new high schools since it was assumed that pupils would be required to spend the second part of the day helping their mothers with domestic and social pursuits.[64] In their avowed intent to provide an atmosphere that was just like home, the new schools had much in common with the older proprietary establishments which continued to cater for three-quarters of all girls receiving secondary education. The Bryce Commissioners, charged with investigating the structure of secondary education in England in 1894-95, reported that in country areas these proprietary schools were all that was available to older girls by way of schooling. Moreover, according to the Assistant Commissioner responsible for Lancashire, these schools seem to have remained quite untouched by the reforms in girls' education which had taken place in the last quarter of the century.[65]

For the British middle and upper classes home education for girls still remained the ideal, even though it might be realised in a variety of different ways. During the last third of the century, for instance, many families sent their daughters to one of the new generation of academically sound schools until mid-teens but preferred to employ a governess thereafter, since it was felt that a home education supervised by a governess was more appropriate for a young lady.[66] Many of those upper-class families whose peripatetic lifestyle made day-school education impractical still preferred to use the services of a governess rather than send their daughters away to a residential public school: even a family as committed to educational reform as the Kay-Shuttleworths found it desirable and more convenient to have their girls educated at home. Girls who were considered too delicate to endure the rough and tumble of public schooling were also likely to receive all their education from a resident governess.[67] Country clergy remained one of the largest employers of governesses in the last two decades of the century – perhaps because a salary of £40 still represented a considerable saving over two or more sets of school fees.[68] Significantly, in those families with unlimited money to spend on their girls, a popular option was to combine the best of both worlds, sending them to school by day but ensuring that their moral and social education continued at home under the watchful eye of a full-time governess. Louisa Martindale, who was sent to Brighton High School in the 1880s, 'much to the dismay of some of our friends',[69] was nonetheless chaperoned to and from the school gates by her resident governess. Similarly, as we have seen, Cynthia Asquith set off for Cheltenham Ladies College once a week, accompanied by the ever-faithful but distinctly unacademic Squidge.[70]

The decision of some upper- and upper middle-class families to provide their daughters with an education which combined supervision by a governess with attendance at an academically-sound school bears witness both to the continuing value attached to home teaching and to the simultaneous recognition that an old-style ornamental education was no longer considered adequate, even for those girls who would never have to make their own living. As a result, from the 1880s onwards, any governess seeking a position in such a household needed to be able to offer either a clutch of certificates from Queen's College, or some passes in the Junior and Senior Local University exams, or even a university degree. Although she was still not obliged to have undergone the vocational training that was now required of the public or high school mistress, the home governess was expected to achieve, in conjunction with visiting masters, a level of instruction which was comparable to that provided by a staffroom of specialist teachers. She had become, in the words of Charlotte Yonge, 'a lady with a profession'.[71]

This is not to suggest that every woman working in the late-Victorian home schoolroom necessarily achieved the sort of standards outlined. As we saw earlier, governessing remained the only resort for the many middle-class girls who continued to be prepared for the drawing-room but unexpectedly found themselves obliged to support themselves in later life. While the introduction of examinations for girls allowed able women such as May Pinhorn to prove their competence and claim a decent salary, there were many who continued to offer no qualification save that of their ladyhood. While a family such as the Kay-Shuttleworths were keenly aware of the various levels of competence represented by different certificates, the vast majority of employers seems to have remained blithely ignorant of these distinctions. According to Alfred W. Pollard, whose article in an 1889 issue of *Murray's Magazine*, provides a useful snapshot of the state of the home schoolroom at the end of the century:

> The Lady Registrar of the best Governess Agency in the kingdom asserts emphatically that between a second class in the most elementary examination of the College of Preceptors and a second class honours in the Cambridge Higher Local Examination most employers are unable to distinguish. How is the average governess

to be persuaded of the necessity of an efficient training, when the market value of the highest and lowest certificates is often a matter of chance?[72]

Such indifference hardly created the conditions in which home education might be professionalised: indeed, continued Pollard, the 1889 schoolroom housed a governess body as confused and chaotic as that of the 1840s:

But while every other profession has established for itself a certain amount of organisation and has won for its members a definite status, the great army of governesses remains an undisciplined mob. Ranked together under one common name we find women with the most diverse qualifications and acquirements, receiving salaries of which the diversities are certainly no less, but whose distribution often bears no kind of proportion to the merits of the receivers.[73]

The little statistical evidence available certainly bears out the main thrust of Pollard's assessment of the late Victorian schoolroom, although it also offers some important qualifications to it. For instance, it does seem to have been the case that by the end of the century the salaries earned by governesses had fanned out to cover a broader range than those of the 1840s and 50s. On the other hand, there was a closer correlation between qualifications offered and remuneration claimed. The fact that May Pinhorn's salary increased four-fold during 1888-99 suggests that by the end of the century a rudimentary career path had opened up, whereby the able governess could expect her growing stock of qualifications and experience to be acknowledged in the form of a salary which increased steadily until she reached her mid thirties.[74] What is not in doubt is that for the uncertificated governess of the late nineteenth century salaries remained as low as they had done fifty years earlier, and that this had a knock-on effect on those of more able women. Throughout this period advertisements from distressed gentlewomen frequently appeared asking for no more than £20 per annum,[75] much to the fury of the members of the elite Union of Private Governesses, who gathered at Queen's College in 1913 to protest at the way in which their own salaries had been dragged down by the low expectations of their incompetent sisters. According to their analysis

the want of such a Society has been felt for many years. English governesses experience difficulties in obtaining well-paid work. Although the cost of living and clothes has so enormously increased of late years, and though wages have risen for every other kind of work, there is a decided tendency in the opposite direction in respect to the salary of the English governess.[76]

The solution, as far as the Union of Private Governesses, which was made up of 'governesses to the children of the influential classes',[77] was concerned, was to attract on to its governing committee society ladies who could be counted upon to recommend individual members to their friends. The idea was to by-pass the need for formal recruitment and to reproduce the word-of-mouth proce-dures of an earlier period.[78]

Although periodical writers maintained that the conditions under which the late-Victorian governess laboured were an improvement on those experienced by her predecessor of the 1840s, they were unable to point to any big shifts. Despite various proposals that neighbouring governesses and pupils in urban areas should meet together every day to set up what was in effect a small private school, home teaching remained an isolated and lonely business.[79] Like commentators of an earlier period, Alfred W. Pollard continued to worry about the fact that the new system of academic qualifications had opened up the way for clever, low-born young women to enter the schoolroom: it was with evident approval that he recorded the case of a certificated yet ill-bred young governess who was unable to achieve a salary of more than £25-40 on account of her vulgarity.[80] Several accounts of late-Victorian governessing suggest that the conception of the governess' relationship to her employers had changed little over the previous fifty years. Written contracts, for instance, were still rare, while questions of leisure and privileges were still open to constant negotiation and confusion.[81] Even those very few governesses who had received vocational training continued to define themselves as family members rather than specialist professionals: one woman who in 1918-19 attended Charlotte Mason's 'House of Education', which aimed to prepare middle-class girls as superior nursery-governesses, recalled that she had been trained to become, above all, 'an active and acceptable member of the household, one who demanded little but could cheerfully co-operate in daily living'.[82]

The question remains as to why those able women who gathered at Queen's College in 1913 had chosen the home schoolroom over the school classroom as their place of employment. Why, indeed, did May Pinhorn, born in 1868 the daughter of a poor clergyman, decide to prepare herself for a career as a governess rather than as a schoolteacher in one of the prestigious new public schools? The fact that well-qualified women continued to chose the home schoolroom over other places of employment suggests that, even by the beginning of the twentieth century, governessing was able to offer some clearly-perceived benefits. At £80 to £100 the salary that the able governess could expect to receive compared favourably with that of the schoolmistress, who had to find her own board and lodging out of £120 or so. Moreover, by the 1890s the oversupply of schoolmistresses (over half of all the women who graduated from Newnham College, Cambridge during 1871 to 1893 went into teaching) meant that salaries were starting to fall.[83] In spite of repeated pleas to set a minimum of £100 p.a., a beginner's wages in a small school could be as low as £70 to £80 non-residential or £40 to £60 residential. As the growth of the new schools slowed down, vacancies became few and far between and the opportunites for promotion started to contract.[84] To make matters worse, a teacher in an independent school had no security of tenure: she could be dismissed without reason, often without notice.

There were, in turn, plenty of advantages which the home schoolroom could offer over the school classroom. Living in the household of a prominent family allowed the governess to participate, albeit vicariously, in the nation's public and political life: such certainly was one of the attractions of the Kay-Shuttleworths to May Pinhorn.[85] Other women entering the home schoolroom may have been drawn by the opportunity to form close emotional bonds with two or three children as opposed to the more superficial relationships which were on offer in the school classroom. There is some suggestion, too, that the first generation of schoolmistresses, having received their own education at home, found the task of keeping order in a classroom of fifteen adolescent girls quite terrifying;[86] a post in a private schoolroom, while not exempt from discipline problems, might prove less traumatic. Other women who chose governessing over schoolteaching may simply have enjoyed feeling that they were 'one of the family' – particularly if their own had recently disintegrated. The fact that the very highest people in the land continued to educate their daughters at home cannot fail to have bestowed on the governess an aura of glamour and refinement, no matter how humble her actual circumstances. That a growing number of governesses now came equipped with paper qualifications allowed home teaching to claim just a little of the prestige associated with the increasingly respected activity of schoolteaching.

The story of the late-Victorian governess is one of polarisation. Those bright daughters of poor professional men who would once have entered the home schoolroom were now equipped with the certificates which allowed them to take their places in the staff rooms of the new high and public schools.[87] Meanwhile, a new generation of those clerks' and tradesmen's daughters, who had endured such scorn for daring to set themselves up as governesses during the middle decades of the century, were increasingly able to find work in the new shops and offices of late nineteenth-century Britain. The women who were left behind in the home schoolroom fell into two categories. On the one hand, they were those distressed gentlewomen, familiar from an earlier generation, who lacked the qualifications for the new type of schoolteaching, yet whose social pretensions prevented them from standing behind a counter in Selfridges. On the other hand, they belonged to that small elite of able and often well-qualified women who catered for those financially and socially privileged families which still prefered to educate their girls at home. The home schoolroom of 1900 contained as wide an array of ability, though not perhaps of social class, as it had done in 1840. Ranked under the label 'governess' one might find women such as Miss Jourdain, who had a degree in classics from Oxford,[88] together with those unfortunate women who had nothing to offer but their ladyhood and their desperation.

The reason women like Charlotte Jourdain and May Pinhorn did not go on to form the core of an elite band of well-paid home teachers is explained, in part, by the fact that no occupation followed overwhelmingly by women has ever managed to win itself the prestige and privilege associated with professional work. The continued attachment of the middle as well as the upper classes to the principles of home education for girls, no matter in what context these were actually realised, suggests that ideas about the nature of femininity and the education and employment appropriate to it remained remarkably constant throughout the second half of the nineteenth century. While the appearance of schoolteaching and nursing as viable alternatives to the home schoolroom appeared to imply a rethinking of the sort of work appropriate to women, this soon turned out to be a chimera. In the last analysis, the new schools and hospitals offered intelligent and well-qualified women nothing more novel than a ghetto of low pay and poor prospects, sustainable only through economic need and a strong service ethic.

Another reason why the late Victorian governess failed to become the prototype of a new sort of professional woman was that, slowly but surely, her numbers were declining. Although there are no figures available, it appears that from the 1890s the middle classes were increasingly taking advantage of the new generation of girls' schools.[89] As their incomes, especially those which were in some way dependent on agricultural revenue, came under pressure from the 1870s, the governess was the first luxury to go. Now that falling birthrates meant that a family was likely to contain only two as opposed to five girls, the governess' salary represented less of a saving over school fees than had been the case earlier in the century. By the end of the century the desire for privacy, always perceived as especially strong in the male members of the household, may have led some families into choosing the visiting governess over her resident sister.[90] Worries about the tarnished image of daily governessing remained: one periodical writer suggested that the solution was simply to pay a sufficiently high salary to ensure that the governess could devote her attentions to a single family.[91] Nannies, by contrast, continued to be much in demand because there was no alternative to the service they provided: genteel mothers would rather have done almost any household task themselves than have to change a nappy. For this reason, the turn of the century onwards saw the gradual professionalisation of the children's nurse, with colleges such as the Norland training middle-class girls in readiness for remunerative and interesing careers.[92] The home schoolroom, by contrast, was staffed by a dwindling number of women working in the households of those men whose unusual, isolated or peripatetic lifestyle made normal schooling for their daughters impossible.

9

Epilogue

The governess continued to be a feature of the British social landscape throughout the inter-war period. Middle-class girls in country areas, especially clergy daughters, were still educated at home, whilst aristocratic families found that employing a private governess was often more convenient and congenial than using the services of a boarding school. The royal family continued its attachment to home education by entrusting the present Queen and her sister to governesses, one of whom – the infamous 'Crawfie' – earned the lasting displeasure of Buckingham Palace by selling her recollections of the young princesses to the popular press.

Yet the fact remains that from 1900 less and less was heard about the governess in the periodicals, novels and domestic literature of the day. It was not that she had faded from view exactly, simply that she was no longer the most conspicuous example of a middle-class woman who worked outside the home. By the turn of the century she had been joined in the employment place by teachers, nurses, clerks and bookeepers, all of whom expected to work until they married. While many of the difficulties which had confronted the governess in 1840 still held true over fifty years later – not least the problem of low pay and limited prospects – the principle of single middle-class women working outside the home had lost its power to shock.

This gradual quietening of the debate over the governess' 'plight' at the end of the century is proof, if any were needed, that what had really stirred up the Victorians was not the specific conditions under which the governess laboured, but the fact that she worked at all. Her very definition – a lady in paid employment – cut across those social codes around which the wealthiest sections of the middle class were obliged to organize themselves if they were to assert their right to be considered the natural rulers of the country. It was the governess' mute and unconscious challenge to this process which roused whole sections of Victorian society into debating with such passion the 'plight' of 25,000 otherwise unremarkable women.

The Victorians were right to be obsessed with the governess. For she marked the point at which the orthodoxies and 'natural' order of things broke down to reveal their man-made origins. While journalists urged individual employers to alleviate the governess' poverty by paying her more, the writers of conduct manuals rushed to smooth away the awkward moments in the household's routine by suggesting intricate ways of normalizing the governess' position. The novelists, too, recognised the figure of the governess as the place where the prevailing cultural norms began to crack. Some chose to use her to shore up those norms as best they could, others to prize the gap apart a little further in order to look at the chaos which lay below.

We, too, need to pay heed to the governess, for she can tell us about much more than the daily routine of the home schoolroom. She marks the point where the ideology of bourgeois feminity began to break down to reveal itself as a pragmatic and provisional set of myths and rules which buttressed the existing political and social order. By attending to the governess' discomforts and occasional joys as she tried to make sense of a set of conventions designed to exclude the possibility of her existence, we can begin to make out the constrictions and possibilities which operated in the lives of all women, of whatever social class, during Victoria's reign.

Appendix

Table 1

Occupation of Heads of Household in Governess-Employing Families in Paddington, Crediton and Edgbaston, (1861)*

Paddington West London		Edgbaston Birmingham		Crediton Devonshire	
Merchant	33	Merchant	7	Farmer	11
Fundholder	17	Manufacturer	6	Landowner	2
Lawyer	11	Tradesman	4	Miller	2
Doctor	10	Proprietor		Clergy	1
Stockbroker/		of Houses	1	JP	1
Insurance Agent	10	Landed Proprietor	1	Widow	1
Civil Servant	10	Bank Manager	1	Annuity	
Widow/Lady/	9	Commission Agent	1	Holder	1
Engineer/					
Surveyor	7				
Army/Navy	7				
No occupation/					
Head absent	6				
Tradesman	6				
Landed Proprietor	6				
MP/JP	6				
Manufacturer	4				
Knight/Baronet	2				
Clergy	1				
Patentee	1				
Actuary	1				
Master Mariner	1				

* Extracted from Enumerators' Handbooks, Census of England and Wales, 1861.

Table 2

Selected Former Occupations of Female Lunatics Compared to Total of Each Occupation in Population, England and Wales (1861)*

Occupation	Total in Occupation	Lunatics	% of Total
Musician	1,618	5	.31
Schoolmistress	58,350	121	.21
Governess	24,770	136	.55
Servant	962,786	2,695	.28
Charwoman	65,273	240	.37
Independent	27,420	631	2.30
No stated occupation		4,026	
Total Listed	10,289,965	13,096	

*Adapted from A. James Hammerton, *Emigrant Gentlewomen: Genteel Poverty and Female Emigration, 1830-1919* (London, 1979).

Notes

Preface

1. Governesses' Benevolent Institution, London, *Reports of the Board of Management for 1843–53* (London, 1844–54).

2. Report of the Schools Inquiry Commission, *Parliamentary Papers* 1867–68, xxviii, 13, pts. 1, 3 and 4.

3. The 1861 census enumerators' handbooks for three areas were subject to detailed analysis. Enumerators' Handbooks, Census of England and Wales, 1861, Public Record Office, London. Crediton: district 292, sub-districts 1–4; RG9/1470–1475. Edgbaston: district 393, sub-district 2; RG9/2122–2124. Paddington: district 1, sub-districts 1–2; RG9/1–12.

4. Three of the foremost writers on middle-class female education during the first half of the Victorian period – Anna Jameson, Mary Maurice and Elizabeth M. Sewell – had all spent part of their working lives as schoolteachers or governesses.

5. Mary Maurice, *Mothers and Governesses* (London, 1847).

6. For a detailed discussion of the literary governess, see Susan A. Nash, '"Wanting A Situation": Governesses and Victorian Novels', unpublished PhD thesis, Rutgers, State University of New Jersey, (New Brunswick, 1980). See also Patricia Thomson, *The Victorian Heroine: A Changing Ideal, 1837–1873* (London, 1956), ch. 2, pp. 37–56; Katharine West, *Chapter of Governesses: A Study of the Governess in English Fiction, 1800–1949* (London, 1949), chs. 2–4, pp. 54–193.

7. Two books which typify this uncritical approach are Bea Howe, *A Galaxy of Governesses* (London, 1954) and, most recently, Alice Renton, *Tyrant or Victim? A History of the British Governess* (London, 1991). Two articles from the early 1970s have proved the only exception to this perfunctory treatment of the historical governess. See M. Jeanne Peterson, 'The Victorian Governess: Status Incongruence in Family and Society', in Martha Vicinus (ed.), *Suffer and Be Still: Women in the Victorian Age* (London, 1980; first pub. Bloomington, 1972), pp. 3–19; and Leonore Davidoff, 'The English Victorian Governess: A Study In Social Isolation', (unpublished article, 1971).

8. A valuable source of information for autobiographical work produced by Victorian women can be found in S. Barbara Kanner's bibliographical essay 'The Women of England in a Century of Social Change, 1815–1914: A Select Bibliography, Part 11' in Martha Vicinus (ed.), *A Widening Sphere; Changing Roles of Victorian Women* (London, 1980; first pub. Bloomington, 1977), pp. 218–21.

9. Elizabeth Ham, *By Herself*, ed. Eric Gillett (London, 1945).

10. Mary Smith, *The Autobiography of Mary Smith, Schoolmistress and Nonconformist*, 2 vols. (London, 1892).

11. Mary Cowden-Clarke, *My Long Life: An Autobiographical Sketch* (London, 1896).

12. Edith Gates, Diary, (manuscript, 1876), Schulte Ms.

13. May Pinhorn, Fore-ward, *Some Account of the Life of Mary Blanche Pinhorn*, unnumbered pages, (typescript, 1926), Walley MS.

14. Mary Bazlinton, Diary, (manuscript, 1854–59, not continuous), House MS.

15. Patricia Clarke, *The Governesses: Letters From The Colonies, 1862–1882* (London, 1985).

16. A. James Hammerton, *Emigrant Gentlewomen: Genteel Poverty and Female Emigration, 1830–1914* (London, 1979).

1.   Reader, I Married Him

1. My discussion of the fictional governess is indebted to Susan A. Nash, '"Wanting A Situation": Governesses and Victorian Novels', unpublished PhD thesis, Rutgers, State University of New Jersey, (New Brunswick, 1980).

2. William Thackeray, *Vanity Fair* (Harmondsworth, 1968; first pub., London, 1848). *Vanity Fair* appeared in monthly installments from January 1847 before being published in novel form in 1848.

3. Charlotte Brontë, *Jane Eyre* (Harmondsworth, 1966; first pub., London, 1847).

4. Ibid., p. 474.

5. For a list of Victorian novels which have either a governess as a main protagonist, or contain a statement about the nature of governessing, see Susan A. Nash, '"Wanting A Situation"', appendix c., pp. 437–44.

6. Ian Watt, *The Rise of the Novel* (London, 1972), pp. 171–72. See also Terry Lovell, *Consuming Fiction* (London 1987).

7. Jane Austen, *Emma* (Harmondsworth, 1966; first pub., London, 1816).

8. Charlotte Brontë, *Jane Eyre,* pp. 140–141.

9. Anne Brontë, *Agnes Grey* (Harmondsworth, 1988; first pub., 1847).

10. Elizabeth M. Sewell, *Amy Herbert* 2 vols. (London, 1844).

11. Mrs Henry Wood, *East Lynne* (London, 1861).

12. Sheridan Le Fanu, *Uncle Silas* (London, 1864).

13. Henry James, *The Turn of the Screw* (Harmondsworth, 1986; first pub., New York, 1907–9).

14. Anne and Charlotte Brontë had both worked as governesses; Elizabeth Sewell ran a school with her sisters; William Thackeray relied on governesses to look after his children, since his wife's ill-health prevented her from doing so.

2.   *A Matter of Necessity*

1. Leonore Davidofff and Catherine Hall, *Family Fortunes: Men and Women of the English Middle Class* (London, 1987), p. 366.

2. F.M.L. Thompson, *The Rise of Respectable Society, 1830–1900* (London, 1988), p. 160.

3. For a full discussion of this, one of the central debates in early modern British history, see Lawrence Stone and Jeanne C. Fawtier Stone, *An Open Elite? England, 1540–1880* (Oxford, 1984); John Cannon, *Aristocratic Century: The Peerage of Eighteenth-Century England* (Cambridge, 1984), chs. 1, 3, pp. 1–38, 71–92.

4. For a classic exposition of the professional ideal, see Harold Perkin, *The Origins of Modern English Society, 1780–1880* (London, 1969), pp. 252–70.

5. Quoted in Martin Wiener, *English Culture and the Decline of the Industrial Spirit, 1850–1980* (Cambridge, 1981), p. 16.

6. Leonore Davidoff and Catherine Hall, *Family Fortunes*, p. 265.

7. Sarah Stickney Ellis, *The Women of England: Their Social Duties and Domestic Habits* (London, 1839), p. 463.

8. Hannah More produced a stream of religious and moral works from 1788 onwards. An adult convert to evangelicalism, she believed fervently that men and women were destined to occupy separate spheres of influence, with women as the natural moral guardians of the human race. Two of her most influential works include *Coelebs in Search of a Wife*, 2 vols. (London, 1807) and *Strictures on the Modern System of Female Education*, 2 vols. (London, 1799). Sarah Stickney Ellis developed Hannah More's ideas in the context of the urban landscape of the 1830s and 40s. Texts like *The Women of England: Their Social Duties and Domestic Habits* (London, 1839) and *The Mothers of England: Their Influence and Responsibility* (London, 1843), located virtue as residing in the modest homes of the middle class.

9. Between 1851 and 1871 the number of cooks, the most prestigious category of female servant, rose by 111.5 per cent compared with an increase of only 35.6 per cent for low-status maids-of-all-work. The data for these calculations is taken from J.A. Banks, *Prosperity and Parenthood: A Study of Family Planning Among the Victorian Middle Classes* (London, 1954), p. 83.

10. Emily Shore, *Journal of Emily Shore* (London, 1891), chs. 3–4, pp. 30–69.

11. J.A. Banks, *Prosperity and Parenthood*, pp. 86–102.

12. Duncan Crow, *The Victorian Woman* (London, 1971), p. 120.

13. Harriet Martineau, *Autobiography*, 3 vols. (London, 1877), 1, p. 100.

14. Lynda Nead, *Myths of Sexuality: Representations of Women in Victorian Britain* (Oxford, 1990; first pub., Oxford, 1988), p. 25.

15. Ibid., p. 34.

16. Leonore Davidoff and Catherine Hall, *Family Fortunes*, p. 235.

17. For a fuller discussion of the part played by the great public schools in the gentrification of the upper middle class, see Brian Simon and Ian Bradley (eds.), *The Victorian Public School: Studies in the Development of an Educational Institution* (Dublin, 1975).

18. Jane Panton, *Leaves from a Life* (London, 1908), p. 59.

19. A frequent pattern in homes where money was tight was to send an elder

daughter away to school until she was considered old enough to take charge of her siblings' education at home: see Harriet M. Jukes, *The Earnest Christian: Memoir, Letters and Journals*, ed. Mrs H.A. Gilbert (London, 1858), p. 6.

20. For a description of Shore's typical day, see Emily Shore, *Journal*, pp. 31–32.

21. William Thackeray, *Vanity Fair*, (Harmondsworth, 1968; first pub., London, 1848), pp. 57–58.

22. For a fuller description of these small boarding schools, see Carol Dyhouse, *Girls Growing up in Late Victorian and Edwardian England* (London, 1981), pp. 46–52.

23. Elizabeth M. Sewell, *The Autobiography of Elizabeth Missing Sewell*, edited by her niece Eleanor L. Sewell (London, 1907), p. 117.

24. Quoted in Carol Dyhouse, *Girls Growing Up*, p. 47.

25. Report of the Schools Inquiry Commission (hereafter SIC), *Parliamentary Papers* (hereafter *PP*), 1867–68, xxviii, 13, pt. 4, p. 234.

26. Elizabeth M. Sewell, *Autobiography*, pp. 33–34.

27. This was a favourite grouse of William Cobbett in *Rural Rides* (Harmondsworth, 1985; first pub., London, 1830), p. 229.

28. Elizabeth M. Sewell, *Autobiography*, pp. 3, 19.

29. Letter from Prudence Hackworth to her sister Jenny Hackworth, 22 January 1852 (Hackworth MS).

30. Fragment of letter from Prudence Hackworth to her sister Jenny Hackworth, undated (Hackworth MS).

31. Sarah Stickney Ellis, *Education of the Heart: Women's Best Work* (London, 1869), pp. 224–25.

32. 'Hints on the Modern Governess System', *Fraser's Magazine*, 30 (November 1844), p. 572.

33. Anna Jameson, *The Relative Social Position of Mothers and Governesses* (London, 1846), pp. 6–7.

34. Bea Howe, *A Galaxy of Governesses* (London, 1954), p. 78.

35. 'The Governess Question', *English Woman's Journal*, 4 (November 1859), p. 166.

36. Anna Jameson, *The Relative Social Position of Mothers and Governesses* (London, 1846); Mary Maurice, *Mothers and Governesses* (London, 1847); Mme Bureau Riofrey, *Private Education; Or, Observations on Governesses* (London, 1836).

37. Mrs Isabella Beeton, *Mrs Beeton's Book of Household Management*, 2 vols. (London, 1861), 1, p. 8.

38. See p. 205. Information extracted from Enumerators' Handbooks, Census of England and Wales, 1861, Public Record Office, London (hereafter PRO), Crediton: district 292, sub-districts 1–4; RG9/1470–1475. Edgbaston: district 393, sub-district 2; RG9/ 2122–2124. Paddington: district 1, sub-districts 1–2; RG9/1–12.

39. This figure is taken from the Census of England and Wales, 1861, vol. 2, *PP* 1863, table xvii, p. xxxiv. Those women who worked within their extended family network were probably not recorded as 'governess' by the census enumerator. Nor is it clear that all those who described themselves as 'governess' were necessarily employed exclusively in teaching childen; in trade and farming households some may well have been involved in more general domestic duties. Those women who worked as daily or visiting governesses were not distinguished from resident governesses by the census enumerator. Consequently, it is difficult to be precise about how many women worked as resident governesses during the middle decades of the century.

40. Patricia Branca, *Silent Sisterhood: Middle-Class Women in the Victorian Home* (London, 1975), p. 55.

41. Patricia Branca is wrong in suggesting that the 1871 census lists 55,000 governesses. This figure included those women who taught in private girls' schools

and were also sometimes known as 'governesses'. 1861 was unfortunately the last year in which private governesses were listed as a separate occupational category in the census. Branca's general argument that, once the upper classes had taken their pick from the pool of available governesses, there would be only a few thousand to service the entire middle class, still holds good. However, I have assumed that one quarter rather than one third of upper-class families had young daughters. Patricia Branca, *Silent Sisterhood*, pp. 46, 58.

42. The ratio of governesses to upper and middle-class girls aged 5–20 (calculated at 20 per cent of all girls aged 5–20) for selected counties is as follows:

County	Middle– and Upper-class girls aged 5–20 years	Governesses	Girls per governess
Middlesex (extra metropolitan)	7322	505	14
Hampshire	17570	759	23
Leicestershire	9829	323	30
N. Riding of Yorkshire	8326	209	40
Derbyshire	11520	191	60
County Durham	21731	206	105

Source: Extracted from the Census of England and Wales, 1861, *PP* 1863, vol. 2.

43. 'Hints on the Modern Governess System', p. 582.

44. SIC, *PP* 1867–68, xxviii, 13, pt. 3, p. 693.

45. Bea Howe, *A Galaxy of Governesses*, p. 115.

46. Enumerators' Handbooks, Census of England and Wales, 1861, PRO, RG 9/1, fo. 107.

47. SIC, *PP* 1867–68, xviii, 13, pt. 3, p. 693.

48. Enumerators' Handbooks, Census of England and Wales, 1861, PRO, RG 9/1470 fo. 7.

49. Enumerators' Handbooks, Census of England and Wales, 1861, PRO, RG9/7, fo. 10.

3. Take a Lady

1. Bessie Rayner Parkes, 'The Profession of the Teacher: The Annual Reports of the Governesses' Benevolent Institution, from 1843 to 1856', *English Woman's Journal* (hereafter *EWJ*), 1 (March 1858), p. 1.

2. The precise figures are: merchant/businessman 9, surgeon 5, military or naval officer 3, civil servant/government officer 3, solicitor 1, architect 1, independent 1, clergyman, 1. Governesses' Benevolent Institution, *Report of the Board of Management* (hereafter *GBI Report*) *for 1848* (London, 1849), pp. 19–35.

3. 'Governesses', *Eliza Cook's Journal*, 1 (September 1849), p. 305.

4. *GBI Report for 1853* (London, 1854), p. 23.

5. Miss Maria N., *GBI Report for 1852* (London, 1853), p. 20.

6. Census of England and Wales, 1861, vol. 2., *Parliamentary Papers* (hereafter *PP*) 1863, table xx, p. lvii.

7. Bessie Rayner Parkes, 'Educated Destitution', in *Essays on Women's Work* (London, 1865), pp. 83–84.

8. *GBI Report for 1848* (London, 1849), p. 28.

9. Harriet Martineau, 'The Governess', *Once a Week*, 3 (September 1860), p. 272.

10. Joan N. Burstyn, *Victorian Education and the Ideal of Womanhood* (London, 1980), p. 120.

11. Millicent Garrett Fawcett, *What I Remember* (London, 1924), p. 48.

12. Mary Smith, *The Autobiography of Mary Smith, Schoolmistress and Nonconformist* 2 vols. (London, 1892), 1, p. 90.

13. May Pinhorn, 'Some Account of the Life of Mary Blanche Pinhorn' (typescript, 1926), p. 47, Walley MS.

14. *GBI Report for 1851* (London, 1852), p. 19.

15. Census of England and Wales, 1861, vol. 2., *PP* 1863, table xx, p. lvii. Unfortunately there is no way of knowing at what age these women first started work.

16. 'The Governess Question', *EWJ*, 4 (November 1859), p. 166.

17. A. James Hammerton, *Emigrant Gentlewomen: Genteel Poverty and Female Emigration, 1830–1914* (London, 1979), p. 29.

18. Ibid., p. 30.

19. *GBI Report for 1853* (London, 1854), pp. 19–30.

20. Lady [Elizabeth] Eastlake, '*Vanity Fair, Jane Eyre*, and the Governesses' Benevolent Institution', *Quarterly Review*, 84 (December 1848), p. 176.

21. Ibid., p. 180.

22. Information extracted from the Enumerators' Handbooks, Census of England and Wales, 1861, Public Record Office, London (hereafter PRO): Crediton, (district 292, sub-districts 1–4); RG9/1470–1475.

23. Theresa M. McBride, *The Domestic Revolution: The Modernisation of Household Service in England and France, 1820–1920* (London, 1976), pp. 84–92.

24. Jessie Boucherett, *Hints on Self-Help: A Book for Young Women* (London, 1863), p. 25.

25. See, for example, the entries for Mary Ann Jennings and Louisa and Elizabeth Marlow. Enumerators' Handbooks, Census of England and Wales, 1861, PRO, RG9/11, fo. 76; RG 9/1, fo. 53.

26. Bessie Rayner Parkes, 'The Profession of the Teacher', p. 1.

27. Theresa M. McBride, *The Domestic Revolution*, p. 98.

28. A. James Hammerton, *Emigrant Gentlewomen*, p. 126.

29. Winifred Peck, *A Little Learning: Or, a Victorian Childhood* (London, 1952), pp. 19–20.

30. Charlotte Brontë, *Shirley* (Hardmondsworth, 1985; first pub. London, 1849), p. 204.

31. Harriet Martineau, 'The Governess', p. 271.

32. Elizabeth Ham, *By Herself*, ed. Eric Gillett (London, 1945), p. 202.

33. John Ruskin, *Praeterita*, 3 vols. (London, 1885–1900), 1, p. 112.

34. Mary Smith, *Autobiography*, 1, p. 65.

35. The *Englishwoman's Domestic Magazine*, published and edited by Samuel Beeton, appeared monthly from 1852 and advised middle-class women, employing little or no domestic help, on all aspects of household management.

36. For more biographical information see Mrs Steuart Erskine, *Anna Jameson: Letters and Friendships, 1812–1860* (London, 1915); *Elizabeth M. Sewell: The Autobiography of Elizabeth M. Sewell*, edited by her niece, Eleanor L. Sewell (London, 1907); Mrs Sarah Stickney Ellis, *The Home Life and Letters of Mrs Ellis*, Compiled by Her Nieces (London, 1893).

37. Deborah Gorham, *The Victorian Girl and the Feminine Ideal* (London, 1982), p. 29.

38. Ibid, p. 28.

39. *The Times*, 10 October, 1850.

40. Mary Bazlinton, Diary (manuscript, 1854–59, not continuous), 4 November 1859, House MS.

41. Bea Howe, *A Galaxy of Governesses* (London, 1954), p. 126.

42. *The Times*, 10 October 1850; *The Times*, 4 April, 1837.

43. Enumerators' Handbooks, Census of England and Wales, 1861, PRO, RG 9/11, fo. 104; RG 9/12, fo. 46.

44. Quoted in Lee Holcombe, *Victorian Ladies at Work* (Newton Abbot, 1973), p. 12.

45. Bessie Rayner Parkes, 'A Year's Experience in Women's Work', *Transactions of the National Association for the Promotion of Social Science* (London, 1860), p. 813.

46. Katharine West, *Chapter of Governesses: A Study of the Governess in English Fiction, 1800–1949* (London, 1949), pp. 31–32.

47. Edith Gates, Diary (manuscript, 1876), 1 February 1876, Schulte MS.

48. Mary Bazlinton, Diary, 15 October 1856, House MS.

49. Mary Smith, *Autobiography*, 1, p. 169.

50. Elizabeth Gaskell, *The Life of Charlotte Brontë* (Harmondsworth, 1985; first pub. London, 1857), p. 97.

51. Barry Turner, *Equality for Some: The Story of Girls' Education* (London, 1974), p. 77.

52. Clement Shorter, (ed.), *The Brontës: Life and Letters*, 2 vols. (London, 1908), 1, p. 82.

53. Report of the Schools Inquiry Commission (hereafter SIC), *PP* 1867–68, vol. xxviii, 13, pt. 4, pp. 625–32.

54. Ibid., p. 238.

55. SIC, *PP* 1867–68, vol. xxviii, 13, pt. 1, p. 562.

56. Elizabeth M. Sewell, *Principles of Education, Drawn from Nature and Revelation and Applied to Female Education in the Upper Classes*, 2 vols. (London, 1865), 2, pp. 258–59.

57. Typically, in *The Times*, 1 February 1876, one governess offered 'French, which she has studied on the continent'.

58. Such was the experience of Edith Gates, Diary, 'written in Germany about the year 1874', Schulte MS.

59. Mrs Steuart Erskine, *Anna Jameson*, p. 48.

60. Mary Maurice, *Governess Life: Its Trials, Duties and Encouragements* (London, 1849), p. 62.

61. Ibid., p. 78.

62. 'Governesses', p. 306.

63. Brenda Colloms, *Charles Kingsley: The Lion of Eversley* (London, 1975), pp. 280–81.

64. Elizabeth Ham, *By Herself*, p. 200.

65. Margot Peters, *Unquiet Soul: A Biography of Charlotte Bronte* (London, 1975), p. 67.

66. Harriet M. Jukes, *The Earnest Christian*, ed. Mrs H. A. Gilbert (London, 1858), pp. 28–29.

67. Mary Bazlinton, Diary, 7 October 1859, House MS.

68. Ibid., 20 July 1856.

69. *GBI Report for 1846* (London, 1847), p. 12.

70. Mme Bureaud Riofrey, *Governesses: or Modern Education* (London, 1842), p. 53.

71. *The Times*, 24 September 1850.

72. *The Times*, 7 October 1830.

73. *The Times*, 13 September 1841.

74. *The Times*, 2 October 1860.

75. 'Sisters of Misery', *Punch*, 15 (July–December 1848), p. 78.

76. Alicia Percival, *The English Miss To-Day and Yesterday* (London, 1939), p. 113.

77. S.Y.E., 'Experiences in Search of a Governess', *Work and Leisure*, 1 (March 1880), p. 88.

78. Ibid., pp. 88–89.

79. For example, The Governesses Institution of 30 Soho Square which advertised in *The Times*, 20 April 1843.

80. 'The Governess Question', p. 167.

81. Lady Kay-Shuttleworth, 'Thoughts on the Relations between Mothers and Governesses', *Work and Leisure*, 1 (June 1880), p. 163.

82. *The Woman's Gazette*, 4 (November 1879), p. 169.

83. *GBI Report for 1847* (London 1848), p. 12.

84. 'Going a Governessing', *EWJ*, 1 (August 1858), p. 396.

85. The precise figures are:

Year	Registered	Engaged
1848	1509	807
1849	1506	866
1850	1370	951
1851	1167	924
1852	1238	803
1853	1446	875

Extracted from *GBI Reports for 1848–1853* (London, 1849–54).

86. 'Going a Governessing', p. 396.

87. Sir George Stephen, *Guide to Service: The Governess* (London, 1844), p. 12.

88. Mme Bureaud Riofrey, *Private Education; Or, Observations on Governesses* (London, 1836), pp. x–xi.

89. The governess was in exactly the same position here as any man, whether professional or labouring, who was applying for a job. Questions to determine 'character' – which included establishing an applicant's family background – always took precedence over enquiries about a candidate's particular suitability for a position.

90. Mary Maurice, *Governess Life*, p. 72.

91. Ibid., p. 70.

92. Elizabeth Ham, *By Herself*, p. 207.

93. Ibid.

94. Mary Bazlinton, Diary, 10 March 1855, House MS.

95. Ibid., 24 February 1856.

96. Elizabeth Ham, *By Herself*, p. 202.

97. Mary Bazlinton, Diary, 20 July 1856, House MS.

98. Lady Kay-Shuttleworth, 'Thoughts on the Relations between Mothers and Governesses, no. 2', *Work and Leisure*, 1 (August 1880), p. 227.

99. K.A., Correspondence, *Work and Leisure*, 1 (June 1880), p. 186.

100. Mary Maurice, *Governess Life*, p. 73.

101. Mary Bazlinton, Diary, 20 November 1855, House MS.

102. William Tait, an Edinburgh surgeon who conducted a survey into the city's prostitute population in 1840 certainly found a number of women who gave their former occupation as 'governess'. While some mention was made of poor economic and employment opportunities to explain why working-class women were obliged to become prostitutes, Tait was anxious to suggest that former governesses came into the category of 'fallen women' who had taken to the streets only once they had been seduced and 'betrayed' by a dishonourable suitor. Lynda Nead, *Myths of Sexuality*, pp. 95, 103. From 1850, veiled references to the fact that middle-class women who were unable to find work might have to resort to prostitution to keep themselves formed part of a standard argument about the need to open up both the professions and new types of work to women. Anna Jameson, *The Communion of Labour: A Second Lecture on the Social Employments of Women* (London, 1856), pp. 11, 82. Ellen Barlee, *Friendless and Helpless* (London, 1863), p. 133. For a discussion of the imaginative association between the governess and the prostitute, see pp. 119–121.

103. Mary Bazlinton, Diary 20 July, 1856, House MS.

104. 'Going a Governessing', p. 397.

105. Harriet M. Jukes, *The Earnest Christian*, p. 29.

106. Elizabeth M. Sewell, *Principles of Education*, 2, p. 233.

107. May Pinhorn, 'Life', pp. 47–48, Walley MS.

4. A Perfect Treadmill of Learning

1. Lynda Nead, *Myths of Sexuality: Representations of Women in Victorian Britain* (Oxford, 1990; first pub. Oxford, 1988), p. 27.

2. Mary Poovey, *Uneven Developments: The Ideological Work of Gender in Mid-Victorian England* (London, 1989; first pub. Chicago, 1988), p. 144. My discussion of Victorian motherhood, and the threat posed to it by the governess, is indebted to Poovey's brilliant chapter on the governess, 'The Anathematized Race: The Governess and Jane Eyre', especially pp. 126–48.

3. Mary Maurice, *Mothers and Governesses* (London, 1847), pp. 3–4.

4. 'Hints on the Modern Governess System', *Fraser's Magazine*, 30 (November 1844), p. 581.

5. Mary Maurice, *Governess Life: Its Trials, Duties and Encouragements* (London, 1849), p. 105.

6. Mary Poovey, *Uneven Developments*, p. 143.

7. L.H.M. Soulsby, *The Home Governess* (London, 1916), p. 6.

8. Charlotte Brontë reported that her employer, Mrs Sidgwick, 'expects me to do things I cannot do – to love her children and be entirely devoted to them'. Letter from Charlotte Brontë to her sister Emily, 8 June 1839, Clement Shorter, (ed.), *The Brontës: Life and Letters* 2 vols. (London, 1908), 1, p. 160.

9. Letter dated 20 April 1854, Nancy Mitford, (ed.), *The Stanleys of Alderley: Their Letters between the Years 1851–1865* (London, 1939), p. 92.

10. Margot Peters, *Unquiet Soul: A Biography of Charlotte Brontë* (London, 1975), p. 72.

11. Edith Gates, Diary (manuscript, 1876), 10 February 1876, Schulte MS.

12. Sybil Lubbock, *The Child in the Crystal* (London, 1939), p. 165.

13. Edith Gates, Diary, 22 February 1876, Schulte MS.

14. The dedication, shared with Lubbock's nanny, reads 'in memory of a tender nurse and a wise governess'. Sybil Lubbock, *The Child in the Crystal*, frontispiece.

15. Lady Dorothy Nevill, *The Reminiscences of Lady Dorothy Nevill*, ed. Ralph Nevill (London, 1906), p. 249.

16. Loelia Ponsonby, *Grace and Favour: The Memoirs of Loelia, Duchess of Westminster* (London, 1961), p. 61.

17. Countess of Oxford and Asquith (ed.), *Myself When Young*, By famous women of to-day (London, 1938), pp. 14–15.

18. J.A. Banks, *Prosperity and Parenthood: A Study of Family Planning among the Victorian Middle Classes* (London, 1954), p. 80.

19. Sir George Stephen, *Guide to Service: The Governess* (London, 1844), p. 109.

20. Cynthia Asquith, *Haply I May Remember* (London, 1950), p. 207.

21. Lady Frederick Cavendish, *The Diary of Lady Frederick Cavendish*, ed. John Bailey, 2 vols. (London, 1927), 1, p. 7.

22. M. Jeanne Peterson, *Family, Love, and Work in the Lives of Victorian Gentlewomen* (Bloomington, 1989), p. 49.

23. Jane Panton, *Leaves from a Life* (London, 1908), pp. 61–62.

24. Lucy Cohen, (ed.), *Lady de Rothschild and her Daughters, 1821–1931* (London, 1935), p. 81.

25. Elizabeth Ham, *By Herself*, ed. Eric Gillett (London, 1945), p. 204.

26. Mary Carbery, *Happy World: The Story of a Victorian Childhood* (London, 1941), p. 222.

27. Cynthia Asquith, *Haply I May Remember*, pp. 222–23.

28. Deborah Gorham, *The Victorian Girl and the Feminine Ideal* (London, 1982), p. 27.

29. Joan N. Burstyn, *Victorian Education and the Ideal of Womanhood* (London, 1980), p. 23.

30. Cynthia Asquith, *Haply I May Remember*, p. 218.

31. Eleanor Acland, *Goodbye for the Present: The Story of Two Childhoods. Milly: 1878–88 & Ellen: 1913–1924* (London, 1935), p. 151.

32. Mary Carbery, *Happy World* (London, 1941), p. 41.

33. Elizabeth Ham, *By Herself*, p. 206.

34. Mary Maurice, *Governess Life*, p. 16.

35. Sybil Lubbock, *The Child in the Crystal*, p. 155.

36. Ibid., p. 156.

37. Ibid.

38. Jonathan Gathorne-Hardy, *The Rise and Fall of the British Nanny* (London, 1972), ch. 4, pp. 105–48.

39. Mrs R.L. Devonshire, 'Resident Governesses', *The Parents' Review*, 13 (November 1902), p. 836.

40. Sonia Keppel, *Edwardian Daughter* (London, 1958), p. 38.

41. Mrs R.L. Devonshire, 'Resident Governesses', p. 836.

42. Angela Forbes, *Memories and Base Details* (London, 1921), p. 15.

43. Mary Carbery, *Happy World*, p. 175.

44. Jonathan Gathorne-Hardy, *The British Nanny*, p. 69.

45. Sybil Lubbock, *The Child in the Crystal*, p. 157.

46. Cynthia Asquith, *Haply I May Remember*, p. 211.

47. C.B. Firth, *Constance Louisa Maynard: A Family Portrait* (London, 1949), p. 25.

48. Edith Gates, Diary, 22 February 1876, Schulte MS.

49. Elizabeth M. Sewell, *Amy Herbert*, 2 vols. (London, 1844), 1, p. 106.

50. Anne Brontë, *Agnes Grey* (Harmondsworth, 1988; first pub. London, 1847), p. 82.

51. Mrs L. Valentine, *The Amenities of Home* (London, 1882), p. 130.

52. Mary Bazlinton, Diary (manuscript, 1854–59, not continuous), 7 April 1854, House MS.

53. May Pinhorn, 'Some Account of the Life of Mary Blanche Pinhorn' (typescript, 1926), p. 65, Walley MS.

54. Daphne Bennett, *Queen Victoria's Children* (London, 1980), p. 133.

55. Harriet Martineau, *Deerbrook* (London, 1983; first pub. London, 1839), p. 22.

56. In a letter to Ellen Nussey, Charlotte Brontë described the dilemma in which her sister Anne, who had started work as governess to the Ingham family, found herself: 'She is requested, when they [her pupils] misbehave themselves, to inform their mama, which she says is utterly out of the question, as in that case she might be making complaints from morning till night. So she alternately scolds, coaxes, and threatens …' Letter from Charlotte Brontë to Ellen Nussey, 15 April 1839, Clement Shorter (ed.), *The Brontës: Life and Letters*, 1, p. 155.

57. Sybil Lubbock, *The Child in the Crystal*, p. 163.

58. Letter from Charlotte Brontë to her sister Emily, 8 June 1839, Clement Shorter (ed.), *The Brontës: Life and Letters*, 1, p. 158.

59. May Pinhorn, 'Life', p. 60, Walley MS.

60. Mary Maurice, *Governess Life*, p. 127.

61. Lady Muriel Beckwith, *When I Remember* (London, 1936), pp. 88–89.

62. Mary Bazlinton, Diary, 10 April 1855, House MS. Bazlinton's handwriting is hard to read and the names, or rather nicknames, of her two pupils difficult to fathom: 'Tiney' and 'Toddy' remain the best approximations.

63. 'Home Schoolroom and Private Governesses, Chapter 1', *Work and Leisure*, 10 (May 1885), p. 129.

64. Jane Panton, *Leaves from a Life*, p. 83.

65. Cynthia Asquith, *Haply I May Remember*, p. 215.

66. Ibid.

67. Juliet Clough, 'A Gentle Fade-Out for the Governess', *Illustrated London News*, 257 (September 12, 1970), p. 17.

68. Angela Forbes, *Memories and Base Details*, p. 14.

69. Jo Manton, *Elizabeth Garrett Anderson* (London, 1958), p. 17.

70. Jane Panton, *Leaves from a Life*, p. 63.

71. Lady Frederick Cavendish, *Diary*, 1, pp. 7–8.

72. Kenneth Rose, *Superior Person* (London, 1969), p. 20.

73. Daphne Bennett, *Queen Victoria's Children*, p. 25.

74. Loelia Ponsonby, *Grace and Favour*, p. 56.

75. Mary Carbery, *Happy World*, p. 193.

76. Osbert Sitwell (ed.), *Two Generations* (London, 1940), p. 27.

77. Lady Frederick Cavendish, *Diary*, 1, p. 11.

78. Winifred Peck, *A Little Learning: Or, a Victorian Childhood* (London, 1952), pp. 21–25.

79. Cynthia Asquith, *Haply I May Remember*, p. 213.

80. Osbert Sitwell (ed.), *Two Generations*, p. 21.

81. Sonia Keppel, *Edwardian Daughter*, p. 86.

82. In the 1830s the Sitwell girls were expected to be out in the fresh air for three to four hours every day. Osbert Sitwell (ed.), *Two Generations*, p. 29.

83. Sybil Lubbock, *The Child in the Crystal*, p. 157.

84. E.M. Almedingen, *Fanny* (London, 1970), p. 50.

85. Osbert Sitwell (ed.), *Two Generations*, p. 29.

86. See, for example, Cynthia Asquith, *Haply I May Remember*, p. 211–12.

87. Lady Muriel Beckwith, *When I Remember*, p. 91.

88. Sybil Lubbock, *The Child in the Crystal*, p. 165.

89. Mary Paley Marshall, *What I Remember* (Cambridge, 1947), p. 6.

90. Margaret Thornley, *The True End of Education and the Means Adapted To It* (Edinburgh, 1846), p. 35.

91. R.M. Mangnall, *Historical and Miscellaneous Questions* (London, 1800).

92. These are all texts mentioned by autobiographers when recalling their schooldays.

93. Sir George Stephen, *Guide To Service*, p. 43.

94. Ibid., p. 51.

95. Ibid., p. 12.

96. L.H.M. Soulsby, *The Home Governess*, p. 9

97. Harriet Martineau, 'The Governess', p. 269.

98. Jane Panton, *Leaves from a Life*, p. 63.

99. Sybil Lubbock, *The Child in the Crystal*, p. 160.

100. C.B. Firth, *Constance Louisa Maynard*, pp. 22–23.

101. Elizabeth M. Sewell, *Principles of Education, Drawn from Nature and Revelation and Applied to Female Education in the Upper Classes*, 2 vols. (London, 1865), 2, p. 256.

102. 'Home Schoolrooms and Private Governesses, Chapter 3', *Work and Leisure*, 10 (July 1885), p. 192.

103. Sara Delamont and Lorna Duffin (eds.), *The Nineteenth-Century Woman: Her Cultural and Physical World* (London, 1978), p. 177.

104. Jane Panton, *Leaves from a Life*, p. 83.

105. Edith Gates, Diary, 10 March 1876, Schulte MS.

106. Sybil Lubbock, *The Child in the Crystal*, p. 186.

107. Anne Brontë, *Agnes Grey*, p. 206.

108. Edith Gates, Diary, 1 February 1876, Schulte MS.

109. Ibid.

110. Bea Howe, *A Galaxy of Governesses* (London, 1954), p. 98.

111. Cynthia Asquith, *Haply I May Remember*, p. 216.

112. Mary Carbery, *Happy World*, p. 184.

113. Sybil Lubbock, *The Child in the Crystal*, pp. 180–81.

114. M. Jeanne Peterson, *Family, Love and Work*, p. 40.

115. Cynthia Asquith, *Haply I May Remember*, p. 220.

116. Sybil Lubbock, *The Child in the Crystal*, p. 174.

117. Edith Gates, Diary, 2 April 1876, Schulte MS.

118. May Pinhorn, 'Life', Walley MS, p. 70.

119. Margaret Thornley, *The True Means of Education*, p. 9.

120. Eleanor Acland, *Good-bye for the Present*, pp. 152–53.

121. M. Jeanne Peterson, *Family, Love and Work*, p. 42.

122. Mary Paley Marshall, *What I Remember*, p. 8.

123. Report of the Schools Inquiry Commission (hereafter SIC), Parliamentary Papers (hereafter *PP*), 1867–68, vol. xxviii, 13, pt. 4, p. 257. Although it is not clear whether the home education of which Buss speaks was supervised by mothers or governesses, the point remains that the concentrated attention of one adult, no matter how ill-prepared for her task, could often bring better results than attendance at an indifferent school.

124. Carol Dyhouse, *Girls Growing Up in Late Victorian and Edwardian England* (London, 1981), p. 45.

125. Jo Manton, *Elizabeth Garrett Anderson*, pp. 15–18.

126. Lady Georgina Peel, *The Recollections of Lady Georgina Peel*, ed. E. Peel (London, 1920), pp. 59–60.

127. Mrs R.L. Devonshire, 'Resident Governesses', p. 837.

128. Lady Frederick Cavendish, *Diary*, 1, p. 10.

129. See, for instance, the Countess of Blessington, *The Governess* (London, 1839); Elizabeth Sewell, *Amy Herbert* (London, 1844); Henry Courtney Selous, *The Young Governess* (London, 1872).

130. Sir George Stephen, *Guide to Service*, p. 106.

131. L.H.M. Soulsby, *The Home Governess*, p. 7.

132. Mary Smith, *Autobiography of Mary Smith, Schoolmistress and Nonconformist*, 2 vols. (London, 1892), 1, p. 180.

133. See pp. 108–9.

134. Cynthia Asquith, *Haply I May Remember*, pp. 207–8.

135. Sybil Lubbock, *The Child in the Crystal*, p. 158.

136. Anna Jameson, *The Relative Social Position of Mothers and Governesses* (London, 1846), p. 22.

137. Edmund Gosse, *Father and Son: A Study of Two Temperaments* (Harmondsworth, 1986; first pub. London, 1907), p. 97.

138. Anna Jameson, *The Relative Social Position of Mothers and Governesses*, p. 4.

139. C.M. Yonge, *Womankind* (London, 1876), p. 35.

140. Carol Dyhouse, *Girls Growing Up*, p. 35.
141. Cynthia Asquith, *Haply I May Remember*, p. 218.
142. Eleanor Farjeon, *A Nursery in the Nineties* (London, 1960; first pub., London, 1935), p. 408.
143. Edith Gates, Diary, 10 February 1876, Schulte MS.
144. Mary Bazlinton, Diary, 16 October, 1859, House MS.
145. Countess of Oxford and Asquith (ed.), *Myself When Young*, p. 191.
146. Cynthia Asquith, *Haply I May Remember*, p. 209.
147. Mary Bazlinton, Diary, 20 November 1855, House MS.
148. Sybil Lubbock, *The Child in the Crystal*, pp. 240–41.

5. They Dwell Alone

1. Letter from Charlotte Brontë to Ellen Nussey, 1 July 1839, Clement Shorter (ed.), *The Brontës: Life and Letters*, 2 vols. (London, 1908). 1, p. 160.

2. The concept of 'status incongruence', and its use in understanding the governess' situation, is taken from M. Jeanne Peterson's pioneering article, 'The Victorian Governess: Status Incongruence in Family and Society', in Martha Vicinus (ed.), *Suffer and Be Still: Women in the Victorian Age* (London, 1980; first pub., Bloomington, 1972), pp. 3–19.

3. Anna Jameson, *The Relative Social Position of Mothers and Governesses* (London, 1846), pp. 35–36.

4. Mrs L. Valentine, *The Amenities of Home* (London, 1886), pp. 131–32.

5. Frances Power Cobbe, *Life of Frances Power Cobbe*, 2 vols. (London, 1894), 1, p. 51.

6. Cynthia Asquith, *Haply I May Remember* (London, 1950), p. 211.

7. Jane Panton, *More Leaves from a Life* (London, 1911), pp. 2–3.

8. Cynthia Asquith, *Haply I May Remember*, p. 145.

9. Lady Frederick Cavendish, *The Diary of Lady Frederick Cavendish*, 2 vols., ed. John Bailey (London, 1927), 1, p. 28.

10. Mary Carbery, *Happy World: The Story of a Victorian Childhood* (London, 1941), p. 186.

11. Mary Maurice, *Governess Life: Its Trials, Duties, and Encouragements* (London, 1849), p. 19.

12. Katharine West, *Chapter of Governesses: A Study of the Governess in English Fiction, 1800–1949* (London, 1949), p. 60.

13. Mary Cowden-Clarke, *My Long Life: An Autobiographical Sketch* (London, 1896), p. 35.

14. May Pinhorn, 'Some Account of the Life of Mary Blanche Pinhorn' (typescript, 1926), p. 53, Walley MS.

15. Letter from Charlotte Brontë to Emily Brontë, 8 June 1839, quoted in Elizabeth Gaskell, *The Life of Charlotte Brontë* (Harmondsworth, 1985; first pub. London, 1857), p. 187.

16. May Pinhorn, 'Life', p. 52, Walley MS.

17. Elizabeth Ham, *By Herself*, ed. Eric Gillett (London, 1945), p. 204.

18. Ibid., p. 224.

19. Ibid., p. 227. Ham's experience seems to confirm the mechanism whereby a governess returning to her own community after several years working for a smart family might find her marriage prospects much improved as a consequence of her association with a high-status household.

20. May Pinhorn, 'Life', p. 93, Walley MS.

21. Katharine West, *Chapter of Governesses*, p. 60.

22. Letter from Charlotte Brontë to Ellen Nussey, 4 May 1841, Clement Shorter (ed.), *The Brontës: Life and Letters*, 1, p. 210.

23. Letter from Charlotte Brontë to her sister Emily, undated July 1839, ibid., p. 162.

24. Elizabeth Ham, *By Herself*, p. 207.

25. Letter from Ellen Weeton to Tom Weeton, 28 January 1810, in Edward Hall, (ed.), *Miss Weeton's, Journal of a Governess Volume 1, 1807–1811* (New York, 1969; first pub., London, 1936), p. 227.

26. Lady [Elizabeth] Eastlake, '*Vanity Fair, Jane Eyre* and the Governesses' Benevolent Institution', *Quarterly Review*, 84 (December 1848), p. 177.

27. Mme Bureaud Riofrey, *Private Education: Or, Observations on Governesses* (London, 1836), pp. 119–120.

28. Countess of Blessington, *The Governess*, 2 vols. (London, 1839), 1, p. 58.

29. 'The Governess Question', *English Woman's Journal* (hereafter *EWJ*), 4 (November 1959), p. 164.

30. Elizabeth Ham, *By Herself*, p. 224.

31. See, for instance, Elizabeth M. Sewell, *Amy Herbert*, 2 vols., (London, 1844), 1, p. 61.

32. Lady Frederick Cavendish, *Diary*, 1, p. 36.

33. Edmund Gosse, *Father and Son: A Study of Two Temperaments* (Harmondsworth, 1986; first pub., London, 1907), p. 96.

34. Juliet Clough, 'A Gentle Fade-Out for the Governess', *Illustrated London News*, 257 (September 12 1970), p. 17.

35. Henry Courtney Selous, *The Young Governess* (London, 1872), p. 24.

36. Ibid., p. 161.

37. Elizabeth M. Sewell, *Amy Herbert*, 1, p. 210.

38. Ibid., 1, p. 234.

39. Sonia Keppel, *Edwardian Daughter* (London, 1958), p. 86.

40. Countess of Blessington, *The Governess*, 1, p. 89.

41. S.S.H., 'The Social Position of Governesses', *Work and Leisure* (October 1893), p. 276.

42. Elizabeth Ham, *By Herself*, p. 223.

43. Mrs L. Valentine, *The Amenities of Home*, p. 134.

44. Letter from Charlotte Brontë to Ellen Nussey, 7 August 1841, quoted in Elizabeth Gaskell, *The Life of Charlotte Brontë*, p. 117.

45. Apprehensive because Mr Rochester has requested her presence in the drawing-room where he is entertaining a large houseparty, Jane Eyre is reassured by Mrs Fairfax, the housekeeper, that 'nobody will notice you'. Charlotte Brontë, *Jane Eyre* (Harmondsworth, 1985; first pub. London, 1847), p. 199.

46. Anne Brontë, *Agnes Grey* (Harmondsworth, 1988; first pub., London, 1847), pp. 161–162.

47. Mary Maurice, *Mothers and Governesses* (London, 1847), p. 56.

48. Harriet Martineau, *Deerbrook* (London, 1983; first pub., London, 1839), p. 397.

49. 'Hints on The Modern Governess System', *Fraser's Magazine*, 30 (November 1844), p. 575.

50. Ibid., p. 582.

51. Sybil Lubbock, *The Child in the Crystal* (London, 1939) p. 164. Miss Cutting's independence was further assured by the fact that, as a daily governess, she returned to her own lodgings every night.

52. Edith Gates, Diary (manuscript, 1876), 1 February 1876, Schulte MS.

53. Ibid., 1 February 1876.

54. Ibid., 17 February 1876.

55. Mary Cowden-Clarke, *My Long Life*, p. 38.

56. Edith Gates, Diary, 12 March 1876, Schulte MS.

57. Letter from Charlotte Brontë to Ellen Nussey, 3 March 1841, Clement Shorter (ed.), *The Brontës: Life and Letters*, 1, p. 204.

58. This is one of Martha Vicinus' central theses in her *Independent Women: Work and Community for Single Women, 1850–1920*, (London, 1985; first pub. Chicago, 1985).

59. 'Hints on the Modern Governess System', p. 575.

60. Mary Smith, *The Autobiography of Mary Smith, Schoolmistress and Nonconformist*, 2 vols. (London, 1892), 1, p. 149.

61. 'The Governess Question', p. 164.

62. S.S.H., 'The Social Position of Governesses', p. 277.

63. Lady Kay-Shuttleworth, 'Thoughts on the Relations between Mothers and Governesses, no. 2', *Work and Leisure*, 1 (August 1980), p. 227.

64. Edith Gates, Diary, 28 February 1876, Schulte MS.

65. Mary Carbery, *Happy World*, p. 89.

66. Edith Gates, Diary, 19 March 1876, Schulte MS.

67. Ibid., 16 February 1876.

68. Ibid., 6 April 1876.

69. Ibid., 23 March 1876.

70. Ibid., 6 February 1876.

71. Ibid., 5 February 1876.

72. Mary Cowden-Clarke, *My Long Life*, p. 34.

73. Edith Gates, Diary, 5 February 1876, Schulte MS.

74. Census of England and Wales, 1861, vol. 2, *Parliamentary Papers* (hereafter, *PP*), 1863, table xxxi, p. xc.

75. Sybil Lubbock, *The Child in the Crystal*, p. 161.

76. Alicia Percival, *The English Miss To-Day and Yesterday* (London, 1939), p. 103.

77. C.M. Yonge, *Womankind* (London, 1876), p. 38.

78. Mary Maurice, *Mothers and Governesses*, p. 13.

79. Elizabeth M. Sewell, *Amy Herbert*, 1, p. 172.

80. Mrs R.L. Devonshire, 'Resident Governesses', *Parents' Review*, 13 (November 1902), p. 843.

81. Daphne Fielding, *Mercury Presides* (London, 1954), p. 43.

82. 'Employment of Women in Germany', *EWJ*, 5 (March 1860), p. 55; 'The Position of Women In France', *EWJ*, 5 (April 1860), pp. 95–96.

83. Winifred Peck, *A Little Learning: Or, a Victorian Childhood* (London, 1952), p. 103.

84. Sonia Keppel, *Edwardian Daughter*, p. 129.

85. Mrs L. Valentine, *The Amenities of Home*, p. 133.

86. Quoted in Clement Shorter, (ed.), *The Brontës: Life and Letters*, 1, p. 157.

87. Mary Bazlinton, Diary (manuscript, 1854–59, not continuous), 4 March 1855, House MS.

88. Ibid., 15 July 1855.

89. Ibid., 10 April 1855.

90. Ibid., 6, 11, 15 April 1855.

91. Ibid., 29 July 1855.

92. Ibid., 12 June 1855.

93. Ibid., 1 March 1855.

94. Ibid., 28 July 1855.

95. Ibid., 20 November 1855.

96. Mrs R.L. Devonshire, 'Resident Governesses', p. 834.

97. Mrs Isabella Beeton, *Mrs Beeton's Book of Household Management*, 2 vols. (London, 1861), 1, p. 9.

98. May Pinhorn, 'Life', p. 94, Walley MS.

99. Lady Frederick Cavendish, *Diary*, 1, p. 11.

100. Cynthia Asquith, *Haply I May Remember*, p. 208.

101. Mrs R.L. Devonshire, 'Resident Governesses', p. 840.
102. Anna Jameson, *The Relative Social Position of Mothers and Governesses*, p. 43.
103. Mrs R.L. Devonshire, 'Resident Governesses', p. 839.
104. C.M. Yonge, *Womankind*, p. 37.
105. May Pinhorn, 'Life', pp. 63–64, Walley MS.
106. Ibid., p. 70.

6.   A Tabooed Woman

1. A. James Hammerton, *Emigrant Gentlewomen: Genteel Poverty and Female Emigration, 1830–1914* (London, 1979), p. 29.

2. Ibid., p. 30.

3. Martha Vicinus, *Independent Women: Work and Community for Single Women, 1850–1920* (London, 1985; first pub., Chicago, 1985), p. 32.

4. 14,476 of the total governess population of England and Wales were under thirty in 1861. Census of England and Wales, 1861, vol. 2, *Parliamentary Papers* (hereafter *PP*) 1863, table xx, p. lvii.

5. Mary Poovey, *Uneven Developments: The Ideological Work of Gender in Mid-Victorian England* (London, 1989; first pub., Chicago, 1988), p. 131.

6. F.M.L. Thompson, *The Rise of Respectable Society, 1830–1900* (London, 1988), p. 258.

7. Harriet Martineau, 'The Governess', *Once a Week*, 3 (September 1860), p. 269.

8. Lynda Nead, *Myths of Sexuality: Representations of Women in Victorian Britain* (Oxford, 1990; first pub., Oxford, 1988), p. 103.

9. For a further discussion of the fallen woman, see ibid., pp. 95–96.

10. 'Hints on the Modern Governess System', *Fraser's Magazine*, 30 (November 1844), p. 574.

11. Bernard Taylor, *Cruelly Murdered: Constance Kent and the Killing at Road Hill House* (London, 1989; first pub., London, 1979), pp. 31–32.

12. Loelia Ponsonby, *Grace and Favour: The Memoirs of Loelia, Duchess of Westminster* (London, 1962), p. 55.

13. Elizabeth Ham, *By Herself*, ed. Eric Gillett (London, 1945), p. 226.

14. Ibid., p. 230.

15. 'The Governess Question', *English Woman's Journal* (hereafter *EWJ*), 4 (November 1859), p. 164.

16. William Thackeray, *Vanity Fair* (Harmondsworth, 1968; first pub. London 1848), p. 96.

17. Augustus Hare, *The Story of My Life*, 6 vols. (London, 1896–1900), 1, p. 176.

18. See ch. 7, pp. 184–88.

19. Lynda Nead, *Myths of Sexuality*, p. 158.

20. Edmund Gosse, *Father and Son: A Study of Two Temperaments* (Harmondsworth, 1986; first pub., London, 1907), pp. 181–82.

21. May Pinhorn, 'Some Account of the Life of Mary Blanche Pinhorn' (typescript, 1926), pp. 53–54, Walley MS.

22. Henry James, *The Turn of The Screw* (Harmondsworth, 1986; first pub. New York, 1907–9).

23. Mme Bureaud Riofrey, *Governesses: Or, Modern Education* (London, 1842), p. 88.

24. Lady [Elizabeth] Eastlake, '*Vanity Fair, Jane Eyre* and the Governesses' Benevolent Institution', *Quarterly Review*, 84 (December, 1848), p. 177.

25. Mary Maurice, *Governess Life: Its Trials, Duties, and Encouragements* (London, 1849), pp. 14–15.

26. Ibid., p. 52.

27. William Thackeray, *Vanity Fair*, p. 135.

28. Mme Bureaud Riofrey, *Private Education; Or, Observations on Governesses* (London, 1836), p. 77.

29. May Pinhorn, 'Life', p. 60, Walley MS.

30. Elizabeth Ham, *By Herself*, p. 207.

31. Mary Smith, *The Autobiography of Mary Smith, Schoolmistress and Nonconformist*, 2 vols. (London, 1892), 1, p. 151.

32. 'Hints on the Modern Governess System', p. 577.

33. Governesses' Benevolent Institution, *Report of the Bord of Management* (hereafter *GBI Report*) *for 1843* (London, 1844), p. 13.

34. Charlotte Brontë, *Jane Eyre* (Harmondsworth, 1985; first pub. London, 1847), p. 146.

35. Mary Cowden-Clarke, *My Long Life: An Autobiographical Sketch* (London, 1896), pp. 37–38.

36. This painting appears as an illustration in the plate section of this book.

37. Theresa M. McBride, *The Domestic Revolution: The Modernization of Household Service in England and France, 1820–1920* (London, 1976), p. 25.

38. May Pinhorn, *Life*, p. 51, Walley MS.

39. Mme Bureaud Riofrey, *Private Education; Or, Observations on Governesses*, p. 72.

40. Anna Jameson, *The Relative Social Position of Mothers and Governesses* (London, 1846), p. 49.

41. Beryl L. Booker, *Yesterday's Child: 1890–1909* (London, 1937), p. 71.

42. E.M. Almedingen, *Fanny* (London, 1970), p. 71.

43. Eleanor Farjeon, *A Nursery in the Nineties* (London, 1960; first pub. London, 1935), pp. 408–9.

44. Jane Panton, *Leaves from a Life* (London, 1908), p. 210.

45. Ibid., p. 82.

46. Osbert Sitwell (ed.), *Two Generations* (London, 1940), p. 28.

47. Letter from May Pinhorn, undated, Walley MS.

48. Edith Gates, Diary (manuscript, 1876), 6 February 1876, Schulte MS.

49. Lucy Cohen (ed.), *Lady de Rothschild and her Daughters, 1821–1931* (London, 1935), p. 100.

50. Winifred Peck, *A Little Learning: Or, a Victorian Childhood* (London, 1952), p. 107.

51. Osbert Sitwell (ed.), *Two Generations*, p. 249.

52. Lucy Cohen (ed.), *Lady de Rothschild and her Daughters*, p. 82.

53. Ibid., p. 84.

54. Ibid., p. 84.

55. May Pinhorn, 'Life', p. 48, Walley MS.

56. The story of Miss Lucy R. is told in Sigmund Freud and Joseph Breuer, *Studies on Hysteria* (Harmondsworth, 1974; first pub. Vienna, 1885), pp. 169–89.

57. The story of Celestine Doudet is told in Mary S. Hartman, *Victorian Murderesses: A True History of Thirteen Respectable French and English Women Accused of Unspeakable Crimes* (London, 1977), ch. 3, pp. 85–129.

58. Edmund Gosse, *Father and Son*, pp. 107–8.

59. This compelling interest in flagellation seems to have been – and continues to be – confined to this country. My discussion of the subject is indebted to Ian Gibson, *The English Vice: Beating, Sex and Shame in Victorian England and After* (London, 1978), chs. 2, 5, pp. 48–98, 194–232; and Steven Marcus, *The Other Victorians: A Study of Sexuality and Pornography in Mid-Nineteenth Century England* (London, 1966), ch. 6, pp. 252–65.

60. Quoted in Ian Gibson, *The English Vice*, pp. 221–22.

61. Steven Marcus, *The Other Victorians*, p. 260.

62. Leonore Davidoff, 'Class and Gender in Victorian England', in Judith L. Newton, Mary P. Ryan and Judith R. Walkowitz (eds.), *Sex and Class in Women's History* (London, 1983), pp. 17–71.

63. Edith Gates, Diary, 14 February 1876, Schulte MS.

64. Information about Edith Gates' subsequent life is drawn from correspondence with her granddaughter, Anne Schulte.

65. Charlotte Brontë, *Shirley* (Harmondsworth, 1985; first pub., London, 1849), p. 367.

66. Information about Blanche Borthwick is drawn from correspondence with Rosemary Shaw.

67. Mary Cowden-Clarke, *My Long Life*, p. 35.

68. Sir George Stephen, *Guide to Service: The Governess* (London, 1844), p. 346.

69. Countess of Blessington, *The Young Governess*, 2 vols (London, 1839), 1, pp. 163–64.

70. Theresa M. McBride, *The Domestic Revolution*, pp. 94–95.

71. Mary Cowden-Clarke, *My Long Life*, pp. 34–35.

72. Bea Howe, *A Galaxy of Governesses* (London, 1954), p. 88.

73. Mary Maurice, *Mothers and Governesses* (London, 1847), p. 34.

74. Charlotte Brontë, *Jane Eyre*, p. 207.

75. May Pinhorn, 'Life', p. 77, Walley MS.

76. Ibid., pp. 84–85.

77. Theresa M. McBride, *The Domestic Revolution*, ch. 5, pp. 82–98.

78. See, for example, the way in which Elizabeth Ham was greeted by local tradesmen when she returned to Bath with her well-placed employers, the Eltons. See ch. 4, p. 92.

79. Katharine West, *Chapter of Governesses: A Study of the Governess in English Fiction, 1800–1949* (London, 1949), p. 121.

80. In the GBI's Report for 1850, twelve of the seventy-five women whose case histories are given are widows. Most of these seem to have worked as governesses prior to their marriage before returning to the schoolroom on the death of their husbands. *GBI Report for 1850* (London, 1851), pp. 19–27.

7.   A Contract Without Equality

1. Nancy Mitford (ed.), *The Ladies of Alderley, 1841–1850* (London, 1938), p. 134.

2. Theresa M. McBride, *The Domestic Revolution: The Modernization of Household Service in England and France, 1820–1920* (London, 1976), p. 62.

3. See ch. 7, p.197.

4. For governesses in *Punch*, see Alison Adburgham, *A Punch History of Modern Manners and Modes, 1841–1940* (London, 1961), pp. 86–87, 99.

5. My discussion of the fears and anxieties which lay behind contemporaries' discussion of the governess' plight is indebted to Mary Poovey's 'The Anathematized Race: The Governess and Jane Eyre', in her *Uneven Developments: The Ideological Work of Gender in Mid-Victorian England* (London, 1989; first pub. Chicago, 1988), pp. 126–63.

6. Select Committee on Factory Children's Labour (Sadler's Committee), 1831–32; Children's Employment Commission, Mines, 1842.

7. Mary Poovey, *Uneven Developments*, p. 128; Jane Rendall, '"A Moral Engine"? Feminism, Liberalism and the *English Woman's Journal* in Jane Rendall (ed.), *Equal or Different: Women's Politics, 1800–1914* (Oxford, 1987).

8. Mary Maurice, *Governess Life: Its Trials, Duties, and Encouragements* (London, 1849), pp. 114–15.

9. Anna Jameson, *The Relative Social Position of Mothers and Governesses* (London, 1846), pp. 7–8.

10. Mary Smith, *The Autobiography of Mary Smith, Schoolmistress and Nonconformist*, 2 vols. (London, 1892), 1, p. 180.

11. Elizabeth Ham, *By Herself*, ed. Eric Gillett (London, 1945), p. 226.

12. Advertisements placed by clergymen employers in *The Times* frequently ask for a governess who would be prepared to undertake these tasks.

13. Mary Smith, *Autobiography*, 1, p. 132.

14. Letter from Charlotte Brontë to Emily Brontë, 8 June 1839, Clement Shorter (ed.), *The Brontës: Life and Letters*, 2 vols. (London, 1908), 1, pp. 158–59.

15. Edmund Gosse, *Father and Son: The Study of Two Temperaments* (Harmondsworth, 1986; first pub., London, 1907), pp. 181–82.

16. Elizabeth Ham, *By Herself*, p. 226.

17. Mary Smith, *Autobiography*, 1, pp. 145–46.

18. Letter from Charlotte Brontë to Ellen Nussey, 7 August 1841, Clement Shorter (ed.), *The Brontës: Life and Letters*, 1, p. 218.

19. Winifred Peck, *A Little Learning: Or, a Victorian Childhood* (London, 1952), p. 59.

20. Letter from Charlotte Brontë to Ellen Nussey, 1 April 1841, Clement Shorter (ed.), *The Brontës: Life and Letters*, 1, p. 207.

21. May Pinhorn, 'Some Account of the Life of Mary Blanche Pinhorn' (typescript, 1926), pp. 50–51, Walley MS.

22. Osbert Sitwell (ed.), *Two Generations* (London, 1940), p. 27.

23. Edith Gates, Diary (manuscript, 1876), 1 April 1876, Schulte MS.

24. 'The Governess Question', *English Woman's Journal* (hereafter *EWJ*), 4 (November 1859), p. 164.

25. Henry Courtney Selous, *The Young Governess* (London, 1872), p. 6.

26. Louisa Anderson, *Elizabeth Garrett Anderson* (London, 1939), pp. 30–31.

27. Mary Bazlinton, Diary (manuscript, 1854–59, not continuous), 18 June 1855, House MS.

28. Sonia Keppel, *Edwardian Daughter* (London, 1958), p. 15.

29. 'Hints on the Modern Governess System', *Fraser's Magazine*, 30 (November 1844), pp. 575–76.

30. Sir George Stephen, *Guide to Service: The Governess* (London, 1844), p. 360.

31. 'Hints on the Modern Governess System', p. 578.

32. By 1861 Harriet Martineau was referring to 'the well-known descriptions and appeals, of which the world's heart is weary, derived from the life and lot of the governess . . .' Harriet Martineau, 'The Governess', *Once a Week*, 3 (September 1860), p. 269.

33. Mary Bazlinton, Diary, 3 August 1856, House MS.

34. Governesses' Benevolent Institution, *Report of the Board of Management* (hereafter *GBI Report) for 1853* (London, 1854), p. 27.

35. Mary Cowden-Clarke, *My Long Life: An Autobiographical Sketch*, (London, 1896), p. 37.

36. May Pinhorn, 'Life', p. 47, Walley MS.

37. Lady Eastlake, for instance, mentions 100 to 120 guineas as being the once-typical governess' salary, a figure to which the best-qualified could not now aspire. Lady [Elizabeth] Eastlake, '*Vanity Fair, Jane Eyre*, and The Governesses' Benevolent Institution', *Quarterly Review*, 84 (December 1848), p. 180.

38. Sir George Stephen, *Guide to Service*, pp. 352–53.

39. Mary Maurice, *Mothers and Governesses* (London, 1847), p. 100.

40. Sarah Lewis, 'On the Social Position of Governesses', *Fraser's Magazine*, 34 (April 1848), p. 413.

41. Lady [Elizabeth] Eastlake, '*Vanity Fair, Jane Eyre*, and the Governesses' Benevolent Institution', p. 179.

42. 'Hints on the Modern Governess System', pp. 578–80.

43. Ibid., p. 579.

44. This figure does seem high. It may be that the writer's desire to stress the discrepancy between the amount that parents were prepared to pay for accomplishments and the figure that they would lay out for a governess led to an exaggeration of the sum generally received by masters.

45. 'Governesses', *Eliza Cook's Journal*, 1 (September 1849), p. 306.

46. Mrs Isabella Beeton, *Mrs Beeton's Book of Household Management*, 2 vols. (London, 1861), 1, p. 8.

47. Sir George Stephen, *Guide to Service*, p. 354.

48. Patricia Branca, *Silent Sisterhood: Middle-Class Women in the Victorian Home* (London, 1975), p. 40.

49. Theresa M. McBride, *The Domestic Revolution*, pp. 57–59.

50. Ibid., p. 62.

51. Ibid.

52. *GBI Report for 1850* (London, 1851), pp. 19–27.

53. Ibid., pp. 21, 22.

54. Mary Cowden-Clarke, *My Long Life*, p. 37.

55. Sir George Stephen, *Guide to Service*, p. 356.

56. *GBI Report for 1843* (London, 1844), p. 15.

57. Sir George Stephen, *Guide To Service*, p. 358.

58. *GBI Report for 1843* (London, 1844), p. 16.

59. 'Hints on the Modern Governess System', p. 578.

60. Mary Cowden-Clarke, *My Long Life*, p. 39.

61. Elizabeth Ham, *By Herself*, p. 206.

62. May Pinhorn, 'Life', p. 51, Walley MS.

63. Mary Cowden-Clarke, *My Long Life*, p. 42.

64. Sir George Stephen, *Guide to Service*, p. 355.

65. Anna Jameson, *The Relative Social Position of Mothers and Governesses*, p. 27.

66. Letter from Charlotte Brontë to Ellen Nussey, 1 July 1839, Clement Shorter (ed.), *The Brontës: Life and Letters*, 1, pp. 160–61.

67. Elizabeth Ham, *By Herself*, p. 208.

68. Harriet Martineau, *Deerbrook* (London, 1983; first pub., London, 1839), p. 254.

69. Lady Frederick Cavendish, *The Diary of Lady Frederick Cavendish*, ed. John Bailey, 2 vols. (London, 1927), 1, p. 11.

70. 'Going a Governessing', *EWJ*, 1 (March 1858), p. 397.

71. Lady [Elizabeth] Eastlake, '*Vanity Fair, Jane Eyre* and the Governesses' Benevolent Institution', p. 177.

72. See Table 2, p. 206. This table is adapted from A. James Hammerton, *Emigrant Gentlewomen: Genteel Poverty and Female Emigration, 1830–1919* (London, 1979), Table 1: 'Selected Former Occupations of Lunatics Compared to Total of Each Occupation in Population, England and Wales, (1861)', p. 26.

73. Leonore Davidoff, 'The English Victorian Governess' (unpublished article, 1971), p. 51.

74. Elaine Showalter, *The Female Malady: Women, Madness and Culture in England, 1830–1980* (London, 1987; first pub., New York, 1985), p. 29.

75. William L. Parry-Jones, *The Trade in Lunacy: A Study of Private Madhouses in the Eighteenth and Nineteenth Centuries* (London, 1972), p. 126.

76. Bea Howe, *A Galaxy of Governesses* (London, 1954), p. 116.

77. Elaine Showalter, *The Female Malady*, pp. 35–40.

78. Anna Jameson, *The Relative Social Position of Mothers and Governesses*, p. 46.

79. Lady [Elizabeth] Eastlake, '*Vanity Fair, Jane Eyre* and the Governesses' Benevolent Institution', p. 177.

80. Ibid., pp. 173–74.

81. Mary Smith, *Autobiography*, 1, pp. 153–54.

82. Mary Bazlinton, Diary, 19 February 1854, House MS.

83. Anne Brontë, *Agnes Grey* (Harmondworth, 1988; first pub., London, 1847), p. 222.

84. Mary Smith, *Autobiography*, 1, p. 220.

85. Mary Maurice, *Governess Life*, p. 40.

86. Report of the Schools Inquiry Commission (hereafter SIC), *Parliamentary Papers* (hereafter *PP*) 1867–68, vol. xxviii, 13, pt. 4, pp. 628–29.

87. *GBI Report for 1853* (London, 1854), p. 23.

88. Letter from Charlotte Brontë to Ellen Nussey, 29 July 1844, Clement Shorter (ed.) *The Brontës: Life and Letters*, 1, p. 283.

89. *GBI Report for 1853* (London, 1854), pp. 27–28.

90. When May Pinhorn retired from governessing in 1914 and set up house with her sister, she found herself quite unprepared for domestic life: '. . . I settled down to learn how to cook and housekeep . . . At first I was rather nervous about the success of my efforts but soon got used to managing our simple regime'. May Pinhorn, *Life*, pp. 97–98, Walley MS.

91. *GBI Report for 1850* (London, 1851), pp. 19–27.

92. 'The Governess Question', p. 166.

93. Mary Maurice, *Mothers and Governesses*, p. 132.

94. See, for example, Elizabeth Ham, *By Herself*, p. 202.

95. Mrs Steuart Erskine, *Anna Jameson Letters and Friendships, 1812–1860* (London, 1915), p. 61.

96. Mary Bazlinton, Diary, 19 June 1855, House MS.

97. Elizabeth Ham, *By Herself*, p. 207.

98. *The Reminiscences of Lady Dorothy Nevill*, ed. R Nevill (London, 1906), p. 9.

99. Harriet Martineau, 'The Governess', p. 270.

100. See, typically, the case of elderly governess Miss Harriet F---R who was described by the GBI to be 'entirely dependent on the kindness of friends', *GBI Report for 1846* (London, 1847), p. 19.

101. Lady [Elizabeth] Eastlake, '*Vanity Fair, Jane Eyre*, and the Governesses' Benevolent Institution', p. 180.

102. *GBI Report for 1846* (London, 1847), p. 12.

103. Winifred Peck, *A Little Learning*, pp. 17–18.

104. Sybil Lubbock, *The Child in the Crystal* (London, 1939), p. 41.

105. Information about Margaret Crockford is drawn from correspondence with her great niece, Margaret Bishop.

106. May Pinhorn, *Life*, p. 89, Walley MS.

107. Ibid., p. 90.

108. Ibid., p. 120.

109. Ibid., p. 89.

110. Ibid., p. 117.

111. Information about May Pinhorn's life is drawn from conversation with her niece, Elisabeth Walley.

112. 'The Governess Question', p. 167.

113. Information about Miss Killick is drawn from correspondence with P.C. Hodson.

114. For example, Miss Priscilla D., *GBI Report for 1843* (London, 1844), p. 18.

115. For example, the case of Miss Catherine J---t, *GBI Report for 1844* (London, 1845), p. 20.

116. For example, Mrs Ellen G., *GBI Report for 1843* (London, 1844), p. 19.

117. Enumerators' Handbooks, Census of England and Wales, 1861, Public Record Office, London (hereafter PRO), R9/12 fo. 77.

118. Enumerators' Handbooks, Census of England and Wales, 1861, PRO, RG 9/9, fo. 104.

119. Census of England and Wales, 1861, vol. 2, *PP* 1863, table xliv, p. cv.

120. For example in 1843 the GBI reported the case of Miss Harriet G. who was described as having seriously weakened her health as a result of her 'dread of destitution', *GBI Report for 1843* (London, 1844), p. 23.

8. A Lady With a Profession

1. Details of May Pinhorn's early life are taken from her unpublished memoirs, 'Some Account of the Life of Mary Blanche Pinhorn' (typescript, 1926), Walley MS.

2. Details of Charlotte Brontë's early life are taken from Elizabeth Gaskell, *The Life of Charlotte Brontë* (Harmondsworth, 1985; first pub., London, 1857).

3. May Pinhorn, 'Life', p. 57, Walley MS.

4. Ibid., p.35.

5. Ibid.

6. Ibid., p. 41.

7. Ibid., p. 43.

8. Ibid., p. 63.

9. Elaine Kaye, *A History of Queen's College, London, 1848–1972* (London, 1972), p. 12.

10. For more information on the Christian Socialists, see Torben Christensen, *The Origin and History of Christian Socialism, 1848–54* (Aarhus, 1962).

11. Mary Maurice, *Mothers and Governesses* (London, 1847), pp. 156–57. For more information on Mary Maurice's involvement with the GBI, see p. 184.

12. Elaine Kaye, *Queen's College*, p. 12.

13. It is impossible to be certain whether the biographical information about governesses given in the annual reports of the Governesses' Benevolent Institution (hereafter GBI) is accurate. On the one hand, some destitute governesses may have exaggerated their circumstances to their sponsors in the hope of being elected to an annuity. On the other, a ladylike revulsion about announcing one's despair to the world may have led others into minimising their hardships.

14. Governesses' Benevolent Institution, *Report of the Board of Management* (hereafter, *GBI Report*) *for 1844* (London, 1845), p. 12.

15. *GBI Report for 1850* (London, 1851), p. 12.

16. See ch. 2, p. 27.

17. *Governess Life: Its Trials, Duties, and Encouragements* (London, 1849); *Mothers and Governesses* (London, 1847.)

18. *GBI Report for 1847* (London, 1848), p. 14.

19. Elaine Kaye, *Queen's College*, pp. 40–41.

20. Ibid., pp. 96–97.

21. Ibid., 46.

22. *GBI Report for 1848* (London, 1849), p. 17.

23. Ibid.

24. Mary Maurice, *Governess Life*, p. 2.

25. *GBI Report for 1847* (London, 1848), unnumbered pages.

26. Elaine Kaye, *Queen's College*, p. 49.

27. *GBI Report for 1849* (London, 1850), p. 19.

28. Elaine Kaye, *Queen's College*, p. 59.

29. Ibid., p. 58.

30. Ibid., p. 59.

31. Ibid.

32. Ibid.

33. Ibid.

34. Ibid.

35. For more information on the nineteenth-century feminist movement, see Ray Strachey, *The Cause: A Short History of the Women's Movement in Great Britain* (London, 1978; first pub., London 1928); Josephine Kamm, *Rapiers and Battleaxes: The Women's Movement and its Aftermath* (London, 1966).

36. Quoted in Margaret Bryant, *The Unexpected Revolution: A Study in the History of the Education of Women and Girls in the Nineteenth Century* (London, 1979), p. 82.

37. For a fuller discussion on the debate which raged between the *English Woman's Journal* (hereafter, *EWJ*) and conservative periodicals such as the *Saturday Review* on this point, see Mary Poovey, *Uneven Developments: The Ideological Work of Gender in Mid-Victorian England* (London, 1989; first pub. Chicago, 1988), pp. 152–57.

38. There was nonetheless a certain amount of dissension amongst the Ladies on this point. In a letter to the *EWJ* Emily Faithfull, the founder of the Victoria Press, maintained that good education and employment opportunities would allow women to make an active choice over whether they wished to marry at all. Jane Rendall, '"A Moral Engine"? Feminism, Liberalism and the *English Woman's Journal*', in Jane Rendall (ed.), *Equal or Different: Women's Politics, 1800–1914* (Oxford, 1987), p. 124.

39. Jessie Boucherett, 'On the Obstacles to the Employment of Women', *EWJ*, 4 (February 1860), p. 367.

40. 'The Society for Promoting the Employment of Women', *EWJ*, 5 (August 1860), p. 395.

41. Lee Holcombe, *Victorian Ladies at Work: Middle-Class Working Women in England and Wales, 1850–1914* (Newton Abbot, 1973), p. 16.

42. For precise statistics on the increase of female employment in five middle-class occupations from 1861 onwards, see ibid., appendix, pp. 203–17.

43. Ibid., p. 18.

44. Quoted in A. James Hammerton, *Emigrant Gentlewomen: Genteel Poverty and Female Emigration, 1830–1914* (London, 1979), p. 42.

45. Ibid., p. 40.

46. Ibid., p. 41.

47. Quoted in ibid., p. 35.

48. Martha Vicinus, *Independent Women: Work and Community for Single Women, 1850–1920* (London, 1985; first pub., Chicago, 1985), p. 172.

49. Ibid.

50. Lee Holcombe, *Victorian Ladies at Work*, pp. 49–50.

51. By 1914, one third of all schoolmistresses in grant-earning schools had both a degree as well as some sort of vocational training. Lee Holcombe, *Victorian Ladies at Work*, p. 53.

52. Ibid., p. 56.

53. Ibid. It was not until 1906 that the G.P.D.S.C. became a trust and was henceforward known as the G.P.D.S.T.

54. 'Home Schoolrooms and Private Governesses, Chapter 3', *Work and Leisure*, 10 (July 1885), pp. 193–94.

55. Martha Vicinus, *Independent Women*, pp. 170–171.

56. Ibid., p. 175.

57. This debate is mapped out in Sara Delamont, 'The Domestic Ideology and Women's Education', in Sara Delamont and Lorna Duffin (eds.), *Nineteenth-Century Woman: Her Cultural and Physical World* (London, 1978), ch. 6, pp. 164–187.

58. Alfred W. Pollard, 'The Governess and her Grievances', *Murray's Magazine*, 5 (April 1889), p. 515.

59. Joan N. Burstyn, *Victorian Education and the Ideal of Womanhood* (London, 1980), p. 26.

60. J.S. Pedersen, 'The Reform of Women's Secondary and Higher Education: Institutional Change and Social Values in Mid- and Late-Victorian England', in *History of Education Quarterly*, 19 (1979), pp. 61–91.

61. Carol Dyhouse, *Girls Growing up in Late Victorian and Edwardian England* (London, 1981), p. 73.

62. See p. 76.

63. Deborah Gorham, *The Victorian Girl and the Feminine Ideal* (London, 1982), p. 114.

64. Carol Dyhouse, *Girls Growing Up*, p. 71.

65. Ibid., p. 50.

66. Ibid., p. 41.

67. May Pinhorn, 'Life', p. 70, Walley MS.

68. Alfred W. Pollard, 'The Governess and her Grievances', p. 509.

69. Sara Delamont, 'The Domestic Ideology and Women's Education', pp. 175–76.

70. Cynthia Asquith, *Haply I May Remember* (London, 1950), p. 220.

71. C.M. Yonge, *Womankind* (London, 1876), pp. 34–35.

72. Alfred W. Pollard, 'The Governess and her Grievances', p. 508.

73. Ibid., pp. 505–6.

74. May Pinhorn, 'Life', p. 63, Walley MS.

75. A. James Hammerton, *Emigrant Gentlewomen*, p. 40.

76. *Women's Employment*, 13 (17 January 1913), p. 8.

77. Ibid., 13 (18 April 1913), p. 6.

78. Ibid., 13 (17 January, 1913), p. 8.

79. Alfred W. Pollard, 'The Governess and her Grievances', pp. 513–14; 'Home Schoolrooms and Private Governesses, Chapter 2', *Work and Leisure*, 10 (June 1885), p. 169.

80. Alfred W. Pollard, 'The Governess and her Grievances', p. 507.

81. Ibid., pp. 512–515; Mary Maxse, 'On Governesses', *National Review*, 37 (May 1901), pp. 400–1.

82. Alice Renton, *Tyrant or Victim? A History of the British Governess* (London, 1991), p. 152.

83. Martha Vicinus, *Independent Women*, p. 177.

84. Ibid., p. 176.

85. At the beginning of her unpublished memoirs, Pinhorn attached a list of 'Some People of Public Interest Whom I Have Met' which included a list of the great and the good from Ramsay McDonald to the daughters of Mrs Gaskell. May Pinhorn, *Life*, pp. 3–6, Walley MS.

86. Martha Vicinus, *Independent Women*, p. 181.

87. 'Home Schoolrooms and Private Governesses, Chapter 3', p. 193.

88. Cynthia Asquith, *Haply I May Remember*, p. 205.

89. Deborah Gorham, *The Victorian Girl*, p. 26.

90. S.E.S., '"Resident" or "Daily"', *Work and Leisure*, 16 (November 1891), pp. 302–305.

91. Mary Maxse, 'On Governesses', pp. 401–2.

92. Jonathan Gathorne-Hardy, *The Rise and Fall of the British Nanny* (London, 1972), p. 178.

Select Bibliography

PRIMARY SOURCES: UNPUBLISHED

1. PRIVATE COLLECTIONS

House MS. (in the possession of Mrs Charis House)

Bazlinton, Mary, Diary, 1854–1859. Manuscript, 6 volumes, not continuous.

Schulte MS. (in the possession of Mrs Anne Schulte)

Gates, Edith, Diary, 1876. Manuscript, 1 volume.

Walley MS. (in the possession of Lady Elisabeth Walley)

Pinhorn, May, 'Some Account of the Life of Mary Blanche Pinhorn'. Typescript, 1926, 1 volume.

Hackworth-Young MS. (in the possession of Miss Jane Hackworth-Young)

The Letters of Prudence Hackworth, 1852–54.

2. OFFICIAL MANUSCRIPT SOURCES

Enumerators' Handbooks, Census of England and Wales, 1861,
Public Record Office, London: Paddington (district 1, sub-districts
1–2); Crediton (district 292, sub-districts 1–4); Edgbaston (district
393, sub-district 2).

PRIMARY SOURCES: PUBLISHED

3. PARLIAMENTARY PAPERS

Schools Inquiry Commission, *PP* 1867–8, xxviiii, 13, pts., 1, 3 and 4.
Census of England and Wales, 1861, *PP* 1863, vols. 1–2.

4. REPORTS OF SOCIETIES

Governesses' Benevolent Institution, *Reports of the Board of
Management, 1843–53* (London, 1844–54).

5. NEWSPAPERS AND PERIODICALS

Eliza Cook's Journal
Edinburgh Review
English Woman's Journal
Englishwoman's Domestic Magazine
Fraser's Magazine
Household Words
Illustrated London News
Murray's Magazine
National Review
Once a Week

Parents' Review
Punch
Quarterly Review
Saturday Review
The Times
Woman's Gazette
Women's Employment
Work and Leisure

6. CONTEMPORARY ARTICLES

Edinburgh Review

Harriet Martineau, 'Female Industry', 109 (April 1859): 293–336.

Eliza Cook's Journal

'Governesses', 1 (September 1849): 305–307.

English Woman's Journal

[Bessie Rayner Parkes], 'The Profession of the Teacher. The Annual Reports of the Governesses' Benevolent Institution, from 1843 to 1856', 1 (March 1858): 1–13.
'Female Education in the Middle Classes', 1 (June 1858): 217–27.
'Going a Governessing', 1 (August 1858): 396–404.
'On The Adoption of Professional Life by Women', 2 (September 1858): 1–10.
'Association for Promoting the Employment of Women', 4 (September 1859): 54–59.
'The Governess Question', 4 (November 1859): 163–170.
[Bessie Rayner Parkes], 'The Market for Female Educated Labour', 4 (November 1859): 145–52.
[Bessie Rayner Parkes], 'What Can Educated Women Do?', 4 (December 1859): 217–27.
[Bessie Rayner Parkes], 'What Can Educated Women Do? Part 11', 4 (January 1860): 289–98.
'The Employment of Women in Germany', 5 (March 1860): 53–55.

'The Position of Women In France', 5 (April 1860): 92–99.

A.R.L., 'Tuition or Trade', 5 (May 1860): 173–83.

'The Society for Promoting the Employment of Women', 5 (August 1860): 388–96.

Bessie Rayner Parkes, 'A Year's Experience in Women's Work', 6 (October 1860): 112–21.

Jessie Boucherett, 'On the Education of Girls, with Reference to their Future Position', 6 (December 1860): 217–224.

Fraser's Magazine

'Hints on the Modern Governess System', 30 (November 1844): 571–583.

Sarah Lewis, 'On The Social Position of Governesses', 37 (April 1848): 411–414.

Illustrated London News

Juliet Clough, 'A Gentle Fade-out for the Governess', 257 (September 12 1970): 16–17.

Murray's Magazine

Alfred W. Pollard, 'The Governess and her Grievances', 5 (April 1889): 505–515.

The National Review

Greg, W.R., 'Why are Women Redundant?', 28 (April 1862): 434–460.

Maxse, Mary, 'On Governesses', 37 (May 1901): 397–402.

Once a Week

Martineau, Harriet, 'The Governess', 3 (September 1860): 267–272.

Select Bibliography

Parents' Review

Devonshire, Mrs R.L., 'Resident Governesses', 13 (November 1902): 833–844.

Punch

'Sisters of Misery', 15 (July-December 1848): 24–25.

Quarterly Review

Eastlake, Lady [Elizabeth], '*Vanity Fair, Jane Eyre* and the Governesses' Benevolent Institution', 84 (December 1848): 153–185.

Woman's Gazette

'Registry Offices', 4 (November 1879): 169.

Work and Leisure

E.C.J., 'Teaching by Governess', 1 (January 1880): 24.
S.Y.E. 'Experiences in Search of a Governess', 1 (March 1880): 88–89.
Kay-Shuttleworth, Lady, 'Thoughts on the Relations between Mothers and Governesses', 1 (June 1880): 161–63.
——, 'Thoughts on the Relations Between Mothers and Governesses. No. 2', 1 (August 1880): 225–29.
'Co-operation among Governesses', 2 (August 1881): 221–25.
K.A., Correspondence, 2 (September 1881): 278–79.
'Home Schoolroom and Private Governesses. Chapter 1', 10 (May 1885): 127–31.
'Home Schoolroom and Private Governesses. Chapter 2', 10 (June 1885): 167–69.
'Home Schoolroom and Private Governesses. Chapter 3', 10 (July 1885): 192–195.
M.L., Correspondence, 16 (April 1891): 109–10.
S.E.S., '"Resident" or "Daily"', 16 (November 1891): 302–5.
S.S.H., 'The Social Position of Governesses', (October 1893): 276–77.

7. BOOKS

The place of publication is London, unless otherwise indicated.

Acland, Eleanor, *Good-Bye for the Present: The Story of Two Childhoods, Milly: 1878–88 & Ellen: 1913–1924*, 1935.

Asquith, Cynthia, *Haply I May Remember*, 1950.

Austen, Jane, *Emma*, Harmondsworth, 1985; first pub. 1816.

Barlee, Ellen, *Friendless and Helpless*, 1863.

Beckwith, Lady Muriel, *When I Remember*, 1936.

Beeton, Isabella, *Mrs Beeton's Book of Household Management*, 2 vols., 1861.

Bodichon, Barbara, *Women and Work*, 1856.

Booker, Beryl L., *Yesterday's Child: 1890–1909*, 1937.

Boucherett, Jessie, *Hints on Self-Help: A Book for Young Women*, 1863.

Blessington, Countess of, *The Governess*, 2 vols., 1839.

Brontë, Anne, *Agnes Grey*, Harmondsworth, 1988; first pub. 1847.

Brontë, Charlotte, *Jane Eyre*, Harmondsworth, 1985; first pub., 1847.

——, *Shirley*, Harmondsworth, 1985; first pub., 1849.

Bureaud Riofrey, Mme, *Private Education; Or, Observations on Governesses*, 1836.

——, *Governesses; Or Modern Education*, 1841.

——, *Governesses: Or Modern Education*, 1842.

——, *Moral and Intellectual Education*, 1843.

Butler, Josephine (ed.), *The Education and Employment of Women*, 1868.

——, *Woman's Work and Woman's Culture*, 1869.

Carbery, Mary, *Happy World: The Story of a Victorian Childhood*, 1941.

Cavendish, Lady Frederick, *The Diary of Lady Frederick Cavendish*, ed. John Bailey, 2 vols., 1927.

Chorley, Katharine, *Manchester Made Them*, 1950.

Cobbe, Frances Power, *Essays on the Pursuits of Women*, 1863.

——, *Life of Frances Power Cobbe*, By Herself, 2 vols, 1894.

Cobbett, William, *Rural Rides*, Haramondsworth, 1985; first pub., 1830.

Cohen, Lucy (ed.), *Lady de Rothschild and her Daughters, 1821–1931*, 1935.

Collet, Clara E., *The Economic Position of Educated Working Women*, 1890.

Collins, Wilkie, *No Name*, 1862.

Cowden-Clarke, Mary, *My Long Life: An Autobiographical Sketch*, 1896.

Craik, Dinah Mulock, *Bread upon the Waters: A Governess's Life*, 1852.

——, *John Halifax, Gentleman*, 1856.

Crawshay, Rose M., *Domestic Service for Gentlewomen: A Record of Experience and Success*, 1874.

Davies, Emily, *On Secondary Instruction as Relating to Girls*, 1864.

Edgeworth, Maria, *Essays on Practical Education*, 2 vols., 1798.

Ellis, Sarah Stickney, *The Women of England: Their Social Duties and Domestic Habits*, 1839.

——, *The Daughters of England: Their Position in Society, Character and Responsibilities*, 1843.

——, *The Mothers of England: Their Influence and Responsibility*, 1843.

——, *Education of the Heart: Woman's Best Work*, 1869.

——, *The Home Life and Letters, of Mrs Ellis*, compiled by her nieces, 1893.

Farjeon, Eleanor, *A Nursery in the Nineties: Portrait of a Family* 1960; first pub. 1935.

Erskine, Mrs. Steuart, *Anna Jameson, Letters and Friendships: 1812–1860*, 1915.

Farr, William, *Remarks on a Proposed Scheme for the Conversion of Assessments Levied on Public Salaries . . . into a 'Provident Fund' for the Support of Widows and Orphans of Civil Servants of the Crown*, 1849.

Fawcett, Millicent Garrett, *What I Remember*, 1924.

Fielding, Daphne, *Mercury Presides*, 1954.

Forbes, Angela S., *Memories and Base Details*, 1921.

Freud, Sigmund, and Breuer, Josef, *Studies on Hysteria*, Harmondsworth, 1974; first pub., Vienna, 1885.

Gaskell, Elizabeth, *The Life of Charlotte Brontë*, Harmondsworth, 1985; first pub., 1857.

——, *Wives and Daughters*, 1866.

Gosse, Edmund, *Father and Son. A Study of Two Temperaments*, Harmondsworth, 1986; first pub., 1907.

Grogan, Mercy, *How Women May Earn a Living*, 1880.

Hadland, Selina, *Occupations for Women Other than Teaching*, London, 1886.

Ham, Elizabeth, *By Herself, 1783–1820*, ed. Eric Gillett, 1945.

Hare, Augustus, *The Story of My Life*, 6 vols., 1896–1900.

Hints to Governesses, By One of Themselves, 1856.

Hoare, Louisa, *Hints for the Improvement of Early Education*, 1819.

Ingelow, Jean, 'Dr. Deane's Governess', in her *Studies for Stories*, 1864.

James, Henry, *The Turn of The Screw*, Harmondsworth, 1986; first pub., New York 1907–9.

Jameson, Anna, *The Relative Social Position of Mothers and Governesses*, 1846.

——, *The Communion of Labour: A Second Lecture on the Social*

Employments of Women, 1856.

Jukes, Harriet M., *The Earnest Christian: Memoir, Letters, and Journals,* ed., Mrs H.A. Gilbert, 1858.

Keppel, Sonia, *Edwardian Daughter*, 1958.

Le Fanu, Sheridan, *Uncle Silas*, 1864.

Lubbock, Sybil, *The Child in the Crystal*, 1939.

Mangnall, R.M., *Historical and Miscellaneous Questions*, 1800.

Marshall, Mary Paley, *What I Remember*, Cambridge, 1947.

Martindale, Hilda, *From One Generation to Another, 1839–1944: A Book of Memoirs*, 1944.

Martineau, Harriet, *Deerbrook*, 1983; first pub., 1839.

——, *Autobiography*, 3 vols., 1877.

Maurice, F.D., *Lectures to Ladies on Practical Subjects*, 1855.

Maurice, F.D., and Kingsley, Charles, *Introductory Lectures Delivered at Queen's College*, 1849.

Maurice, Mary, *Mothers and Governesses*, 1847.

——, *Governess Life: Its Trials, Duties, and Encouragements*, 1849.

Mitford, Nancy, *The Ladies of Alderley, 1841–1850*, 1938.

Mitford, Nancy, (ed.), *The Stanleys of Alderley: Their Letters between the Years 1851–1865*, 1939.

More, Hannah, *Strictures on the Modern System of Female Education*, 2 vols., 1799.

——, *Coelebs in Search of a Wife*, 2 vols., 1807.

Nevill, Dorothy, *The Reminiscences of Lady Dorothy Nevill*, ed. Ralph Nevill, 1906.

Oxford, The Countess of Asquith (ed.), *Myself When Young, By famous women of to-day*, 1938.

Panton, Jane, *From Kitchen to Garret: Hints for Young Householders*, 1893.

——, *Leaves from a Life*, 1908.

——, *More Leaves from a Life*, 1911.

Parkes, Bessie Rayner, *Remarks on the Education of Girls*, 1854.

——, *Essays on Women's Work*, 1865.

Peart, Emily, *A Book for Governesses: By One of Them*, 1869.

Peck, Winifred, *A Little Learning; Or, a Victorian Childhood*, 1952.

Peel, Georgina, *Recollections of Lady Georgina Peel*, compiled by her daughter, Ethel Peel, 1920.

Ponsonby, Loelia, *Grace and Favour: The Memoirs of Loelia, Duchess of Westminster*, 1962.

Ruskin, John, *Sesame and Lilies*, 1865.

——, *Praeterita*, 3 vols., 1885–1900.

Selous, Henry Courtney, *The Young Governess*, 1872.

Sewell, Elizabeth M., *Amy Herbert*, 2 vols., 1844.

——, *Principles of Education, Drawn from Nature and*

Revelation, and Appplied to Female Education in the Upper Classes, 2 vols., 1865.

——, *The Autobiography of Elizabeth Missing Sewell*, ed., Eleanor L. Sewell, 1907.

Shireff, Emily, *Intellectual Education and its Influence on the Character and Happiness of Women*, 1858.

Shore, Emily, *Journal of Emily Shore*, 1891.

Smith, Mary, *The Autobiography of Mary Smith: Schoolmistress and Nonconformist*, 2 vols., 1892.

Soulsby, L.H.M., *The Home Governess*, 1916.

Stephen, George, *Guide To Service: The Governess*, 1844.

Thackeray, William, *Vanity Fair*, Harmondsworth, 1968; first pub., 1848.

——, *Book of Snobs*, 1852.

——, *The Newcomes*, 1855.

Thornley, Margaret, *The True End of Education and the Means Adapted to It*, Edinburgh 1846.

Trollope, Anthony, *The Eustace Diamonds*, 1873.

Valentine, Mrs L., *The Amenities of Home*, 1882.

Weeton, Ellen, *Miss Weeton's Journal of a Governess, 1807–1825*, ed. Edward Hall, 2 vols., New York, 1969; first pub., 1936.

Wood, Mrs Henry, *East Lynne*, 1891; first pub., 1861.

Yonge, Charlotte M., *The Daisy Chain*, 1856.

——, *Womankind*, 1876.

SECONDARY SOURCES

8. BOOKS

Place of publication is London, unless otherwise indicated.

Adburgham, Alison, *A Punch History of Manners and Modes, 1841–1940*, 1961.

Almedingen, E.M., *Fanny*, 1970.

Anderson, Louisa, *Elizabeth Garrett Anderson*, 1939.

Anderson, Michael, *Approaches to the History of the Western Family 1500–1914*, 1980.

Ariès, Philippe, *Centuries of Childhood*, Harmondsworth, 1973; first pub., Paris, 1960.

Armstrong, Nancy, *Desire and Domestic Fiction: A Political History of the Novel*, Oxford, 1987.

Banks, Joseph, *Prosperity and Parenthood: A Study of Family Planning among the Victorian Middle Classes*, 1954.

Banks, Joseph and Olive, *Feminism and Family Planning in Victorian England*, Liverpool, 1964.

Banks, Olive, *Faces of Feminism: A Study of Feminism as a Social Movement*, Oxford, 1981.

Basch, Francoise, *Relative Creatures: Victorian Women in Society and the Novel, 1837–67*, New York, 1974.

Beatty, J.W., *The Story of the Governesses' Benevolent Institution* (private circulation only), 1961.

Bennett, Daphne, *Queen Victoria's Children*, 1980.

Best, Geoffrey, *Mid-Victorian Britain, 1851–75*, 1971.

Binfield, Clyde, *So Down to Prayers: Studies in English Nonconformity, 1780–1920*, 1977.

Bradley, Ian, *The Call to Seriousness: The Evangelical Impact on the Victorians*, 1976.

Branca, Patricia, *Silent Sisterhood: Middle-Class Women in the Victorian Home*, 1975.

Bryant, Margaret, *The Unexpected Revolution: A Study in the History of Education of Women and Girls in the Nineteenth Century*, 1979.

Burman, Sandra (ed.), *Fit Work For Women*, 1979.

Burn, W.L., *The Age of Equipoise: A Study of the Mid-Victorian Generation*, 1968.

Burstyn, Joan, N., *Victorian Education and the Ideal of Womanhood* 1980.

Cannon, John, *Aristocratic Century: The Peerage of Eighteenth Century England*, Cambridge 1984.

Christensen, Torben, *The Origin and History of Christian Socialism, 1848–54*, Aarhus, 1962.

Clarke, Patricia, *The Governesses: Letters from the Colonies, 1862–1882*, 1985.

Colloms, Brenda, *Charles Kingsley: The Lion of Eversley*, 1975.

Cook, Edward, *The Life of Florence Nightingale*, 2 vols., 1913.

Crossick, Geoffrey, *The Lower Middle Class in Britain, 1870–1914*, 1977.

Crow, Duncan, *The Victorian Woman*, 1971.

Davidoff, Leonore, *The Best Circles: Society, Etiquette and the Season*, 1973.

——, and Hall, Catherine, *Family Fortunes: Men and Women of the English Middle Class*, 1987.

Delamont, Sara, and Duffin, Lorna (eds.), *The Nineteenth-Century Woman: Her Cultural and Physical World*, 1978.

Dunbar, Janet, *The Early Victorian Woman: Some Aspects of Her Life, 1837–1857*, 1953.

Dyhouse, Carol, *Girls Growing Up in Late Victorian and Edwardian England*, 1981.

Elshtain, Jeanne B., *The Family in Political Thought*, Brighton, 1982.

Finch, Janet, *Married to the Job: Wives' Incorporation in Men's Work*, 1983.

Firth, C.B., *Constance Louisa Maynard, Mistress of Westfield College: A Family Portrait*, 1949.

——, *The History of Sexuality, Volume 1: An Introduction*, Harmondsworth, 1981; originaly published, New York, 1978.

Fraser, Flora, *The English Gentlewoman*, 1987.

Gallop, Jane, *Feminism and Psychoanalysis: The Daughter's Seduction*, 1982.

Gathorne-Hardy, Jonathan, *The Rise and Fall of the British Nanny*, 1972.

Gibson, Ian, *The English Vice: Beating, Sex and Shame in Victorian England and After*, 1978.

Gilbert, Sandra M., and Gubar, Susan, *The Madwoman in the Attic: The Woman Writer and the Nineteenth-Century Literary Imagination*, Yale 1979.

Gorham, Deborah, *The Victorian Girl and the Feminine Ideal*, 1982.

Grisewood, H., *Ideas and Beliefs of the Victorians*, New York, 1966.

Hall, Catherine, *White, Male and Middle-Class: Explorations in Feminism and History*, Cambridge, 1992.

Hammerton, A. James, *Emigrant Gentlewomen: Genteel Poverty and Female Emigration, 1830–1919*, 1979.

Harrison, J.F.C., *The Early Victorians, 1832–1851*, 1971.

Hartman, Mary S., *Victorian Murderesses: A True History of Thirteen Respectable French and English Women Accused of Unspeakable Crimes*, 1977.

Heath, Stephen, *The Sexual Fix*, 1982.

Hobsbawm, Eric J., *The Age of Capital, 1848–1875*, 1975.

Holcombe, Lee, *Victorian Ladies at Work: Middle-Class Working Women in England and Wales, 1850–1914*, Newton Abbot, 1973.

Horn, Pamela, *The Rise and Fall of the Victorian Servant*, Dublin, 1975.

——, *Education in Rural England*, 1800–1914, Dublin, 1978.

Houghton, Walter E., *The Victorian Frame of Mind*, New Haven, 1957.

Howe, Bea, *A Galaxy of Governesses*, 1954.

Hudson, Derek, *Munby, Man of Two Worlds: The Life and Diaries of Arthur J. Munby, 1828–1910*, 1972.

Hunt, Linda D., *A Woman's Portion: Ideology, Culture and the British Female Novel Tradition*, New York, 1988.

Jacobus, Mary, *Reading Women: Essays in Feminist Criticism*, 1986.

Jeffreys, Sheila, *The Spinster and her Enemies: Feminism and Sexuality, 1880–1930*, 1985.

Jelinek, Estelle C. (ed.), *Women's Autobiography: Essays in Criticism*, Bloomington, 1980.

John, Angela, *Unequal Opportunities: Women's Employment in England, 1800–1918*, Oxford, 1987.

Kamm, Josephine, *Hope Deferred: Girls' Education in English History* 1965.

——, *Rapiers and Battleaxes: The Women's Movement and its Aftermath*, 1966.

Kaye, Elaine, *A History of Queen's College, London, 1848–1972*, 1972.

Lewis, Jane, *Labour and Love: Women's Experience of Home and Family, 1850–1940*, Oxford, 1986.

Levine, Philippa, *Victorian Feminism, 1850–1900*, 1987.

Lovell, Terry, *Consuming Fiction*, 1987.

McBride, Theresa M., *The Domestic Revolution: The Modernization of Household Service in England and France, 1820–1920*, 1976.

Manton, Jo, *Elizabeth Garrett Anderson*, 1958.

Marcus, Steven, *The Other Victorians: A Study of Sexuality and Pornography in Mid-Victorian Britain*, 1966.

Mingay, G.E., *Rural Life in Victorian England*, 1977.

Mitchell, Juliet, and Oakely, Ann (eds.), *The Rights and Wrongs of Women*, Harmondsworth, 1976.

Nead, Lynda, *Myths of Sexuality: Representations of Women in Victorian Britain*, Oxford, 1990; first pub. Oxford, 1988.

Neale, R.S., (ed.), *Class and Ideology in the 19th Century*, 1972.

Neff, Wanda F., *Victorian Working Women, 1832–1850*, New York, 1929.

Newton, Judith L., Ryan, Mary P., Walkowitz, Judith R. (eds), *Sex and Class in Women's History*, 1983.

Newton, Judith L., *Women, Power, and Subversion: Social Strategies in British Fiction, 1778–1860*, Athens, GA, 1981.

Ortner, Sherry and Whitehead, Harriet, *Sexual Meanings: The Cultural Construction of Gender and Sexuality*, Cambridge, 1981.

Owen, Alex, *The Darkened Room: Women, Power and Spiritualism in Late Victorian England*, 1989.

Palmegiano, Eugenia, *Women and British Periodicals, 1832–1867: A Bibliography*, 1976.

Parry-Jones, William L., *The Trade in Lunacy: A Study of Private Madhouses in England in the Eighteenth and Nineteenth Centuries*, 1972.

Pearsall, Ronald, *The Worm in the Bud: The World of Victorian Sexuality*, 1969.

Percival, Alicia, *The English Miss, To-Day and Yesterday*, 1939.

Perkin, Harold, *The Origins of Modern English Society, 1780–1880*, 1969.

Perkin, Joan, *Women and Marriage in Nineteenth-Century England*, 1989.

Peters, Margot, *Unquiet Soul: A Biography of Charlotte Brontë*, 1975.

Peterson, Linda, H., *Victorian Autobiography*, 1986.

Peterson, M. Jeanne, *Family, Love, and Work in the Lives of Victorian Gentlewomen*, Bloomington, 1989.

Poovey, Mary, *Uneven Developments: The Ideological Work of Gender in Mid-Victorian England*, 1989; first pub. Chicago, 1988.

Porter, Roy, *English Society in the Eighteenth Century*, Harmondsworth, 1982.

Prochaska, Frank, *Women and Philanthropy in Nineteenth-Century England*, Oxford, 1980.

Reader, W.J., *Professional Men: The Rise of the Professional Classes in 19th Century England*, 1966.

Rendall, Jane, *The Origins of Modern Feminism: Women in Britain, France and the U.S., 1780–1860*, 1985.

—— (ed.), *Equal or Different: Women's Politics, 1800–1914*, Oxford, 1987.

Renton, Alice, *Tyrant or Victim? A History of the British Governess*, 1991.

Roberts, David, *Paternalism in Early Victorian England*, 1979.

Roberts, Elizabeth, *Women's Work, 1840–1940*, New York, 1988.

Rose, Kenneth, *Superior Person*, 1969.

Rosman, Doreen M., *Evangelicals and Culture*, 1984.

Rubinstein, W.D., *Men of Property: The Very Wealthy in Britain Since the Industrial Revolution*, 1981.

——, *Elites and the Wealthy in Modern British History*, Brighton, 1987.

Sanders, Valerie, *The Private Lives of Victorian Women*, Hemel Hempstead, 1989.

Shorter, Clement (ed.), *The Brontës: Life and Letters*, 2 vols., 1908.

Showalter, Elaine, *A Literature of Their Own: British Women Novelists from Brontë to Lessing*, 1982; first pub. Princeton, 1977.

——, *The Female Malady: Women, Madness and Culture in England, 1830–1980*, 1987; first pub. New York 1985.

Siefert, Susan, *The Dilemma of the Talented Heroine: A Study in Nineteenth Century Fiction*, Montreal, 1978.

Simon Brian, and Bradley, Ian (eds.), *The Victorian Public School: Studies in the Development of an Educational Institution*, Dublin 1975.

Sitwell, Osbert (ed.), *Two Generations*, 1940.

Stone, Lawrence, and Stone, Jeanne C. Fawtier, *An Open Elite? England, 1540–1880*, Oxford, 1984.

Strachey, Ray, *The Cause: A Short History of the Women's Movement in Great Britain*, 1928.

Taylor, Barbara, *Eve and the New Jerusalem: Socialism and Feminism in the Nineteenth Century*, 1983.

Taylor Bernard, *Cruelly Murdered: Constance Kent and the Killing at Road Hill House*, 1989; first pub. 1979.

Thompson, Dorothy, *Queen Victoria: Gender and Power*, 1990.

Thomson, Patricia, *The Victorian Heroine: A Changing Ideal, 1837–1873*, 1956.

Thompson, F.M.L., *English Landed Society in the Nineteenth Century*, 1963.

——, *The Rise of Respectable Society, 1830–1900*, 1988.

Tilly, Louise, and Scott, Joan W., *Women, Work and Family*, New York, 1978.

Trudgill, Eric, *Madonnas and Magdalens: The Origins and Development of Victorian Sexual Attitudes*, 1976.

Turner, Barry, *Equality for Some: The Story of Girls' Education*, 1974.

Vicinus, Martha, *Independent Women: Work and Community for Single Women, 1850–1920*, 1985.

Vicinus, Martha (ed.), *Suffer and Be Still: Women in the Victorian Age*, 1980; first pub, Bloomington, 1972.

—— (ed.), *A Widening Sphere: Changing Roles of Victorian Women*, 1980; first pub. Bloomington, 1977.

Vidler, Alexander R., *F.D. Maurice and Company: Nineteenth Century Studies*, 1966.

Walkowitz, Judith R., *Prostitution and Victorian Society: Women, Class and the State*, Cambridge, 1980.

Waterson, Merlin, *The Servants' Hall: A Domestic History of Erddig*, 1980.
Weeks, Jeffrey, *Sex, Politics and Society: The Regulation of Sexuality Since 1800*, 1981.
West, Katharine, *Chapter of Governesses: A Study of the Governess in English Fiction, 1800–1949*, 1949.
White, Cynthia, *Women's Magazines, 1693–1968*, 1970.
Wiener, Martin J., *English Culture and the Decline of the Industrial Spirit, 1850–1980*, Cambridge, 1982.
Wilson, Elizabeth, *Adorned in Dreams: Fashion and Modernity*, 1985.
Wohl, Anthony (ed.), *The Victorian Family: Structure and Stresses*, 1978.
Young, G.M., *Victorian England: Portrait of An Age*, 1936.

9. PUBLISHED ARTICLES

Alexander, Sally, 'Women, Class and Sexual Difference in the 1830s and 1840s: Some Reflections on the Writing of a Feminist History', *History Workshop Journal*, 17 (Spring, 1984): 125–49.
Amies, Marion, 'The Victorian Governess and Colonial Ideals of Womanhood', *Victorian Studies*, 31 (Summer 1988): 537–565.
Beales, H.L., 'The Victorian Family', in H. Grisewood, *Ideas and Beliefs of the Victorians*, New York, 1966: 345–50.
Cominos, Peter T., 'Innocent Femina Sensualis in Unconscious Conflict', in Martha Vicinus (ed.), *Suffer and Be Still*, 1980; first pub., Bloomington, 1972: 155–172.
Davidoff, Leonore, 'Class and Gender in Victorian England', in Judith L. Newton, Mary P. Ryan, Judith R. Walkowitz (eds.), *Sex and Class in Women's History*, 1983: 17–71.
——, Jean L'Esperance, and Howard Newby, 'Landscape with Figures: Home and Community in English Society', in Juliet Mitchell and Ann Oakley (eds.), *The Rights and Wrongs of Women* Harmondsworth, 1976: 139–75.
Delamont, Sara, 'The Contradictions in Ladies' Education', in Sara Delamont, and Lorna Duffin (eds.), *The Nineteenth-Century Woman: Her Cultural and Physical World*, 1978: 134–163.
——, 'The Domestic Ideology and Women's Education', in Sara Delamont, and Lorna Duffin (eds.), *The Nineteenth-Century Woman: Her Cultural and Physical World*, 1978: 164–187.

Hall, Catherine, 'The Early Formation of Victorian Domestic Ideology', in Sandra Burman (ed.), *Fit Work for Women*, 1979: 15–32.

Kanner, S. Barbara, 'The Women of England in a Century of Social Change, 1815–1914: A Select Bibliography', in Martha Vicinus (ed.), *Suffer and Be Still*, 1980; first pub., Bloomington, 1972: 172–206.

——, 'The Women of England in a Century of Social Change, 1815–1914: A Select Bibliography, Part 11', in Martha Vicinus (ed.), A *Widening Sphere*, 1980; first pub., Bloomington, 1977: 199–270.

McBride, Theresa M., '"As The Twig is Bent": The Victorian Nanny', in Anthony Wohl (ed.), *The Victorian Family*, 1978: 44–58.

Musgrove Frank, 'Middle-Class Education and Employment in the Nineteenth Century', *Economic History Review*, 2nd series, 12, 1 (1959–60): 99–111

Neale R.S., 'Class and Class Consciousness in Early 19th Century England: Three Classes or Five?', in Neale R.S. (ed.), *Class and Ideology in the 19th Century*, 1972: 15–40.

Pedersen, Joyce S., 'The Reform of Women's Secondary and Higher Education: Institutional Change and Social Values in Mid– and Late- Victorian England', in *History of Education Quarterly*, 19, 1 (1979): 61–91.

Peterson, M. Jeanne, 'The Victorian Governess: Status Incongruence in Family and Society', in Martha Vicinus (ed.), *Suffer and Be Still*, 1980; first pub., Bloomington, 1972: 3–19.

Roberts, Helene E., 'Marriage, Redundancy or Sin: The Painter's View of Women in the First Twenty-Five Years of Victoria's Reign', in Martha Vicinus (ed.), *Suffer and Be Still*, 1980; first pub., Bloomington, 1972: 45–76.

10. UNPUBLISHED ARTICLES AND THESES

Davidoff, Leonore, 'The English Victorian Governess: A Study In Social Isolation', unpublished article, 1971.

Nash, Susan A., 'Wanting A Situation, Governesses and Victorian Novels', unpublished PhD thesis, Rutgers, State University of New Jersey, 1980.

Index